OutSmarting Wall Street

A Profit-Proven System for Picking Stocks, Mutual Funds & Timing the Market

Daniel Alan Seiver

Third Edition

IRWIN
Professional Publishing®
Chicago • London • Singapore

This publication is designed to provide accurate and authoritative information in regard to the subject matter covered. It is sold with the understanding that the author and the publisher are not engaged in rendering legal, accounting, or other professional service.

ISBN 1-55738-583-1

Printed in the United States of America

BB

 3 4 5 6 7 8 9 0

TAQ/BJS

For my parents, to whom I owe so much

TABLE OF CONTENTS

PREFACE

As the Gipper said, "There you go again!" Yes, another edition of *Outsmarting Wall Street*, complete with a new title and new "bells and whistles." Can't I leave well enough alone? No, I can't. The world, including the financial world, continues to change rapidly, and we must change with it. In particular, today's investors need a rules-based system to build a mutual fund portfolio from among the vast and growing array of over 4,000 funds. Now they have it in Chapter 5: the PAD System applied to mutual funds. I have also demystified short selling (for the experienced investor) and demonstrated how this much-maligned and little-understood tactic can fit into my system (Chapter 11).

Aside from these all-new chapters, I have updated and revised every other chapter of the book. Case Histories have been either added or updated to show how the rules of *Outsmarting Wall Street* have continued to guide investors to big profits in both bull and bear markets.

This flurry of change should not obscure the fact that the two keys to successful investing remain the same: Patience and Discipline. These two keys, applied with the rules set out in this book, will unlock the door marked "investment success."

PREFACE TO THE FIRST (1986) EDITION

This book is designed to help the serious investor make money. I believe it is the only book a serious investor needs to achieve his or her financial goals in the stock market. I have followed the rules laid out in the following chapters with much success, multiplying my investment capital many times over in the past 10 years. There is little danger of this approach failing to operate in the future; neither do I fear that disclosing my "system" will make it useless because everyone will be able to use it. These dangers are minimal because investors in general are never going to be willing to submit themselves to the discipline required by my methods, nor will they be willing to exercise the patience, which is equally important. This book is written for those investors with the requisite patience and discipline, who need only to be shown how to apply those traits to make money.

I learned the lessons in this book over a period of 28 years of bull and bear markets. The book should help others succeed without spending as many years as I did in the school of experience. Before being nominated for sainthood, I should point out that I expect to make money from this book. So will you.

ACKNOWLEDGMENTS

This book was "stric'ly my own idea." The idea could not have become a book without some important help and encouragement, however. My father, Theodore J. Seiver, read drafts of the entire manuscript of all three editions and made many useful comments. My colleague Dennis Sullivan has provided encouragement from "day one" and has made numerous suggestions that have improved all three editions. My colleagues Donald Cymrot, William McKinstry, and Gerald Flueckiger have also made valuable suggestions that have been incorporated into the text.

Numerous readers of the first and second editions have written to me with their comments and suggestions, which have led me to make a number of changes. Two of them deserve special mention for helping me collect most of the data for the charts and tables in the book: Todd Klein (third edition) and Christopher Mason (second edition). Jim Feldhouse did an excellent and timely job of writing the computer code for versions I and II of the PAD Stock Selector Program. John Willig, my former editor at Prentice-Hall, encouraged me to revise the book yet again and helped me find a new publisher.

I also wish to thank Kevin Commins, Jim McNeil, and Michael Jeffers of Probus Publishing for their support of the third edition.

My wife Barbara, who also serves as "magician's assistant" for my "road shows," and my children, Elizabeth and Robert, deserve medals (with oak-leaf clusters) for understanding that "Dad has to work on his book." Heartfelt thanks to all.

ACKNOWLEDGMENTS

CHAPTER 1
INTRODUCTION

"He that can have patience can have what he will."
—Benjamin Franklin

THE SECRET: PATIENCE AND DISCIPLINE (PAD)

The secret of *Outsmarting Wall Street* is simple: Patience and Discipline. These two traits are so important I have elevated them to a "system": the P(atience) A(nd) D(iscipline) System, or the PAD System for short. If you have patience and can discipline yourself to follow rules, you have the two most important qualities of a successful investor. These traits cannot be learned. Everything else you need can be learned from this book.

OUTLINE OF THE BOOK

The first foundation stone of stock market success is individual stock selection. Picking stocks that outperform the market is half the battle, albeit a difficult one. In Chapters 2 and 3, I set out the rules I use to pick stocks that will outperform the market over the long run, that is, the next three to five years. (I explain in Chapter 9 why I believe this is the only time horizon that will permit the ordinary investor to consistently beat the market.) The rules are objective criteria that a company's stock must satisfy before it can be included in a PAD investor's portfolio.

The stocks that end up in your portfolio will normally stay there for a number of years. This is why patience is so important. Many investors buy good growth stocks and then do not wait for them to grow.

The stock-selection rules of the first part of Chapter 2 comprise the "classic" original version of the PAD System, which is now part of PAD-A, the "Aggressive" PAD approach. It is designed to ferret out future winners in the technology sector (computer hardware and software, electronics, precision instruments, and biotechnology), using the *Value Line Investment Survey*. Many of my most successful investments were selected with this set of rules.

Investors with a high tolerance for risk might prefer the modification of the "classic" PAD System described in the second part of Chapter 2. In it, I show a PAD investor how to construct a high-return/high-risk portfolio from the small-company growth stocks reviewed by the *Value Line OTC Special Situations Service*. I have also had success (and some spectacular failures) with this variant of the basic system.

Many investors, especially conservative ones, may be unwilling to limit themselves to PAD-A technology stocks, even though they want to use the PAD System. In Chapter 3, I present another modified set of rules that preserves the spirit of the original PAD System while applying it to a much wider universe of stocks. I have had much success in recent years with this version of the system, called PAD-C (for Conservative). PAD investors who also seek current income should not despair: the last part of Chapter 3 is devoted to a new variant of the system, called PAD-I, which is specifically designed to meet the needs of income-oriented investors.

There are a number of "Case Histories" in Chapters 2 and 3 that illustrate the application of the PAD rules to specific stocks. These are almost all drawn from my own investment experience. Each of these chapters is also followed by an Appendix containing an annotated list of my favorite PAD stocks in each category. Some of these favorites, however, will probably not meet all of the PAD selection criteria when this book is read. The best use of these lists is as "starter sets" for the stock-selection process.

Chapter 4 explains the best way to buy a stock that has passed all the tests of Chapters 2 or 3. I recommend using discount brokers, and an Appendix to the chapter contains information and advice on choosing a discount broker.

I also present rules for selling stocks, both those that have done well and those that have not. Neither selling decision is easy, and most investment advice is geared toward finding winners, rather than dealing with the inevitable losers.

Mutual fund investors now have their very own version of the PAD System in Chapter 5. PAD-M (for Mutual Funds) is a mutual fund selection system based on *Morningstar Mutual Funds*, the leading source of mutual fund data.

In Chapter 6, I describe my techniques of long-term market timing (a fancy name for this is "tactical asset allocation"), the other foundation stone of successful PAD investing. I draw on fundamental, technical, and psychological indicators to try to avoid either buying during periods of market overvaluation or selling during periods of market undervaluation. This is a very difficult task, mainly because it is so hard to avoid being swept along with the herd of ordinary investors, whose panic selling creates buying opportunities and whose greed drives stocks to unsustainable levels. The herd instinct is not confined to the lower echelons of the investing world, either. The "Nifty Fifty" of the early 1970s were the overpriced darlings of institutional investors until the bubble burst in 1974.

The health of the economy has a crucial impact on the health of the stock market. To understand all the interrelationships among money, credit, interest rates, deficits, inflation, and economic growth requires more than the 20 pages I devote to it in Chapter 7. But my brief discussion should be sufficient to direct you toward real knowledge of how the economy works, which should put you near the top of Wall Street's knowledge pyramid. In addition, your understanding of economic trends should improve your long-term timing decisions in the stock market.

The long-run trend of economic growth in the United States is just as important to the PAD investor, since the superior returns of stocks in the long run, compared to bonds or other fixed-income investments, will not hold if our economy does not continue to grow in future decades. In Chapter 8, I present my scenario for the United States and the world economy in the 21st century. It is basically a rosy view, although I do discuss many of the current and future difficulties we must face. The bright future I see is in part a result of the electronic and biologic revolution that is taking place right now. My forecast for the future is the basis for investing in PAD-A technology stocks.

Although economists have made significant contributions to our understanding of the economy, many of them believe in the "efficient markets" theory. A key inference of the main variant of this theory is that it is virtually impossible for any investor to beat the market consistently. Obviously I disagree. Yet it would be a mistake to dismiss the theory out of hand, as many on Wall Street have done, since another variant of the theory is probably true. I explain both variants in a nontechnical fashion in Chapter 9, and point out the various flaws in the theory, using recent research by economists themselves as my chief weapon of attack. This recent research serves double duty, since it also provides a theoretical justification for the PAD System itself.

In Chapter 10, I describe the essential elements of stock options and index options trading. I recommend conservative strategies that enable a PAD investor to "insure" his or her portfolio against a market decline without being forced to sell stock from the portfolio. This strategy is recommended only for the experienced PAD investor with a substantial portfolio.

Chapter 11 presents still another new variant of the PAD System: short selling. While this technique is for the experienced investor only, I believe short selling offers still another way to improve performance without increasing risk. Bear markets still lurk in our future, and a well-planned short selling program can ease the pain considerably.

In Chapter 12, I have collected a useful and diverse set of odds and ends. These are little tidbits of knowledge and advice that are helpful, but don't really fit in to the basic story: tax strategy, IRAs, record-keeping, etc. Chapter 13 contains some concluding comments. All of the PAD rules and all of the Case Histories are collected in subsequent sections for easy reference.

CAUTIONS

A few words of caution before we begin. You cannot buy stock without money. This is not a "nothing down" book. If you do not have at least $5,000 to invest, you cannot take full advantage of the PAD System. And the money has to be invested for a number of years. That means you can't invest the rent money! I also do not recommend that any investor put all of his or her assets in the stock market, no matter how much you love this book. Your own home is a good long-term investment, and a rainy-day fund kept in a money-market mutual fund is an excellent investment. While this advice has certainly become a cliche, it is still true. I also do not recommend that you devote all of your free time to the stock market. Having other hobbies will help you maintain the detachment necessary for patience and discipline. Applying the basic PAD System of Chapters 2–6 should only take a few hours per week. Additional time can be spent monitoring the economy (Chapters 7 and 8), insuring a large portfolio (Chapters 10 and 11), and minimizing taxes (Chapter 12).[1]

A LITTLE TEST

A final word of caution: Some readers will have great difficulty becoming PAD investors. To test your potential, answer the following four questions honestly:

1. Does your spending regularly exceed your income?
2. Do you agonize over small decisions?
3. Do you think a person's income and assets are the best measures of what a person is "worth" in life?
4. Is the stock market your only hobby?

If you answered with four resounding "no's," this book should suit you perfectly. If you answered "yes" four times, you may have to change your way of life before you can profit from this book. If you answered both "yes" and "no," read on and decide for yourself.

---

1. Investors wishing to reduce time requirements to one hour per month can subscribe to my monthly market letter, the *PAD System Report*. See Chapter 12, under the section "Managing the Information Flow: A Time-Saving Alternative."

CHAPTER 2
INDIVIDUAL STOCK SELECTION: THE AGGRESSIVE APPROACH (PAD-A)

The two great investment battles you must fight are (1) finding stocks that tend to do better than the market over the long run, and (2) buying when stocks are cheap and selling when they are dear. It is not necessary to win both battles all the time, but regular losses on one battlefront can cost you the war for investment success. Almost all stocks fall sharply in a bear market, whether they are good, bad, or ugly. Chapters 2 through 4 are designed to help you buy and sell individual stocks that will outperform the market. Chapter 5 will help you build a portfolio of no-load mutual funds that have earned good total returns with moderate risk. Chapter 6 is designed to improve your long-term market timing, that is, to help you identify periods of undervaluation and overvaluation in the market as a whole. Selection and timing are obviously not exact sciences, but with patience and the discipline of the rules I will set out, you can improve your chances of success. If you feel you are already accomplished in one category or the other, you should just skim the relevant chapter(s) to see whether you might have overlooked an idea or two that might improve your performance further. If you are regularly winning both these battles, you should be writing a book on the stock market yourself!

Chapters 2 and 3 lay out three versions of the PAD stock-selection system. In the first part of this chapter, I present the original, or "classic," version, which limits the stock-selection universe to technology stocks culled from the *Value Line Investment Survey*. The second part of the chapter limits stock selection to the small technology stocks followed by the *Value Line OTC Special Situations Service*. These two parts of the system, now dubbed PAD-A (A for Aggressive), have been, in the memorable words of Chico Esquela, "berry berry good to me" for many years. However, technology stocks as a group under-performed the market for a significant portion of the 1980s. This long dry spell convinced me (and many other technology investors) that sole reliance on a technology stock portfolio, no matter how carefully selected, does not provide sufficient diversification. There are many excellent growth stocks outside the technology area that can provide the same levels of long-term total return that I aim for with technol-ogy stocks.

The solution to this diversification problem is straightforward: Modify the stock-selection rules in this chapter to fit low- or no-technology growth stocks. I have done this in Chapter 3, which presents PAD-C (C for Conservative) rules that can be applied to companies in *any* industry. I have also modified the PAD-C stock-selection rules to make them suitable for PAD investors seeking current income. This new version of the system, dubbed PAD-I (I for Income), is presented at the end of Chapter 3.

My portfolio contains stocks selected with every variant of the PAD System, but this is clearly not a requirement. I believe PAD investors can achieve long-term success with any or all of the variations. My own "life-cycle" experience may be a useful guideline: In my youth, I sought out the high-risk/high-return technology stocks of Chapter 2, and I spurned any company that paid a dividend. Now that I am firmly established in the "middle ages," I am irresistibly drawn to the more conservative growth stocks of Chapter 3. As I contemplate re-tirement, low-risk income stocks are developing their own allure.

THE FUNDAMENTAL APPROACH

What Wall Streeters mean by "fundamentals" is the study and evalu-ation of stocks in terms of their current and future earnings and divi-dends, and their balance sheets. Studying stocks in this manner is beyond the means of the nonprofessional investor. The time require-ments and the skills necessary to decode published reports of income statements and assets and liabilities are substantial. For these reasons, masses of analyses are carried out by professionals and sold to the public, both by brokerage firms, which publish research reports, and by firms that produce only research.

While many brokerage firms produce valuable research and do a good job for their clients, their commission structure is much higher than discount brokers, who provide the customer with fewer services.

"Deep" discounters have the lowest commission charges and sometimes provide their customers with only two services: (1) the execution of buy and sell orders, and (2) market quotations. The full-service brokerage firm and its brokers make money when clients trade, and this creates a conflict of interest when they are also providing advice. Since this book is designed to help you make your own decisions, it follows naturally that you should deal with a discount broker to save commissions, and use research services to help you select stocks. Discount brokers and the PAD approach to buying and selling are discussed in Chapter 4 and its appendix.

Where do we get access to the research we need to make informed stock decisions? In my 35 years of investment experience, I have never found a better source of data and interpretation than the *Value Line Investment Survey* (VLIS).[1]

In recent years I have subscribed to this investment service, which has more subscribers (100,000) than any other, although it is available in many public and university libraries around the country. If you are not familiar with VLIS, I suggest you look at a recent weekly issue before reading any further, because Value Line forms the basis of the PAD fundamental approach to stock selection.

My high regard for Value Line is shared by many others. Professor Fischer Black of M.I.T., who once espoused the view that no one can either predict or "beat" the markets, once stated that research departments should fire all their stock analysts except one, and give that one a subscription to Value Line. (Black left M.I.T. for a job on Wall Street with Goldman, Sachs. I do not know if he subscribes to Value Line.) The basis for this high praise from a skeptical academic is Value Line's consistent ability to predict which groups of stocks will perform better than others.[2] In addition to forecasting the relative short-term performances of all of the companies it covers, Value Line also provides and interprets masses of individual company and economy-wide data, which are beyond any individual's capability to analyze.

The weekly VLIS comes in three parts. First, there is the "Value Line View," which reviews general trends in the market, picks a "Stock of the Week," and usually covers some special topic in brief. The second

1. I have never had any financial relationship with Value Line, Inc., or any of its employees. I do keep some IRA and TSA money in Value Line mutual funds. In 1987, I met Arnold Bernhard, founder and chairman of Value Line. Subsequently, Value Line purchased a number of copies of the first edition of this book.
2. The *Hulbert Financial Digest* concurs: for the 13 1/2-year period ending in December 1993, Value Line was ranked #1 of the 20 advisory services rated for that period.

and most important part is the full-page reviews of the 1,700 stocks covered by VLIS, each reviewed four times a year. Since new developments can affect Value Line's opinion about a company at any time, there are supplementary reports on a number of different stocks every week, usually those involved in mergers or buyouts, or those reporting unexpectedly good or bad profits. The third part, called the "Summary Index," includes current rankings for every stock every week.

While Value Line has demonstrated that it is capable of predicting the relative price performances of groups of stocks, I do not believe the firm has shown much ability to forecast general trends in the market. (The company admits as much, but also asserts that no one else can, either.) Thus, the real value of Value Line to the PAD investor is the sifting and analyzing of all the fundamental information about a stock, resulting in a forecast for the given company over the following year and a projection for the three- to five-year time horizon, which is the time horizon for the PAD investor. It is not necessary, however, to review all 1,700 stocks monitored by Value Line. The PAD-A technology investor can concentrate on just a few high-growth industries, which I discuss below.

As I point out in Chapter 8, the next century will witness truly dramatic changes in the American economy. In general, we tend to underestimate the amount of change that will take place. Many of the most important changes will be technological, and those companies that supply the products that fuel those changes will see their sales and earnings rise dramatically if they are not mismanaged. It should be no surprise that computer hardware and software, electronics, precision instruments, and biotechnology are four industries that I think will continue to grow rapidly for the foreseeable future, and long-term investors in these industries will be suitably rewarded. Value Line can help you select and monitor the stocks in these industries so that you participate fully in future growth.

Over the last decade, Wall Street has responded to this view of the future with periodic bouts of excessive enthusiasm, which have been inevitably followed by periods of deep disillusionment. In 1983, for example, Wall Street was in full agreement with the rosy scenario, and bid up all electronic technology stocks to unsustainable levels. By the spring of 1985, a true slowdown in the rate of growth of these industries, combined with falling profits and even losses for some companies, changed the sentiment on Wall Street completely, and electronic technology stocks were driven down to unreasonably low levels. This created a buying opportunity for those who could resist the violent mood swings and herd instinct of Wall Street. Another complete cycle followed: overvaluation in 1987 was the precursor of poor market performance in 1988 and 1989. The early 1990s witnessed still another resurgence of interest in technology stocks, which will inevitably be followed by another period of disappointing performance. (Biotechnology stocks have also been bid up and beaten down in similar patterns.) The 1983–86 and 1988–89 technology bear markets should serve as cautionary notes to PAD-A investors: There will be violent ups and downs and trying times in the future. You must keep your head while others are losing theirs.

This chapter is divided into two parts. In Part 1, I lay out the original PAD rules for technology stock selection using the *Value Line Investment Survey*. In Part 2, I present a modified set of rules for the smaller and riskier technology stocks followed by the *Value Line OTC Special Situations Service*.

PART 1: STOCK SELECTION RULES USING THE *VALUE LINE INVESTMENT SURVEY*

How can you tell which technology stocks will be tomorrow's winners? The most important considerations are (1) future growth of earnings, and (2) the valuation of those earnings, i.e., the so-called price-earnings (P/E) ratio. Let me illustrate with a simple example. Suppose stock X is selling for $10 a share. Suppose also that Value Line is estimating that the company will earn $1.00 per share this year. Then the stock's current P/E ratio, which is just price divided by per share earnings, is 10. Now, if this company were to double its earnings next year to $2.00 a share, and were to still sell for 10 times earnings (P/E = 10), the company's stock would then sell for $20 a share. If, on the other hand, the company earned only $1.00 a share next year, but its P/E ratio rose to 20, the stock would also sell for $20. In either case, we have the happy result that the stock has doubled. But in the second case, this is only because the market is valuing the earnings at a much higher level. Price-earnings ratios for stocks in general tend to rise during bull markets and fall during bear markets. Thus, the stock of a company earning $1.00 a share year after year will tend to rise and fall with the market, but after several years it will still probably sell for about the same price. On the other hand, a company with growing earnings, although it will also be buffeted by bull and bear markets, should eventually sell for a higher price, based on its higher earnings.

Now it is of course true that the market valuation should reflect what the company's prospects are for the future, but this is not always the case. Often during bull markets, price-earnings ratios for many stocks expand beyond reason, such that investors pay $50 or $100 or more for $1.00 of earnings today. Future earnings would have to rise at an almost impossible rate for the current price to make sense. Turning the P/E on its head, that is, inverting it to make it become an earnings-price ratio, makes this clearer: $1.00 of earnings divided by a price of $20 is .05, or 5 percent. We can think of this as the earnings yield on our investment of $20. When the same stock is selling for $100, the earnings yield is a minuscule 1 percent, incredibly small, and acceptable to investors for only short periods of time. If the company does achieve earnings of, say, $2.00 a share two years later, but the P/E drops to 20, or an earnings yield of 5 percent, the stock will fall from $100 to $40!

During bear markets, P/E ratios often shrink to very low levels, which are just as unrealistic and temporary. When the mood of extreme pessimism ends, stocks rise as P/E's expand, and those companies with rising earnings will thus get a double boost to their prices.

Of course, it is impossible for the individual investor to forecast the earnings or the price/earnings ratios of individual stocks. But Value Line does do this for about four years into the future, which is beyond the time horizon of most investors. Combining future earnings and a price/earnings ratio, Value Line estimates a future average price and a range around it, reflecting the changing moods of Wall Street. This range, called the "three- to five-year appreciation potential," is one of the most important numbers in the Value Line full-page report on an individual stock (see Figure 2.1, line A). While this potential is clearly an educated guess, it provides an objective technique for selecting those stocks that should do well during the next several years.

RULE 1: Appreciation potential must be at least 100 percent to the low end of the range.

A first rule for selecting stocks that will grow substantially is to find stocks that have at least a 100 percent appreciation potential to the low end of the range. While it is all right to hold on to stocks that you already own with appreciation potentials below this benchmark, do not commit new funds to stocks that cannot meet this criterion.

RULE 2: Estimated future earnings must be at least 100 percent higher than earnings of the most recently completed year (or the estimate for the year in progress).

Satisfying Rule 1 is only the first hurdle the prospective company must clear before you vote "yes" with your dollars. Some stocks with high appreciation potential are not forecast to have much higher earnings, but just a much higher price-earnings ratio. These stocks are immediately suspect, because their future appreciation is dependent mainly upon the market placing a higher valuation on the current level of earnings, rather than on a significant rise in earnings. Value Line will often project a higher P/E ratio than the current one if the historical data show that the P/E ratio tended to be higher in the past than at the current time. But betting on a change in the P/E ratio means betting on a change in mood on Wall Street, and that, in my opinion, is too much of a gamble.

Future earnings are marked in Figure 2.1 at line B. Estimated future earnings should be at least twice the level for the most recently completed year to ensure that a large portion of the appreciation potential represents growth rather than revaluation of earnings.

This level test cannot be applied if the most recently completed year resulted in a loss or abnormally low earnings. In such a situation, the Value Line estimate for the year in progress, which appears in a column adjacent to the data for the previous year, should be used as a base for performing the 100 percent test. If both years are abnormally depressed, the stock is disqualified from consideration for purchase.

The ability of management is a key ingredient in reaching the doubling goal. Many technology companies produce exciting new products with great prospects and no earnings growth to show for it, reflecting the inability of management to bring the sales dollars down to the bottom line. How can you detect management problems? There are two hints in the history of earnings section of the Value Line stock report: if there have been either repeated years of losses in the past, or frequent wild fluctuations in earnings, I would be cautious, although I have not formalized this notion into a rule.

RULE 3: A financial strength rating below "B" or a safety rating of "5" (lowest) disqualifies the company.

We also want to sift out firms that could not survive a temporary setback in their fortunes. Toward that end, VLIS reports a financial strength rating and a safety rating (Figure 2.1, lines C and D). These

Figure 2.1: Coherent, Inc.

COHERENT INC. NDQ-COHR

RECENT PRICE	12	P/E RATIO 11.4 (Trailing 14.6 / Median NMF)	RELATIVE P/E RATIO 0.70	DIV'D YLD Nil	VALUE LINE 137

TIMELINESS ③ Average
(Relative Price Perform-ance Next 12 Mos.)

SAFETY ③ Average
(Scale: 1 Highest to 5 Lowest)

BETA .80 (1.00 = Market)

1997-99 PROJECTIONS

	Price	Gain	Ann'l Total Return
High	40	(+235%)	35%
Low	25	(+110%)	20%

Insider Decisions

	J	J	A	S	O	N	D	J	F
to Buy	0	0	0	0	0	0	0	0	0
Options	0	0	0	0	1	0	0	0	0
to Sell	2	0	0	2	0	1	0	0	0

Institutional Decisions

	2Q93	3Q93	4Q93
to Buy	15	12	13
to Sell	6	9	7
Hld'g(000)	5113	5127	5247

Percent shares traded: 24.0 / 16.0 / 8.0

Relative Price Strength

Target Price Range 1997 | 1998 | 1999

15.0 x "Cash Flow" p sh

3-for-2 split / 3-for-2 split / 2-for-2 split

Shaded areas indicate recessions

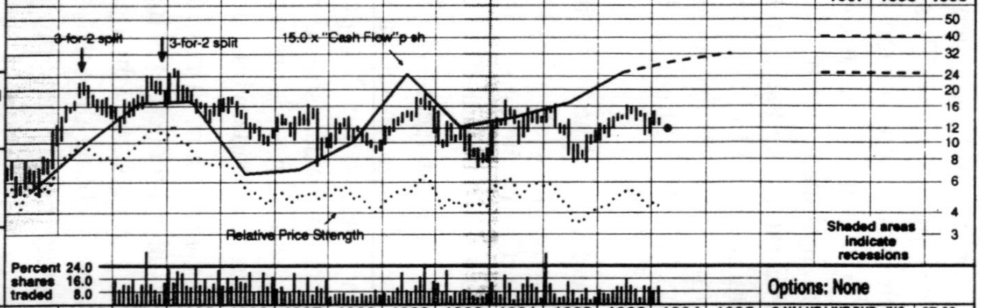

Options: None

1978	1979	1980	1981	1982	1983	1984	1985	1986	1987	1988	1989	1990	1991	1992	1993	1994	1995	© VALUE LINE PUB., INC.	97-99
7.97	11.86	13.28	11.89	13.63	12.43	14.61	16.84	17.43	19.56	22.09	22.63	21.57	22.82	22.83	19.82	21.50	22.55	Sales per sh A	28.65
.61	.89	.60	.62	.35	.64	1.11	1.14	.44	.47	.67	1.65	.81	.93	1.12	1.62	1.95	2.15	"Cash Flow" per sh	2.65
.45	.66	.29	.28	d.12	.37	.79	.81	.11	d.14	.16	.81	d.05	.02	.28	.93	1.05	1.20	Earnings per sh B	1.85
																Nil	Nil	Div'ds Decl'd per sh	Nil
.28	.04	1.57	1.00	.96	.39	.59	1.08	1.12	1.04	1.06	.68	.78	.77	1.66	1.30	.85	.85	Cap'l Spending per sh	.90
2.54	3.36	3.73	5.33	5.21	7.42	9.12	10.28	10.46	10.30	9.76	10.64	10.86	10.64	10.97	11.78	12.00	14.70	Book Value per sh C	19.55
4.11	4.38	4.62	5.84	5.90	7.35	7.63	7.82	7.93	8.13	8.52	8.91	8.87	9.11	9.44	9.93	10.00	10.20	Common Shs Outst'g D	11.00
9.4	13.0	32.2	39.0			21.0	24.0				15.7		NMF	43.5	13.6	Bold figures are		Avg Ann'l P/E Ratio	18.0
1.28	1.88	4.28	4.74	d.12	3.44	1.96	1.95				1.19		NMF	2.64	.80	Value Line estimates		Relative P/E Ratio	1.40
																Nil	Nil	Avg Ann'l Div'd Yield	Nil

CAPITAL STRUCTURE as of 12/25/93

Total Debt $19.8 mill. Due in 5 Yrs $16.4 mill.
LT Debt $12.0 mill. LT Interest $1.5 mill.
(LT interest earned: 4.6x; total interest coverage: 4.0x)

(13% of Cap'l)

Leases, Uncapitalized Annual rentals $4.1 mill.

Pension Liability None

Pfd Stock None

Common Stock 10,106,560 shs.
as of 1/31/94 (87% of Cap'l)

	1982	1983	1984	1985	1986	1987	1988	1989	1990	1991	1992	1993	1994	1995		97-99
Sales ($mill) A	13.63	12.43	111.4	131.7	138.2	159.0	188.1	201.7	191.3	207.8	215.4	196.9	215	230	Sales ($mill)	315
Operating Margin			10.1%	8.6%	3.7%	5.0%	3.5%	9.7%	5.6%	4.9%	6.2%	10.8%	12.0%	12.5%	Operating Margin	13.0%
Depreciation ($mill)			2.3	2.4	4.4	4.9	7.0	7.3	7.7	8.2	7.9	7.3	9.0	9.5	Depreciation ($mill)	11.5
Net Profit ($mill)			6.2	6.5	d.9	d1.1	d1.3	7.4	d.5	NMF	2.6	9.3	10.5	12.5	Net Profit ($mill)	20.0
Income Tax Rate			46.8%	42.0%	NMF	NMF	50.6%	50.6%	NMF	NMF	51.6%	34.0%	35.0%	37.0%	Income Tax Rate	37.0%
Net Profit Margin			5.6%	5.0%	NMF	NMF	NMF	3.7%	NMF	.1%	1.2%	4.7%	5.2%	5.4%	Net Profit Margin	6.4%
Working Cap'l ($mill)			67.6	68.8	60.9	51.6	50.3	68.9	70.2	74.5	78.1	88.3	100	110	Working Cap'l ($mill)	170
Long-Term Debt ($mill)			4.6	2.9	4.2	4.2	3.5	6.3	7.0	6.6	15.6	14.1	12.0	10.0	Long-Term Debt ($mill)	4.0
Net Worth ($mill)			69.5	80.4	82.9	83.7	83.1	94.8	96.3	96.9	103.5	117.0	120	150	Net Worth ($mill)	215
% Earned Total Cap'l			8.6%	8.0%	NMF	NMF	NMF	7.6%	NMF	.5%	2.6%	7.7%	8.5%	8.0%	% Earned Total Cap'l	9.5%
% Earned Net Worth			8.9%	8.1%	NMF	NMF	NMF	7.8%	NMF	.2%	2.6%	8.0%	9.0%	8.0%	% Earned Net Worth	10.0%
% Retained to Comm Eq			8.9%	8.1%	NMF	NMF	NMF	7.8%	NMF	.2%	2.6%	8.0%	9.0%	8.0%	% Retained to Comm Eq	10.0%
% All Div'ds to Net Prof													Nil	Nil	% All Div'ds to Net Prof	Nil

CURRENT POSITION	1992	1993	12/25/93
Cash Assets	29.7	37.1	36.5
Receivables	53.3	43.8	42.2
Inventory (FIFO)	47.3	35.8	37.1
Other	10.7	27.5	25.4
Current Assets	141.0	144.2	141.2
Accts Payable	8.7	9.5	6.6
Debt Due	15.8	7.0	7.8
Other	38.4	39.4	36.4
Current Liab.	62.9	55.9	50.8

ANNUAL RATES of change (per sh)	Past 10 Yrs.	Past 5 Yrs.	Est'd '91-'93 to '97-'99
Sales	5.5%	2.0%	5.0%
"Cash Flow"	8.5%	18.5%	5.0%
Earnings	8.5%	--	28.5%
Dividends	--	--	Nil
Book Value	6.5%	2.0%	10.0%

Fiscal Year Ends	QUARTERLY SALES ($ mill.) A				Full Fiscal Year
	Dec.31	Mar.30	Jun.30	Sep.30	
1991	48.3	54.5	48.3	56.7	207.8
1992	54.7	55.4	50.5	54.8	215.4
1993	46.8	51.3	47.2	51.6	196.9
1994	47.0	57.0	57.0	54.0	215
1995	54.0	59.0	52.0	65.0	230

Fiscal Year Ends	EARNINGS PER SHARE A B				Full Fiscal Year
	Dec.31	Mar.30	Jun.30	Sep.30	
1991	.03	.10	d.23	.12	.02
1992	.11	.14	d.10	.13	.28
1993	.25	.29	.17	.22	.93
1994	.14	.35	.26	.30	1.05
1995	.28	.31	.27	.34	1.20

Cal- endar	QUARTERLY DIVIDENDS PAID				Full Year
	Mar.31	Jun.30	Sep.30	Dec.31	
1990					
1991		NO DIVIDENDS BEING PAID			
1992					
1993					
1994					

(A) Fiscal year ends Sept. 30th.

BUSINESS: Coherent, Inc. designs, manufactures, and markets lasers, laser systems, precision optics, and related accessories (59% of total sales). Medical instruments, incl'd eye care products and surgical laser systems, acent for the balance. Also sells electrical and optical components to other laser systems manufacturers. Acq'd Vinten Electro-Optics '93, sold Coherent General and Coherent Hull in '93. International business, 27% of sales; R&D, 11.0%; wage costs, about 31%. '93 depr. rate: 10.2%. Est'd plant age: 4.5 years. Has 1217 empls, 2,863 stockholders. Insiders own 6.2% of stock; institutions, 19.6% ('93 proxy). Chrmn.: J.L. Hobart. Pres.: H.E. Gauthier. Inc.: CA. Address: 5100 Patrick Henry Drive, PO Box 54980, Santa Clara, CA 95056-0980. Tel.: 408-764-4000.

We believe Coherent Incorporated will have another record breaking year (year ends September 30th). Despite weak first quarter earnings, due primarily to higher research and development costs, late business bookings, and higher currency exchange losses, the company may be primed for its first year of triple digit share-net earnings. The late 1993 sale of Coherent General and Coherent Hull cut expenses significantly, boosting the operating margin almost 75% over the fiscal 1992 figure. With approximately $60 million more product orders already booked, most of which will be shipped in the second quarter, we believe Coherent can earn $1.05 a share in fiscal 1994 and $1.20 in fiscal 1995.

The company has found a delivery system for its erbium laser. In February, Coherent purchased a 37% interest in Infrared Fiber Systems (IFS). Although the price paid for the company was negligible, the payoff could be significant, as IFS currently retains the exclusive rights to a patented fiber needed to transport erbium light. Working together, the laser and fiber can be used for ultra precise cutting or ablation of diseased membrane without damaging surrounding healthy tissue in the neurological, dental, and optical fields. Currently going through Federal Drug Administration clinical trials, the laser could provide an additional 5¢-10¢ a share in earnings by 1996, if all goes as planned.

Sales abroad continue to show good growth prospects. Despite an ongoing recession in Europe and Japan, more than half the company's revenues in the first quarter came from exports. Coherent Electro-Optical realized a 6% increase in revenue, primarily due to the company's November acquisition of its British unit, Vinten Electro-Optics, on a pro-forma basis. We believe that once the overseas market recovers, it will likely contribute 60% of total sales, up from the fiscal 1993 proportion of about 50%.

These shares are ranked 3 (Average) for the next six to 12 months. With a strong European presence established and the divestiture of the two failing subsidiaries, the stock has above-average appreciation potential to 1997-99.
Alex Silverman　　　*March 18, 1994*

(B) Primary earnings. Excl. nonrecurring gains (losses): '83, 21¢; '84, 86¢; '85, 11¢; '89, 13¢; '93, (44¢), 56¢. Next earnings report due mid-April.
(C) Incl. intangibles. In '93: $4.8 mill., $.48/sh.
(D) In millions, adjusted for stock splits.

Company's Financial Strength	B
Stock's Price Stability	25
Price Growth Persistence	10
Earnings Predictability	25

To subscribe call 1-800-833-0046.

ratings reflect detailed analyses of cash flow, composition of debt and its size relative to equity (leverage), and other balance-sheet items which I find are best left to Value Line to interpret. If either of these ratings are at the low end for all VLIS stocks, the company is probably too risky.

RULE 4: Research and Development (R&D) percentage must be at least 7.5 percent.

If a particular stock is still in the running, the next important statistic is the percentage of sales going to research and development (R&D). This crucial statistic is buried in the center of the full-page report (Figure 2.1, line E). For most growing technology companies, the products that will make up the bulk of sales five years from now are not on the market yet. The best indication of the probability of suc-

---

CASE HISTORY: Fairchild Camera and Instrument

Figure 2.2: Fairchild Camera (NYSE-FCI) 1974–1979
I first purchased FCI in 1974. It was my first PAD investment. This company was one of the original high-technology companies of Silicon Valley, and always spent a generous portion of revenues on R&D. Many of its employees went on to start successful electronics companies, but FCI's earnings foundered in spite of its technological excellence. I purchased additional shares in 1977, when the stock was depressed, partly by negative reports in *The Wall Street Journal*. Patience and discipline paid off when FCI was purchased by Schlumberger in 1980. See Chapter 4's merger and buyout section for a discussion of strategies for these situations.

CASE HISTORY: Intel Corporation

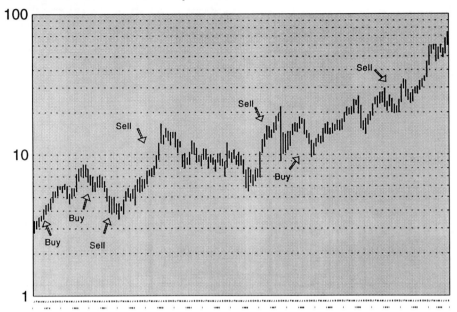

Figure 2.3: Intel Corp. (NDQ-INTC) 1979–1993
Intel, one of my 10 favorite PAD-A stocks, provides an excellent illustration of the PAD-A rules at work over many years and several stock market and technology stock cycles. I first purchased Intel at 3¾ in May 1979, when it met all of the PAD-A requirements for purchase. I purchased additional shares in 1981, half of which I sold for a tax loss at the end of 1981. (I was still getting the bugs out of the system.) I sold additional shares in 1983, when the long-term market-timing indicator of Chapter 6 was signaling a decline. I held the remaining shares patiently until 1987, when the surging market pushed Intel to a triple from original purchase price (see Selling Rule 1, Chapter 4). By April 1987, I had sold all of my Intel shares at a handsome profit. Then I waited. In November 1988, with the stock at 11¼, I pounced. I sold out at exactly 33¾ in February 1992, for another triple. The stock has continued to rise, but I will wait patiently before I pounce yet again. (All prices adjusted for 2-for-1 splits in 1980, 1983, and 1993, and 3-for-2 split in 1987. Vertical axis is logarithmic for clarity.)

cessful new products and innovations is the percent set aside today to create tomorrow's products. My rule here is that R&D must be at least 7.5 percent of sales, or the company is disqualified on the grounds that its competitive chances are weakened and its growth prospects are reduced significantly. Some companies have significant amounts of customer-sponsored research and development. This is not

CASE HISTORY: Microsoft Corporation

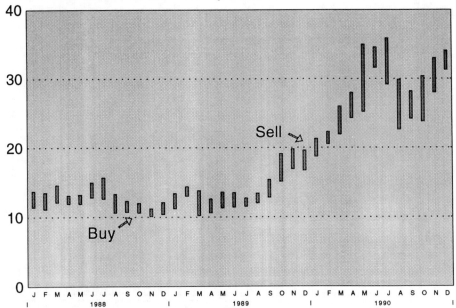

Figure 2.4: Microsoft (NDQ-MSFT) 1988–1990
The PAD-A stock selection rules led me right to Microsoft in 1988. I purchased the stock at 10½ in November 1988, when appreciation potential was about 100 percent. This was one of the few times the stock has ever been cheap enough to buy under the PAD rules. Microsoft had been pushed down by a spate of bad publicity about a delayed rollout of its flagship word-processing software. Up to that time, Microsoft had been the only software house that always met its deadlines, but I felt (correctly) that one delayed product was no reason to panic. I sold my Microsoft shares in 1989 and 1990 at a substantial profit. (With hindsight, it is obvious I sold too soon.) I have been looking for the next Microsoft ever since, and I am counting on the rules of this chapter to help me find it. (All prices adjusted for 100 percent stock dividend in 1990, and 3-for-2 splits in 1991 and 1992.)

nearly as valuable a sign of technological commitment, since the company is not putting aside its own funds for the future. Thus, only company-funded R&D should be counted toward satisfaction of this rule. (Value Line usually reports the two R&D figures separately.)

Even in hard times, companies should maintain the 7.5 percentage if they have confidence in the future. Thus, there should be no exception to this rule. If, however, a company whose stock you have purchased reduces its R&D spending below this level, it should not be sold immediately, but should be considered a candidate for sale when

CASE HISTORY: Quantum Corporation

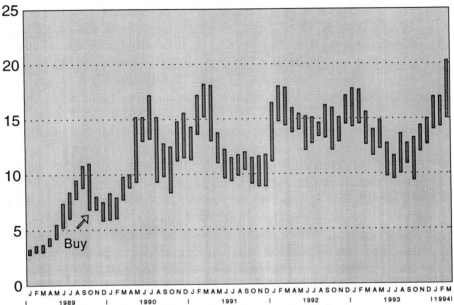

Figure 2.5: Quantum Corporation (NDQ-QNTM) 1989–1994
I created the exception to the 7.5 percent rule to make room for companies like Quantum, a computer disk-drive maker that has experienced several episodes of sales growth so rapid that R&D could not possibly keep up. I established a position in Quantum with three purchases during the period November 1989–January 1990, at an average price of 7. Since that time, Quantum has had two separate years of sales growth that exceeded 50 percent. R&D did periodically fall below 7.5 percent, but I felt that the company was maintaining cutting-edge technology and should be forgiven. The stock has gradually moved higher, and by early 1994 reached 20, close to a "triple" (see Selling Rule 1, Chapter 4). (All prices adjusted for 3-for-2 split in 1991.)

market conditions match those discussed in Chapter 6. The only exception I would make to this rule occurs if the company's sales rise so fast that R&D spending, while rising, falls below 7.5 percent for several quarters.

If 7.5 percent is good, isn't 15 percent better? Perhaps, but at some point a company can be spending too much on R&D. This may be a result of poor management of the R&D function, or it may be traced to a sharp decline in sales. Neither case increases the appeal of the stock. While I have no hard-and-fast rule on this point, once R&D spending reaches 20 percent of sales, I become very cautious.

RULE 5: Short-term performance ranking must be higher than "5" (lowest).

Stocks that meet all of these stringent requirements will be in your portfolio at some time. But clearing these hurdles is still not sufficient to merit an immediate buy. First we must consider long-term market timing, which is discussed in Chapter 6. Buying PAD-A technology stocks when the market is about to begin a major decline is not going to be very profitable. They will decline with the rest of the market, and perhaps even faster. So you must review timing considerations. Just as important, the current prospects of these PAD companies may be especially clouded, leading you to avoid them until a more appropriate time. How can one tell? Value Line also computes a timeliness (Figure 2.1, line F) or short-term (one-year) performance rating for all stocks, from 1 (highest) to 5 (lowest). Stocks that are rated 5 for year-ahead performance should probably be avoided. There is usually a good reason for this low ranking: a severe earnings decline or uncertain prospects over the next few months (new competition, major litigation, or internal restructuring, for example).

As mentioned above, Value Line's reputation has been built partly on its ability to discriminate among stock groups over a period of a year or less. Since it has repeatedly demonstrated that stocks with low rankings tend to do worse on average than stocks with high rankings, it is wise to use this information in timing your PAD purchases, even though you plan to hold stocks much more than one year. Stocks ranked 1, 2, or 3 can be bought without hesitation if long-term market timing suggests that the market is not overvalued. Stocks ranked 4 are more problematic. I would go ahead if everything else about the company is satisfactory. For those stocks ranked 4 or 5 for year-ahead performance, but with future possibilities that are good, it is possible to use a form of technical analysis, discussed below in the section "Technical Analysis," to buy before the performance ranking improves and before the stock moves up in price substantially.

It has been true in recent years that stocks ranked 4 and 5 have done very well in the first weeks of a new year. This is no doubt the result of tax-loss selling at the end of the year, driving these stocks down to unreasonable levels. This is obviously a good time to buy them. Tax-loss selling and strategy are discussed further in Chapter 12.

It is a good idea to scan Value Line every week, even though your current and future portfolio stocks are reviewed only once every three months. Value Line's opinions, particularly for short-term perform-ance, often change more frequently than that. Supplementary reports, which may involve substantial changes in opinion, can be issued at any time. But as a PAD investor, you will not be influenced by short-term changes in either your stocks, the market, or Value Line opin-ions. Additional uses of the VLIS are discussed in the following chapters.

Dividends

I have not discussed dividends for good reason. The technology stocks the PAD-A investor will buy often pay no dividends. None will ever be paying out a large portion of earnings as dividends to stock-holders because the earnings are being reinvested in the business. I consider a large share of earnings paid out in dividends to be a sure sign of a technology company in trouble. PAD-A stocks are purchased for long-term capital gains, and low or zero current income is the price one must pay for this potential. Rapid earnings growth will eventually drive up the stock price even if no dividends are ever paid to shareholders. For example, before Digital Equipment fell on hard times, its stock rose from under $20 to almost $200 without ever paying a dividend (see Figure 4.7).

It is true, however, that many good growth stocks, especially outside the technology sector, pay moderate dividends, which do provide cur-rent income to investors. These stocks can be selected using the rules in Chapter 3. Investors seeking still more current income from their stock portfolios can use the modified rules at the end of Chapter 3 to find good income stocks with the potential to produce rising earnings and dividends.

Other Fundamental Approaches

I have purposely avoided any detailed discussion of balance sheets and net worth à la Graham and Dodd. Value Line will alert you if there are serious problems in this area (see Rule 3). On the other hand, it is unlikely that a good growth stock will sell below book value, for example, but that does not matter. The PAD system is not designed to uncover "turnaround" or especially undervalued stocks.

I am not suggesting that other fundamental methods of stock analysis and selection are worthless. Clearly, they are not. There are many groups of stocks that are undervalued at one time or another, depending on the mood on Wall Street. In general, out-of-favor stocks usually come back into favor, rewarding investors who go against the trend. Even companies in Chapter 11 bankruptcy may be quite profitable as investments, but they will not qualify as PAD stocks.

Technical Analysis

Technicians on Wall Street are not at all interested in the foregoing discussion. It is their belief that movements of a stock's price, volume of trading, relative strength of a stock compared to the market in general, and other even more obscure measures are the best indications of the future trend of a stock's price. A true technician does not even need to know the name of the company or its business. I was once, at a very impressionable age, a technician of the chartist persuasion. Now older and wiser, I have very little faith in the ability of technical analysis alone to help investors. The only situation in which I think it can be useful is in timing purchases of those stocks, selected with the rules listed above, that are poorly ranked for year-ahead performance. It should be no surprise that insiders and sophisticated investors will detect a turnaround in a company's fortunes before the general public or even Value Line is aware of it. To take advantage of their knowledge, those who know often buy the stock, and the price pattern of the stock may reveal this buying. Stripping away all the mysticism surrounding charting, we can note that stocks usually fall, then stop falling, then start going up, then stop going up, and then start falling. Most of technical analysis is designed to determine when these major changes in direction will take place. A PAD stock that is suffering earnings reversals will probably stop falling and start going up before there is an announcement of higher earnings. A chart of the price can reveal this pattern, and justify a *buy* even though Value Line may still rate the company a 4 for near-term performance.

Two of the most common kinds of charts are point-and-figure and bar charts. Many others exist, each with its loyal following. There are many books available in libraries that explain how to construct these charts, and I will restrict the discussion here to one example based on my own experience.

The key feature to look for in a bar chart or a point-and-figure chart is the appearance of sideways movement after a decline. Then, when the stock starts to move up, it is time to *buy*.

For those readers who find this approach irresistibly appealing, as I did in my callow youth, total immersion in technical analysis, fol-

CASE HISTORY: Genrad

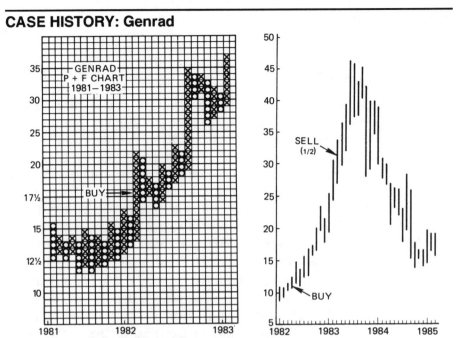

Figure 2.6: Genrad (NYSE-GEN) 1982–1985
Genrad, Inc., is a technology stock which in the past met all of the preceding fundamental criteria. I purchased it first, however, in April 1982, when it was not favor-
ably ranked by VLIS for short-term performance, but the stock chart suggested that
the earnings turnaround was coming. The arrows on the point-and-figure chart and
the bar chart mark my purchase decision. I sold half of my holding 11 months later,
after the stock had almost tripled. The stock continued to rise for a while, but then
retraced all of its rise. (Bar-chart prices adjusted for 3-for-2 split in 1983.)

lowed by complete disillusionment, is probably the best medicine.
One can purchase a compendium of technical analysis from Chartcraft, Inc., which should satisfy the appetite of even the truest gnome
or elf of Wall Street. However, with the one exception I have discussed, I cannot recommend technical analysis for a PAD investor.
Many stocks have short, violent downswings during the course of a
long-term rise to much higher levels. Thus, even if the bar chart turns
bearish, relative strength weakens, and the candlestick chart forms a
pattern called "investor gets mugged," you should continue to hold.
There are too many false signals given by every technical method I
know for them to be of any general use. Note that the point-and-figure chart of Genrad (Figure 2.6) gave several sell signals during its
rapid ascent. Technical indicators of *general* market trends are much
more useful. They are discussed in Chapter 6.

Portfolio Management

Diversification

RULE 6: Diversify!

Any stock that qualifies as a PAD technology stock is a somewhat risky investment for two reasons: (1) the stock is likely to fluctuate more than the general market, so that if the market goes down, it will fall by a greater percentage; and (2) the prospects for the company's future are more uncertain than for other firms in mature industries, which are subject to much slower rates of technological change. For these reasons, you should not put all your eggs in one basket; that is, you need to hold a portfolio of several stocks almost all the time, unless, in anticipation of a bear market, you have been switching to cash, as explained in Chapter 6.

The benefits of diversification can be understood without recourse to serious mathematics. Consider the following example. You have selected five stocks, using the rules listed above. Let's call them stocks A, B, C, D, and E. Suppose that in fact four of these stocks will double in the next two years, and one will drop to zero. (You must be prepared to take some losses when you make a mistake.) If you bought just one of the five, your portfolio would have a 4-out-of-5 chance to increase by 100 percent and a 1-in-5 chance to fall by 100 percent. So if you played this game over and over, you would average gains of 60 percent. Not bad, but you only get to play the game once, and either you gain 100 percent or lose it all. If, instead, you buy all five of the stocks, you will certainly have one that falls to zero, but you will have four that double, so you will make 60 percent every time! You have diversified away the risk of a disaster in this simple example, although you have given up the chance to make a 100 percent killing.[3]

This example is oversimplified, but it still shows the benefits of diversification. I believe you can diversify with as little as $5,000 spread over five stocks, although $20,000 spread over five to ten stocks would probably be better.

If you have a $50,000 portfolio, or your $5,000 portfolio grows to $50,000, you can achieve greater diversification by holding more

---

3.   We have assumed in this example that what happens to Stock A has no effect on
      Stocks B through E, which will clearly not hold for the PAD technology investor, but
      we have also assumed that the portfolio cannot be managed to weed out losers. The
      example is meant strictly for exposition.

Table 2.1:　Recommended Diversification

Portfolio Size	Number of Stocks	$ per Stock
$5,000–$10,000	5	$1,000–$2,000
$10,000–$50,000	5–10	$2,000–$5,000
$50,000–$200,000	10–20	$5,000–$10,000
over $200,000	20	over $10,000

stocks. I have set out some rough guidelines in Table 2.1, which relates size of portfolio to number of stocks held when fully invested. If you keep within the guidelines for your portfolio size, in terms of both number of stocks held and dollar amount per stock, you can be diversified without being spread too thinly. I would initially invest roughly equal amounts in each stock; for example, a 10-stock portfolio bought with $50,000 should have about $5,000 invested in each stock. This rough equality will no doubt disappear as your stocks follow divergent paths, but when you add new stocks, you can again invest a proportional amount. For example, if your $50,000 portfolio has grown to $75,000, and you have $15,000 in cash ready to invest, you could buy two new stocks, putting about $7,500 in each, or three new stocks, putting about $5,000 in each. You would buy at least enough new stocks to maintain a 10-stock portfolio, the minimum for this size portfolio, and you would not let your total number of stocks rise above 15, which, if it did, would put your dollars per stock ($75,000/15) below the minimum of $5,000 for this portfolio size. The limits are broad enough to make it easy to stay within the recommended ranges for number of stocks and dollars per stock for your portfolio size. I have set a maximum of 20 stocks for any size portfolio, in the belief that this is more than enough to reap all the benefits of diversification while still keeping investing as a hobby.

The Buy List

The stocks you buy will come from your "Buy List," comprised of those stocks that satisfy all the rules of Part 1 or Part 2 of this chapter. Those that nearly satisfy all of the rules should be watched carefully, because minor market movements could make them full-fledged buys. With the one exception of "switches" (see Chapter 4), you will buy your Buy List stocks only when the long-term market timing indicator of Chapter 6 is favorable. If the size of the list corresponds to the range of stocks matching your portfolio size (see Table 2.1), you can buy all of your Buy List stocks following the rules of Chapter 4.

It may happen, however, that there are only two or three stocks on your Buy List when the long-term market timing indicator signals "buy" and you have a high level of cash reserves. Committing all of your cash reserves to these few stocks could then drive your dollars-per-stock level above the maximum in the table. While this is an unlikely problem, the solution is straightforward: Buy only those on the Buy List, in amounts consistent with Table 2.1, and hold cash reserves until more stocks appear on the Buy List.

It is also possible that the purchase of all Buy List stocks would make your portfolio exceed the maximum recommended number of stocks. In this situation, you must be more selective. Although I present no rules for this pleasant dilemma, I have solved it by raising my standards until the number of stocks on the Buy List has dropped to the point where I can buy all of them. Rule 5 is my first choice for upgrading, making either a "3" or a "2" (truly picky) a requirement for short-term performance. This upgrade will normally be sufficient, but if not, I would upgrade Rule 1 until the list has shrunk sufficiently.

Mutual Funds as an Alternative

A representative group of PAD technology stocks is included in the appendix to this chapter. While many of these stocks are, and will continue to be, in my PAD portfolio, circumstances change. The reader can use the discussion of each stock in the appendix to see how I have applied the rules of this chapter in the past, but purchase decisions must be based on current Value Line reports. If this still seems too daunting a task, or if the risks of individual stock selection seem too great, consider "no-load" mutual funds as an alternative. There are a number of them that invest in technology stocks exclusively, and the charges made for managing your money are quite small. Investing in a mutual fund family that also has a cash fund would enable you to use the long-term timing techniques of Chapter 6, switching to cash to try to avoid the worst parts of the inevitable bear markets of the future. *A complete set of PAD rules for mutual fund selection is set out in Chapter 5.* In fact, a blend of mutual funds and individual stocks may be ideal until you have demonstrated to yourself that you are a talented stock picker.

SUMMARY OF RULES FOR PART 1

1. Appreciation potential must be at least 100 percent to the low end of the range.

2. Estimated future earnings must be at least 100 percent higher than earnings of the most recently completed year (or the estimate for the year in progress).

3. A financial strength rating below "B" or a safety rating of "5" (lowest) disqualifies the company.

4. Research and development (R&D) percentage must be at least 7.5 percent.

5. Short-term performance ranking must be higher than "5" (lowest).

6. Diversify!

SOURCES FOR THE PAD INVESTOR

Black, Fischer, "Yes, Virginia, There Is Hope: Test of Value Line Ranking System," *Financial Analysts Journal* (Sept.–Oct. 1973). The first academic test of the Value Line ranking system.

Broughton, John B. and Don M. Chance, "The Value Line Enigma Extended: An Examination of the Performance of Option Recommendations," *Journal of Business* (Oct. 1993). Yup, they do options too.

Copeland, Thomas E. and David Mayers, "The Value Line Enigma (1965-1978)," *Journal of Financial Economics* (Nov. 1982). There is still hope!

Encyclopedia of Stock Market Techniques. Published by Chartcraft/Investors Intelligence, 30 Church Street, P.O. Box 2046, New Rochelle, NY 10801. Includes several supplements.

Huberman, Gur and Shmuel Kandel, "Value Line Rank and Firm Size," *Journal of Business* (Oct. 1987). Not only is there still hope, but the "firm size" effect cannot explain the Value Line anomaly.

Value Line Investment Survey. Published weekly by Value Line, Inc., 220 E. 42nd St, New York, NY 10017-5891. My bible. Available at many public and university libraries, or by subscription for about $500 a year. A must.

PART 2: STOCK SELECTION RULES USING
THE *VALUE LINE OTC SPECIAL SITUATIONS SERVICE*

Big technology companies generally start out small. Their most rapid growth in earnings (and often stock price) generally occurs before they achieve the coveted NYSE listing, media coverage, and Wall Street following. Rather than wait for these companies to grow large enough to be covered by the *Value Line Investment Survey*, and thus be eligible for PAD-A investors to add to their portfolios, the "special situation" PAD approach targets these companies when they are still very young. Of course, many small companies remain small, or even shrink (I have owned my share of these "dwarfs"), so careful stock selection and good long-term market timing are as crucial as ever. A very large dose of patience and discipline is required too, since the risks of small-company PAD-A investing are greater than the risks in any other PAD variation. The risks are worth taking for many investors, however, since the potential rewards are great.

I first began developing the "special situation" variation of the PAD System in 1983. I did not make my first investments until 1984, however, since I was willing to be governed by the long-term market timing rules of Chapter 6, which suggested (correctly) that 1983 was not a good year to buy stock. Since 1984, I have monitored and bought a number of PAD "specials" with a steadily rising degree of success. A carefully selected group of these aggressive growth companies will complement well a portfolio of PAD stocks and mutual funds selected with the rules of this and other chapters.

The basic source of investment information for PAD-A stocks is the *Value Line OTC Special Situations Service* (VLSS), published by Value Line, Inc., the publishers of the *Value Line Investment Survey*. Each stock recommended and reviewed by the VLSS is called a "special situation," which Value Line defines as:

. . . a security whose market price stands to rise sharply as a result of a major prospective gain in underlying earning power. This increased potential may result from the introduction of new products or processes, from the particularly rapid expansion of a market in which the company has a strong position, from a change in management or from other unusual—and frequently non-recurring—developments.

These special situations are often small technology companies, but some are as "no-tech" as Cracker Barrel Old Country Stores. The rules below do not eliminate a company such as Cracker Barrel, and no-tech companies can prosper mightily. Nonetheless, I restrict my PAD specials search to technology companies in the belief that the greatest successes will be found in this group. Technology companies can be easily identified in the Business section of the Value Line reports (Figure 2.7, line A).

The VLSS is published 24 times a year, on the second and fourth Mondays of each month, and is available in a limited number of public libraries. Each issue contains a detailed report on a newly recommended special situation, regular supervisory reviews of previously recommended special situations, a general news summary for all stocks covered by the service, and a summary index with current advice on all special situations still under review. Once each quarter, VLSS issues an updated report on all recommended specials that have been closed out, that is, recommended for sale by subscribers. After closeout, the stocks are not reviewed again.

VLSS has only four categories of advice for each special situation: (1) especially recommended, (2) buy/hold, (3) hold, and (4) switch, which is the sale and closeout advice. Each new special situation starts out in the "especially recommended" category and eventually ends up in the "switch" category. In the interim, which in many cases spans several years, Value Line's advice can fluctuate between "especially recommended" and "hold" many times. VLSS recommends that subscribers commit new funds to "especially recommended" stocks, although "buy/hold" stocks can also be purchased. "Hold" stocks are to be held with no new commitments made until the ranking improves. VLSS also projects a three- to five-year average price, but does not report a range of future prices that would be comparable to that reported in the VLIS.

A sample quarterly report on a special situation has been reproduced as Figure 2.7. It is instructive to compare this report with the full-page VLIS report of Figure 2.1. Special-situation firms like Komag, Inc., often have fairly short operating histories compared to most companies, and thus safety, financial strength, short-term performance, and other rankings are not calculated for them. No doubt, almost all of the technology special situations would be classified as above average in volatility and below average in safety. Some additional data are available on these companies in their original four-page recommendation reports, which subscribers can obtain from Value Line. If this report is more than two years old, however, it is preferable to write to the company itself for the latest 10-K report. Company addresses appear at the end of the Business section of the

Figure 2.7: Komag, Inc. (NDQ-KMAG)

The Value Line OTC Special Situations Service/**Supervisory Reviews**/ Mar. 14, 1994

KOMAG, INC. (OTC—KMAG)

(B) BASIS FOR|BUY/HOLD|RECOMMENDATION

The near-term outlook for Komag brightened substantially when the company announced recently that its Dastek unit would exit the thin-film recording head business. Dastek, a joint venture with Asahi Glass America, has been a drain on earnings for the past two years as it struggled to gain a foothold in the thin-film head market. Now, with the attractiveness of this market on the decline due to competitive pressure from older technologies, Komag has decided to focus on its core thin-film media business. The good news for investors is that Komag's media operations have been highly successful through the years and posted solid growth in 1993 despite the turmoil in the disk drive market. And though intense price competition is a constant in the media market, Komag, with its low-cost manufacturing capacity, looks poised to deliver steady sales growth and solid profits in the current year. Though the company's shares have staged an impressive run of late, we think there is more room to the upside; hence, we've raised our rating on these shares to Buy/Hold. Investors should note, however, that the ups and downs of the disk drive industry make this situation one not without risk.

Business: Komag, Inc. is the world's largest supplier of computer hard disks for high-performance disk drives. The company produces disks in the United States and Malaysia and supplies the Japanese market through its joint venture with Asahi Glass. Dastek Inc., Komag's recording head joint venture with Asahi Glass America, has supplied thin-film heads since 1991, but is now exiting that business. Pres: Stephen C. Johnson. Address: 275 South Hillview, Milpitas, CA 95035 (408-946-2300).

Recommendation: Buy/Hold
Recent Price: 25½   (A)
Estimated Dividend Yield: Nil
1996–98 Potential Value:|60 (+140%)| (C)
Originally Recommended at 12⅝ on October 12, 1987
Performance Record: +102%
Corresponding Dow Jones Change: +51%

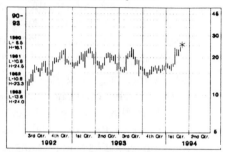

1996–98 PROJECTED VALUATION

Sales: $625 mill.	**Shs outstanding:** 23,500,000 (11% increase)
Profit Margin: 16%	**Projected growth rate:** 31% (1992 to 1996–98)
Earnings per share: $3.00	**Price-earnings multiple:** 20.0
	Normal Average 3- to 5-Year Price: 60

ANALYSIS

Komag reported a fourth-quarter loss of $1.35 a share on revenues of $91.2 million. The bottom line included a one-time charge of $35.4 million, or $1.61 a share, related to Dastek's recently announced exit from the thin-film head business. Excluding the charge, Komag posted a profit of $5.7 million, or 26¢ a share, compared with a profit of $4.4 million, or 20¢ a share, a year ago. For the full year, Komag's bottom line showed a loss of 45¢ a share, compared to a profit of 79¢ last year, and revenues came in at $385.4 million, compared with $326.8 million in 1992.

Komag expects to have fulfilled Dastek's existing customer commitments by the midpoint of the year. The charge covers the costs of finishing off these contracts, paring the bulk of Dastek's U.S.-based work force, and any related asset sales. Meanwhile, approximately 70 people remain in Dastek's research department working on magneto-resistive heads, a next-generation technology that could become marketable next year. Komag is presently seeking additional sources of financing for these efforts and hopes to have announcements forthcoming in the not-too-distant future.

Without the expenses of Dastek's thin-film head efforts, Komag's earnings should show a dramatic rebound this year. The media business was solidly profitable last year and should remain so in 1994 despite an expected narrowing of gross margins. We look for revenues to reach $385 million this year, compared with media sales of $334.4 million in 1993. At the bottom line, we're looking for earnings of $2.00 a share.   *S.M.B.*

CAPITAL STRUCTURE as of 10/3/93

Debt: $51.7 mill.   Pfd Stock: None
Shareholders' Equity $282.6 mill. (21,574,154 shares)

	1990	1991	1992	1993	1994
Sales ($mill)	149.9	279.2	326.8	385.4	*390*
Profit Margin ❶	12.1%	10.2%	6.9%	--	*16.5%*
Tax Rate	37.1%	51.0%	81.2%	--	*30%*
Earn'gs per sh ❷	.88	.74	.79	d.45	*2.00*
Shs Outst'g (mill)	14.7	20.5	21.1	21.8	*22.3*
Div'ds per sh	--	--	--	--	*Nil*
Book Value sh	7.85	9.86	11.80	11.65	*13.60*
% Earn'd Tot Cap	11%	8%	3%	--	*13%*
% Earn'd Net W	12%	8%	7%	--	*15%*
W'rk'g Cap ($mill)	58.1	97.8	97.9		
Current Ratio	3.4	2.9	2.8		
Avg Ann'l P/E	.3 0	23.4	20.3		

Cal-ender	QUARTERLY SALES ($mill.)				Full Year
	Mar. 31	June 30	Sept. 30	Dec. 31	
1991	64.2	72.7	70.0	72.3	279.2
1992	71.1	76.5	82.9	96.3	326.8
1993	93.6	103.2	97.5	91.2	385.4
1994					*390*

Cal-ender	QUARTERLY EARNINGS (Per Share)				Full Year
	Mar. 31	June 30	Sept. 30	Dec. 31	
1991	.38	.24	.10	.04	.74
1992	.14	.16	.29	.20	.79
1993	.35	.37	.19	❸d1.35	❸d.45
1994					*2.00*

❶ -Pretax. ❷ -Excludes extraordinary income: 2¢/sh. in 1990, 1¢/sh in 1991. ❸ -Includes one-time restructuring charge of $35.4 million ($1.61/sh.)

S-846   Factual material is obtained from sources believed to be reliable, but the publisher is not responsible for any errors or omissions contained herein.

To subscribe call 1-800-833-0046

quarterly review (Figure 2.7, line A). If the quarterly review is abbreviated, as is sometimes the case, refer back to the original recommendation report for the address.

The difference in format and reporting between the *Value Line Investment Survey* and the *OTC Special Situations Service* forces us to modify significantly the rules of Part 1. These modifications are spelled out below.

RULE 1S: A special situation must be rated at least a "buy/hold."

One of the ways of reducing the risk of special-situation investing is to follow the Value Line advice on new purchases. If the VLSS current opinion on a special is "hold" (Figure 2.7, line B), it is advising against new commitments. Heed this advice. Either appreciation potential is relatively low, or the company's growth rate is temporarily impaired. Of course, it is quite likely that any special-situation stock you purchase will at some time be rated a "hold." I would continue to hold the stock, unless the market rules of Chapter 6 call for a general selling program. Then stocks in the "hold" category are prime candidates for your Sell List (see the special PAD sell rules below).

RULE 2S: A special situation must have a three- to five-year appreciation potential of at least 200 percent.

Since special-situation stocks are much riskier than other stocks, potential appreciation must be greater than the 100 percent of Part 1 to justify the risks. The rule I use is that the special stock must have three- to five-year appreciation potential of at least 200 percent (Figure 2.7, line C). This rule serves an additional purpose beyond weeding out stocks with subpar potential: many of the newly recommended specials have appreciation potentials of 120–180 percent. Thus, a PAD special investor will rarely buy any special-situation stocks when they are first recommended, waiting instead until they have declined below their initial recommendation price. It is usually impossible to buy a special-situation stock at the initial recommendation price anyway, since many VLSS subscribers rush out and buy the stock immediately. This rush forces up the price and drives the appreciation potential even lower. Rule 2S will keep you from "running with the crowd."

Total return on a special situation will come almost exclusively from this projected price appreciation. A few companies may pay token dividends, in part to broaden interest in their stocks. I would not count the dividend return for a special situation except as a last "tie breaker" when selecting these stocks for purchase. The dividends themselves are small enough to be a good source of "mad money." Indulge yourself, on a small scale, of course.

RULE 3S: Purchase one-half of your eventual investment when Rules 1S and 2S are satisfied. Then wait at least three months before completing your investment.

Value Line itself recommends spreading out purchases of special-situation stocks. This is sage advice. Buy only half of your eventual position when the special stock first qualifies under Rules 1S and 2S. Then wait three months before committing the remainder of your funds. If the stock no longer meets purchase requirements, find another that does. If long-term market timing (Chapter 6) forbids a purchase, continue to wait. Some stocks may "get away" from a PAD special investor with these rules, but that is the price of patience and discipline.

RULE 4S: Do not purchase additional shares more than once.

The urge to continue averaging down is always strong, and it must be stoutly resisted. Some specials will decline to the neighborhood of zero before Value Line recommends "switch." Do not compound your error by adding to your position more than once.

I apply this rule even if I have liquidated the stock entirely and have repurchased at a later date. Given the high degree of risk involved, two chances are enough. A second purchase must be the last; the investing game is not a fight to the death.

Special PAD Sell Rules

In Chapter 4, "Buying and Selling Stocks," I list and discuss rules for buying and selling PAD stocks covered by the *Value Line Investment Survey*. These rules are vitally important for PAD success. The rules for buying stock and maintaining a Buy List can be applied without modification to PAD special-situation investing. Selling rules, however, must be substantially modified, since there is a qualitative difference in the information available. PAD-A investors holding special situations should substitute the selling rules listed below for those of Chapter 4.

RULE 5S: Sell all of your holdings of a stock that is rated "switch" by Value Line.

CASE HISTORY: Autodesk

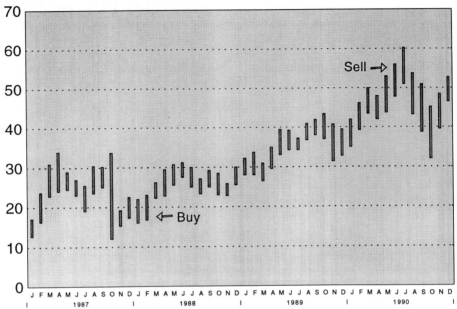

Figure 2.8: Autodesk (NDQ-ACAD) 1987–1990

Autodesk, Inc., is a case in point. I first purchased this stock in 1988 at a price of 17⅝, when it was "dividend-free." Autodesk paid a special one-time $1.50 per share dividend in the summer of 1989. The company's sales and earnings growth was so rapid that the cash was piling up faster than it could be put to use. One analyst stated that "they could buy the city of Sausalito." Instead they gave stockholders a bonus payment, which this stockholder promptly spent. (PAD investors should be able to have some fun!) The company then initiated a regular, albeit small, quarterly dividend payment, which I also spent. The dividends were just the icing on a good-sized cake, since I sold my Autodesk shares for triple my cost in June 1990.

"Switch" advice is similar to a Value Line "5" for short-term performance, but it is more serious, since Value Line coverage will cease and it will become impossible to apply PAD special rules to your holding. Just as important, Value Line does not issue a "switch" recommendation lightly. Trust them. If the long-term market timing indicator of Chapter 6 permits, invest the proceeds from your sale in another special situation satisfying Rules 1S–4S.

RULE 6S: Sell one-fourth to one-half of your holding when the stock has tripled in price.

CASE HISTORY: Silicon General

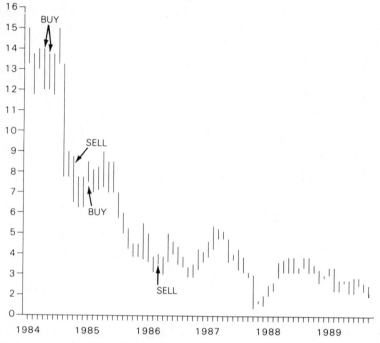

Figure 2.9: Silicon General (OTC-SILN) 1987–1989
My unpleasant experience with Silicon General convinced me that Rule 4S should not be violated. I first purchased this stock at 13 in early 1984, sold out at 7 for a big loss in October 1984, and then tried again with a second purchase at 7 in December 1984. While Value Line remained neutral to optimistic during much of this period, and the three- to five-year projected appreciation was enormous, the company seemed to be going nowhere fast, and the stock performed worse than that. Once I had made my second purchase, however, I wisely decided to spread my risk among other PAD stocks. By February 1986, I was willing to throw in the towel for the last time at a price of (gulp) 4. Value Line continued to review the company until June 1989, when VLSS changed its ranking to "switch" (see Rule 5S). By the time they threw in the towel, the stock was down to 2⅜, untouched by the bull market of the 1980s. (The stock subsequently fell to 1⅜ before recovering. This is a risky business!)

This rule is identical to the standard PAD selling rule and is a crucial one for maintaining patience. Specials often take years to blossom, but when they grow, the growth can be astounding. A number of Value Line specials have eventually appreciated more than 1,000 percent.

RULE 7S: Sell additional fractions of your holding at higher multiples of your cost.

These trees will not grow to the sky either, and sometimes big trees are felled in the forest. Bank some of those profits!

RULE 8S: Sell all of your shares when a merger or buyout is announced.

The announcement of a merger or buyout is almost always accompanied by a rapid run-up in price. Since the target company will soon go out of existence, congratulate yourself on finding it first and take your profit.

RULE 9S: Select stocks rated "hold" with low appreciation potential for your Sell List.

When the market-timing rules of Chapter 6 require you to make up a Sell List and begin selling stock and increasing cash reserves, specials qualifying under Rule 9S should be among your prime candidates, since they are the most vulnerable to a major market decline. Specials rated "hold" but with high appreciation potential are next in line after all Rule 9S stocks have been sold, but these are clearly less desirable sell candidates. I would search the rest of my PAD portfolios carefully for Sell List stocks before selling these "holds."

RULE 10S: Do not "churn" your specials portfolio.

It is tempting to consider switching out of specials that have been downgraded to "hold" and into new or existing specials that are "especially recommended." Resist this temptation. A "hold" means just that. The potential is still there, and specials often require much patience.

RULE 11S: Diversify!

You can achieve a small reduction in risk by purchasing several specials. I am comfortable with four to six of them. Although many of these stocks will tend to move together in the short run, eventually the market sorts them out into winners and losers. Do not bet the farm on just one. The lesson of diversification from Part 1 of this chapter applies.

In recent years, VLSS has expanded its coverage to include biotechnology companies, which makes diversification a little easier. Biotech companies like Mycogen (see the appendix to this chapter) march to

CASE HISTORY: Cognex Corporation

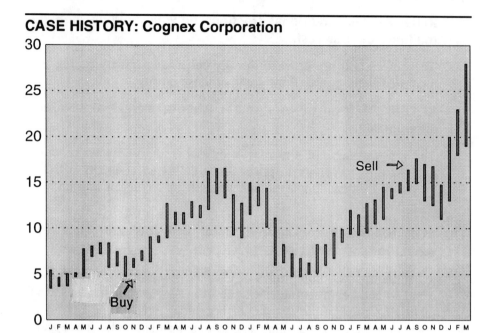

Figure 2.10: Cognex (NDQ-CGNX) 1990–1994
Cognex is an excellent illustration of the rewards and risks of special-situation investing. The stock's price history also demonstrates the vital importance of both
patience and discipline. I bought Cognex at 6¼ in November 1990, when the stock
had 200 percent appreciation potential, and the long-term timing indicators of
Chapter 6 were favorable. I was rewarded with a rapid rise in the stock which
almost reached a "triple" in 1992. The stock then nosedived, losing almost half its
value in a matter of months. Rather than panic, I waited patiently for a comeback,
since the company's growth prospects were as bright as ever. I was rewarded with
a big rally in 1993: I sold half my shares at 15⅜ in August (a little shy of a triple,
but long-term market timing suggested the market would be weak and I needed to
raise my cash percentage); the stock then rallied as high as 28 in early 1994, and
it was time to sell additional shares (Rule 7S). (All prices adjusted for 2-for-1 stock
splits in 1992 and 1993.)

the beat of a different drummer: These companies often have no current earnings, and their stock prices depend crucially on prospects for
products still "in the pipeline" and future R&D successes. Thus the
high degree of risk associated with biotechnology is offset to some
degree by stock price movements, which are not highly correlated
with the electronic technology stocks followed by VLSS.

Specials investing is bound to exact a greater toll than standard PAD
technology investing, since the price swings are even more violent.
Thus, it is only for those PAD investors who have enough patience

CASE HISTORY: Xilinx

Figure 2.11: Xilinx (NDQ-XLNX) 1992–1994
Xilinx also illustrates the patience required while waiting for a triple. I purchased the stock at 18¾ in June 1992, when this electronics special situation had 200 percent appreciation potential. For months the stock was stuck in a trading range between 16 and 23. Then the rising earnings trend finally got Wall Street's attention, and Xilinx began riding the wave of OTC high-tech fever: The stock zoomed to 54½, and I was about to call my broker. But Xilinx turned on a dime and fell to 40. So I waited. My patience was rewarded when the stock reached my target of 56¼ in March 1994.

and discipline to resist the euphoria at the top and the gloom and doom at the bottom. To be safe, a new PAD investor should probably limit holdings of stocks covered by the VLSS to no more than 10 percent of his or her portfolio. Even an experienced PAD investor should probably devote a maximum of 20 percent of his or her portfolio to these stocks.

Occasionally, a special-situation stock is successful enough over the years to be promoted to review by the *Value Line Investment Survey*. Novell (see the appendix and Figure 4.3) is just one of several such stocks that have received this dual coverage. If you own such a stock, be governed by the *Value Line Investment Survey* and the standard PAD rules, since the coverage in the VLIS is much more detailed and frequent.

CASE HISTORY: Caere Corporation

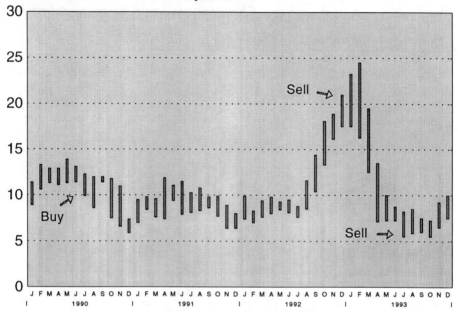

Figure 2.12: Caere Corporation (NDQ-CAER) 1990–1993
Caere unfortunately shows that what goes up can often come back down. And fast.
Model Portfolio-A of the *PAD System Report* purchased Caere, a leader in optical
scanning software, in July and August 1990, at an average price of 10¼. The stock
was mostly "underwater" until the summer of 1992, when it exploded from 8 to 27
in a few short months. At this point, the speed and extent of the run-up, coupled
with a fresh market-timing sell signal (see Chapter 6), convinced us to lighten up a
bit. We sold one-fifth of our holding in December 1992. At this point Caere's earnings growth hit a brick wall and the stock went into a "sumo high dive." It hit the
bottom of the pool at 6. The *PAD System Report* then sold the rest of its holding.
Another investing stripe, right across the shoulders!

SUMMARY OF RULES FOR PART 2

1S. A special situation must be rated at least a "buy/hold."

2S. A special situation must have a three- to five-year appreciation
potential of at least 200 percent.

3S. Purchase one-half of your eventual investment when Rules 1S
and 2S are satisfied. Then wait at least three months before
completing your investment.

4S. Do not purchase additional shares more than once.

CASE HISTORY: Silicon Systems (SIL)

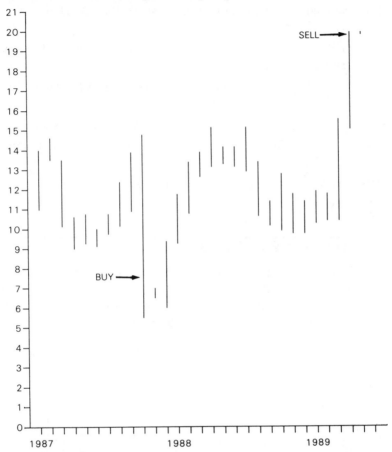

Figure 2.13: Silicon Systems (NYSE-SIL) 1987–1989
Silicon Systems is a perfect example of a "chalkboard touchdown." Everything went just as planned. I began monitoring SIL closely in 1987, although the long-term market-timing rule of Chapter 6 forced me to wait patiently for the market to return to saner levels. When the stock market crashed, taking Silicon Systems with it, I pounced. I purchased two sizable blocks at 7¾ in October 1987. The stock then began an immediate but slow recovery. I was content to hold on as long as the company prospered in its electronics niche, even though the shares languished for months at a time. After the company moved to the NYSE, the big play occurred. First came the vague rumors, with increasing volume and sharp rallies. Then, as John Madden would say, "Boom!": TDK announced they would pay $20 per share hard cash for the company. I sold at 19½, and began looking for the next Silicon Systems.

Summary of Special Pad Sell Rules

5S. Sell all of your holdings of a stock that is rated "switch" by Value Line.

6S. Sell one-fourth to one-half of your holding when the stock has tripled in price.

7S. Sell additional fractions of your holding at higher multiples of your cost.

8S. Sell all of your shares when a merger or buyout is announced.

9S. Select stocks rated "hold" with low appreciation potential for your Sell List.

10S. Do not "churn" your specials portfolio.

11S. Diversify!

SOURCE FOR THE PAD INVESTOR

The *Value Line OTC Special Situations Service.* Published by Value Line, Inc., 220 E. 42nd St, New York, NY 10017-5891. The service is available in some libraries. Subscribers to the regular Value Line receive a substantial discount.

APPENDIX 2
MY TEN FAVORITE PAD-A STOCKS

The 10 stocks listed below have often qualified as PAD technology stocks. All of them have been in my portfolio or the portfolio of the *PAD System Report* in the past, and many will no doubt be in these portfolios in the future. But this list can in no way substitute for the application of the PAD rules to current Value Line and Value Line Special Situations reports. A PAD technology investor should review *all* of the stocks in PAD industries at least occasionally.

Autodesk

Autodesk is tops in the field of PC-based CAD (computer-aided design) software. Its flagship product, called AutoCAD, dwarfs all others in sales, and the company continually revises and upgrades this award-winning product to stay ahead of the competition. Although earnings growth can be temporarily derailed when "glitches" appear in a new release of AutoCAD, the company has always recovered and then forged ahead again. Diversification efforts, through acquisitions and R&D, are finally beginning to pay off, too.

Cognex

Whether or not machines can be made to think, Cognex can make machines see. The company is the world leader in machine-vision systems and is constantly introducing new and better versions of its equipment. As Cognex's products become ever more versatile and less costly, the potential market for these systems will grow rapidly.

Hewlett-Packard

HP is still a major force in electronics, computers, and precision instruments. HP made a well-timed bet on RISC technology for its chips, and the company remains a world leader in computer peripherals. Many other technology giants have fallen by the wayside (IBM, Digital), but Hewlett-Packard has continued to grow and prosper in spite of its large size and the fierce competition in all of its product lines.

Intel

This is the gem of the semiconductor industry. Other old favorites of ours (Advanced Micro Devices) have fallen behind in the technology race while Intel has forged ahead with chips like the 486 and Pentium families. These chips and their brethren will power many millions of desktop machines in the 1990s. Intel's R&D effort guarantees that long before these chips are obsolete, the "P6" and then the "P7" will appear. It will be difficult for other chip makers producing alternative PC "platforms" to hit such a fast-moving target.

Microsoft

High-powered PC hardware is useless without the software to make it run, and Microsoft is the premier software house, led by one of the industry's true visionaries. Their broad product line includes excellent spreadsheet, word-processing, and recreational software. Microsoft also has a near stranglehold on operating-system software, for IBM and clone PCs, which is necessary to make the application software work. While nobody likes DOS, millions of us still use it. The natural "upgrade" path for most of us still leads to some form of Windows, also a Microsoft product. Although competition in operating systems is gradually intensifying, Microsoft spends enough on R&D to stay on top.

Mycogen

The biotechnology revolution will revolutionize food production, and may save our planet's environment as well. Mycogen's part in this rosy scenario is the production of "biopesticides," biologically engineered pesticides that destroy agricultural pests and then degrade quickly without harming the soil or humans. In addition, Mycogen has made an acquisition that has put it in the race to "bioengineer" plants with built-in resistance to pests. Mycogen thus offers tremendous promise, although the risks are also significant, since the company has yet to earn an annual profit.

Novell

Personal computers (PCs) will soon be as common as telephones. Many of them, especially in offices, are already linked together. Novell is one of the leading firms in this "network" effort, which has led to rapid growth for the company. Although this growth was temporarily interrupted in 1993, it should resume by mid-decade.

Octel

Telephones will become more like PCs. Voice mail, voice messaging, and yes, "press '1' now" will become even more common and useful, and perhaps less frustrating. Octel is the world leader in voice information systems, and high R&D spending should keep it on the cutting edge of the information revolution.

Stratus Computer

Stratus is a major manufacturer of "fault-tolerant" computers, which are machines that suffer almost no downtime. This feature is crucial for many business applications, such as On-Line Transactions Processing (OLTP). Although IBM is no longer a big buyer of Stratus machines, the company has upgraded and broadened its product line and found many new customers to replace the lost IBM business.

Thermo Instrument

Thermo is a subsidiary of Thermoelectron, one of my 10 favorite PAD-C stocks (see the appendix to Chapter 3). Thermo Instrument has built an enviable growth record serving three markets: monitoring instruments, used for worker safety and measuring air pollution; analytical instruments, which can test for minute amounts of pesticides in food and measure toxic substances; and environmental services, with a nationwide network of laboratories and engineering consulting offices that are helping clean up polluted water and soil. All of these markets should grow rapidly for many years to come.

CHAPTER 3
INDIVIDUAL STOCK SELECTION: THE CONSERVATIVE APPROACH (PAD-C)

INTRODUCTION

While holding a variety of technology stocks helps reduce the risk of PAD investing, it provides no protection against either general slowdowns in the growth of technology companies, or extended visits by technology stocks to Wall Street's "doghouse" of undervaluation. Investors holding only technology stocks were hit with both a general slowdown and undervaluation during much of the 1980s. A recurrence of this unfortunate combination cannot be ruled out in the future, since technology stocks often boom when the market is rising and drop sharply when the market is weak. These stocks are also more sensitive to earnings disappointments, since investors are buying future earnings growth with little or no dividend to help prop up the price.

While a PAD investor willing to live and die with technology can do so, and do well, the chastening experience of the late 1980s, and the excellent performance of many PAD-C stocks, have convinced me that the typical PAD investor should hold more than just the technology stocks selected with the rules of Chapter 2. Indeed, a conservative investor may want to use the rules in this chapter to create and manage a portfolio that contains no technology stocks at all, although even a conservative investor should be willing to hold technology stocks that meet all the criteria set out below. On the other hand, a PAD investor sold on technology can also use the PAD-C rules to manage a portfolio of non-technology stocks, while gradually shifting funds into PAD-A stocks.

RULES FOR CONSERVATIVE PAD INVESTING

The sections below present a modified set of rules that expand the PAD system to nontechnology growth stocks. Chapter 2 (Part 1) rules are included for comparison. A special section at the end of this chapter is designed for conservative PAD investors for whom current income is of primary importance.

RULE 1: Appreciation potential must be at least 100 percent to the low end of the range.

RULE 1C: Average annual total return must be at least 19 percent to the low end of the range.

While it would be possible to keep Rule 1 intact, it does severely penalize any stock that pays a substantial dividend. Even though dividend payments may not be as valuable after tax as capital gains are, they do provide current income and probably some price stability. A moderate-growth dividend payer may then provide a total return (dividends plus capital gains) equal to a fast-growth firm paying no dividend. Dividends and capital gains are the two factors that determine the annual total return reported by Value Line. These numbers appear just to the right of the three- to five-year price range (see Figure 2.1).

I have selected 19 percent as a minimum annual total return to stay as close to the original PAD System rules as possible, since an 18.9 percent annual total return for four years (midway between three and five years) will turn $1 into $2, which is the doubling requirement of Rule 1. The one drawback of Rule 1C is that the annual total return numbers do not appear in the Value Line weekly summary index, and thus individual full-page stock reports must be examined to find suitable candidates for satisfaction of the rule and, hence, purchase. If the current price of a stock under consideration is different from the one in the full-page report, which will almost certainly be the case, it will be necessary to recalculate the annual total return based on the current price. A shorthand procedure that will give an approximate annual total return is described in Appendix B to this chapter. (This calculation is done automatically by the PAD Stock Selector software.)

I do believe that at least half of the total return should come from capital gains. Many very high-yield companies may face great difficulties in maintaining the dividend, especially if the dividend exhausts the lion's share of earnings (a caution flag). Another caution flag is occasionally raised by Value Line when they report a range for the

CASE HISTORY: Sigma-Aldrich (SIAL)

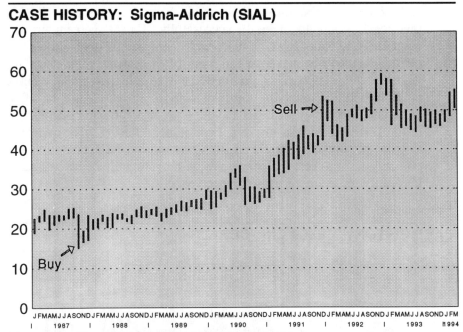

Figure 3.1: Sigma Aldrich (OTC-SIAL) 1987–1994
Sigma-Aldrich is one of my 10 favorite PAD-C stocks. The first cash reserves I committed to the stock market after the crash of 1987 went into SIAL shares at a price of 16. Using the technique outlined in the Appendix A to this chapter, it took me only a few minutes to determine that Sigma met the 19 percent rule after the crash. The stock did not quite meet the 100 percent rule of Chapter 2, however, so without the modifications of Rule IC, I would have missed an excellent opportunity. The shares recovered almost immediately and rose to new all-time highs long before the general market did. I sold part of my holding in January 1992 at a price of 51¾, since the stock had tripled (see Selling Rule 1, Chapter 4). Never have I been so thankful for such a small dividend! (All prices adjusted for 2-for-1 split in 1991.)

---

dividend yield rather than a single number. This is only done when a dividend cut is a serious possibility. Be warned.

RULE 2: Estimated future earnings must be at least 100 percent higher than earnings of the most recently completed year (or the estimate for the year in progress).

RULE 2C: Estimated future earnings must be at least 50 percent higher than earnings of the best year of the last five years (including the year in progress).

Rule 2 needs to be substantially modified if the conservative PAD investor is going to diversify successfully. The 50 percent growth mentioned in Rule 2C is a reasonable compromise that allows for dividend growth to make up for some of the capital gains shortfall, while still limiting appreciation tied solely to a higher price-earnings ratio. In addition, applying the rule to the best year of the last five years should keep cyclical stocks with little or no growth potential out of the portfolio. In bear markets, I recommend raising this percentage to trim the size of your Buy List. Conservative PAD investors will probably want to rule out companies with abnormally depressed earnings or a loss in any of the reference years.

CASE HISTORY: Circuit City (CC)

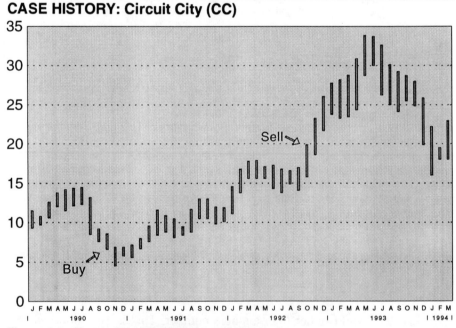

Figure 3.2: Circuit City (NYSE-CC) 1990–1994
Conservative PAD investors should not rule out a company, like Circuit City, which has an occasional earnings setback. CC was in the midst of one in the fall of 1990, when the stock market was taking no prisoners. I bought the stock at 6¾ in October 1990 when it met all of the PAD-C requirements. The earnings setback was indeed temporary, and the subsequent bull market and record company earnings drove the stock to triple my cost in October 1992, at which point I sold my shares. The stock continued to rise (the *PAD System Report* sold shares at much higher prices) but then the dreaded "earnings setback" struck again in 1993, and pushed the stock back down to an attractive level. It was, as Yogi Berra said, "deja vu all over again." (All prices adjusted for 2-for-1 stock split in 1993.)

RULE 3: A financial strength rating below "B" or a safety rating of "5" (lowest) disqualifies the company.

RULE 3C: A financial strength rating below "B++" or a safety rating below "3" (average) disqualifies the company.

The adjustments in Rule 3C may help a conservative PAD investor sleep better at night. All those Value Line stocks that are below average in safety or financial strength are now removed from consideration.

This is one of the few rules that I am willing to bend slightly. I will not rule out a stock that meets all the criteria of this chapter but only has a financial strength rating of "B+" to go along with a safety rating of "3." I do not venture below "B+," however, and I strictly limit the number of stocks in my PAD-C portfolio with a "B+" financial strength rating. I always have a liberal sprinkling of "A" and higher financial strengths in this portfolio, so the addition of a few "B+" stocks does not even bring the average for the entire portfolio down to "B++."

RULE 4: Research and development (R&D) percentage must be at least 7.5 percent.

RULE 4C: Research and development (R&D) percentage must be at least 2 percent.

A high percentage of sales plowed back into R&D is one of the cornerstones of the original PAD selection system. Rather than scrap it altogether, a conservative PAD investor can retain the spirit of the PAD System with Rule 4C. Even companies in mature industries like autos, food, and consumer goods cannot afford to stand still while the world changes. Spending on R&D is evidence that a firm is willing to invest in the future.

While many companies in a variety of industries spend at least 2 percent of revenues on R&D, there are still a number of market sectors, containing high-quality growth stocks, which will be unjustly excluded by this rule from a PAD-C portfolio. A successful bank, for example, does not spend any money on R&D. In order to make room for a few stocks with essentially no R&D, I consider the spirit of Rule 4C satisfied if the average level of R&D for the entire portfolio equals or exceeds 2 percent, while the number of companies with no recognizable R&D is small. In addition, these "no-R&D" companies must compensate for a Rule 4C violation by compiling outstanding

CASE HISTORY: Thermoelectron (TMO)

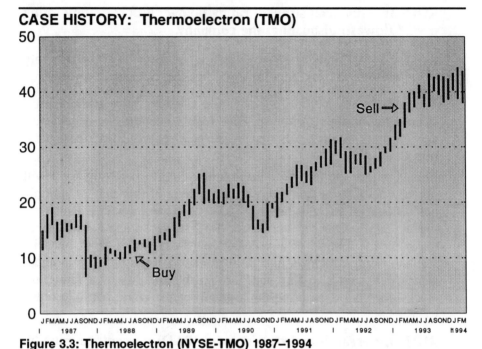

Figure 3.3: Thermoelectron (NYSE-TMO) 1987–1994
Thermoelectron is one of my 10 favorite PAD-C stocks (see Appendix A of this chapter). I purchased Thermoelectron in mid-1988 at a price of 12⅝ *(The PAD System Report,* which is sometimes smarter than I am, purchased it in December 1987 at 10). At the time, the stock easily satisfied all the rules of this chapter, with the exception of Rule 3C, since TMO had a "B+" financial strength rating. I decided to bend the rule slightly and never lost any sleep over it. I sold a part of my holding in March 1993 at a price of 36⅞, since the stock had tripled (see Selling Rule 1, Chapter 4). By that time, Value Line had raised the financial strength rating to B++. (All prices adjusted for 3-for-2 split in 1993.)

growth records. The measure I use for this alternative hurdle is called "price growth persistence" and is reported by Value Line in small print under the financial strength rating (see Figure 2.1). This measure ranges from 5 (lowest) up to 100 (highest) in increments of 5 units, which are actually percentiles. The top 5 percent of all Value Line stocks are rated 100, the next 5 percent are rated 95, and so on. I expect a no-R&D stock to rate at least 80 on this scale, which means that the price has shown a more persistent long-term upward trend than three-fourths of all stocks covered by Value Line.

I use this alternative form of Rule 4C to build a truly well-diversified portfolio of PAD-C stocks, since no industry is ruled out before the search for individual stocks begins. In fact, several of my 10 favorite

CASE HISTORY: Fifth Third Bank

Figure 3.4: Fifth Third Bank (NDQ-FITB) 1987–1994

I first purchased Fifth Third in November 1987 at a price of 14¾. At the time, I was concerned with the zero R&D status of the banking industry, but I felt this deficiency was overwhelmed by the other features of the stock. Here was a bank with a superb balance sheet (financial strength of "A+," safety rank "1") and price growth persistence of 90. How long would it be available at a price that satisfied the 19 percent rule too? Not very long, I suspected, and I was right. Fifth Third participated fully in the recovery after the crash. When the stock reached the low end of its three- to five-year appreciation potential in May 1991, I sold part of my holding (see discussion of Selling Rule 8, Chapter 4). I made additional sales in 1992 and 1993 in accordance with Selling Rule 1 (Chapter 4). My experience with Fifth Third, and other stocks like it, has convinced me that price growth persistence can be safely substituted for R&D for part of my PAD-C portfolio. (All prices adjusted for 3-for-2 stock splits in 1987, 1990, and 1992.)

PAD-C stocks listed at the end of this chapter are no-R&D companies with outstanding growth records and future prospects.

RULE 5: Short-term performance ranking must be higher than "5" (lowest).

RULE 5C: Short-term performance ranking must be higher than "4" (below average).

Stocks ranked "4" for short-term performance are risky to buy, but for a PAD technology investor concentrating on long-term performance, the risk is often worthwhile (see the discussion of Rule 5 in Chapter 2). For a conservative investor, it is probably better to play it safe and restrict purchases to stocks ranked 1, 2, or 3.

RULE 6: Diversify!

RULE 6C: Diversify!

This rule bears repeating without modification. Cast your net over a wide variety of industries. Fifth Third Bank, for example, has a very low beta; that is, the stock price is much less responsive to market fluctuations than the average stock. A very comforting thought in a market downturn.

INCOME STOCK SELECTION (PAD-I)

In my youth I never knowingly bought a stock that paid a dividend. As I now march through the "middle ages" of life, with relentlessly rising expenditures always threatening to outrun current income, I have seen the light: Current income can be good. Even a PAD investor moves through an investing life cycle, beginning with a youthful time of rapid accumulation and high-risk investing, and ending with the mature years of capital preservation and low-risk investing. At some point during this life cycle, the need for current income becomes paramount. This section is designed for the PAD investor who has recognized this need for current income, while still seeking the capital gains so crucial to long-run investment success. In the paragraphs that follow, I explain the relatively minor modifications I have made to the set of PAD-C rules in order to give extra weight to current income. (Young PAD investors can safely skip this section until they are married with children and a house payment.)

Rules 1C through 6C can be relabeled as Rules 1I to 6I and used to build an equity income portfolio, with a few minor adjustments. First, I would not alter Rule 1C at all, since it plays such a vital role in finding good values among stocks with growth potential. However, a high current yield will sharply reduce the amount of three- to five-year appreciation potential necessary to pass this rule. For example, a stock yielding 6 percent will need appreciation potential to the low end of its range of about 60 percent, rather than the 100 percent required by a stock with no dividend at all.

CASE HISTORY: Food Lion "B"

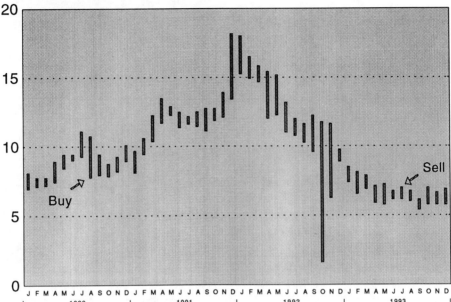

Figure 3.5: Food Lion B (NDQ-FDLNB) 1990–1993
The story of Food Lion B is a reminder that the real reason for diversification is that at least a few of the stocks that pass all of the rules of this chapter will nonetheless go down instead of up. I bought Food Lion at 9¼ in August 1990. This supermarket chain had a superb earnings growth record at that point, while weakness in the overall stock market drove the stock price down far enough to pass all of the rules of this chapter. By the end of 1991 the stock was close to a double, although almost all of Food Lion's appreciation potential had been realized (the *PAD System Report* did sell some of its shares as a result). Then the stock began a slow decline, which gradually accelerated in 1992 and 1993. What almost no one foresaw was that Food Lion would be hit with a spate of very bad publicity at the same time a major expansion program was under way. In short order the company went from king of the jungle to toothless tabby. I sold my shares at 6¼ in August 1993; I walked away from this "accident" with only a scratch, though, since I had most of my eggs in other baskets.

Second, I am willing to let a stock that violates *one* of Rules 2C–5C be in my income portfolio. While a stock like Washington REIT may pass Rules 1C–5C with flying colors, these proven-growth/high-income/high-quality stocks are few and far between. Perhaps the riskiest rule violation is Rule 3C, which checks for financial strength. Since many income stocks will pay out a high proportion of earnings as dividends, a financially strong company provides important extra protection against a dividend cut in hard times. On the other hand, a

CASE HISTORY: Washington Real Estate Investment Trust (REIT)

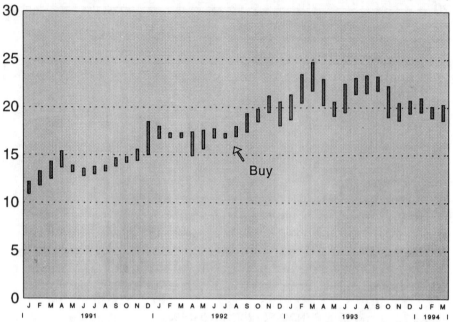

Figure 3.6: Washington Real Estate Investment Trust (ASE-WRE) 1991–1994
Washington REIT is my favorite PAD-I stock, because it meets or exceeds all of the requirements for a PAD-C stock, in addition to paying a healthy dividend. I first purchased the stock in June 1992 at 17; the *PAD System Report* purchased Washington REIT for its income portfolio at the same time. Since that time, the company has increased the dividend twice and set new earnings records. While real estate investment trusts may be Wall Street darlings this year and Wall Street dogs next year, a consistent performer like Washington REIT will no doubt be a core holding in my PAD income portfolio for many years.

violation of Rule 2C, which checks for future earnings growth, or Rule 4C or its substitute, which measures R&D or "price growth persistence," is less worrisome, since it will be nearly impossible to build a good income portfolio without some cyclical stocks in mature industries.

RULE 7I: If the dividend is not covered by earnings for two consecutive years, the company is disqualified.

Although some financially strong firms can pay dividends in excess of earnings for many years, remember that even mighty IBM was eventually humbled (twice). For an income investor, the dividend cut is the unkindest cut of all. I will avoid a stock if the company has not earned enough to cover its dividend for the most recent two-year pe-

CASE HISTORY: Hanson PLC (ADR)

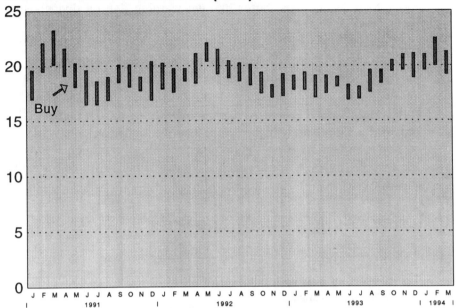

Figure 3.7: Hanson PLC (ADR) (NYSE-HAN) 1991–1994
Hanson PLC, a British conglomerate, was one of the first high-dividend stocks I ever purchased. (This is an example of the investing "life cycle," since the funds to purchase the stock came from a sale of Digital Equipment, one of my old favorite technology stocks, which never paid a dividend.) Hanson is a cyclical growth company that has always paid out a generous share of its earnings in the form of dividends. By May 1991, I found the generous dividend, coupled with substantial appreciation potential, too good to pass up. (The *PAD System Report* income portfolio purchased the stock in December 1991.) Although the stock has not made a lot of forward progress since that time, the large dividend, now paid on a quarterly basis, provides current income while keeping a "floor" under the price of the stock during market weakness. Although Hanson's dividend is more secure than many high-yield stocks, the company has had years in which reported earnings barely exceeded the dividend. If this phenomenon persists for two years in a row, I would certainly look for alternative income stocks (see Rule 7I).

riod. I also consider this rule to be a good income-stock selling rule: Sell any income stock that has not covered its dividend for two straight years. (Note that this rule does not apply to a stock like Washington REIT, which is a trust that pays out just about all of its earnings every year.)

RULE 8I: If Value Line suggests a dividend cut is possible, the company is disqualified.

Some firms cut dividends even when their earnings are sufficient to cover them. Value Line raises its own warning flag on dividends by listing two projected annual yields for a stock for which a dividend cut is a real possibility. Value Line is often right. Unless you would be happy with the *lower* of the two numbers Value Line estimates for the future yield, heed the warning flag and avoid the approaching storm.

Rules 1I–8I should enable an income investor to build a portfolio that provides a significantly higher yield than stocks on average, while not sacrificing potential capital gains. Income stocks are often less volatile than the average stock, which is an added plus for a conservative investor.

SUMMARY OF RULES FOR THIS CHAPTER

PAD-C

1C. Average annual total return must be at least 19 percent to the low end of the range.

2C. Estimated future earnings must be at least 50 percent higher than earnings of the best year of the last five years (including the year in progress).

3C. A financial strength rating below "B++" or a safety rating below "3" (average) disqualifies the company.

4C. Research and development (R&D) percentage must be at least 2 percent.

5C. Short-term performance ranking must be higher than "4" (below average).

6C. Diversify!

PAD-I

7I. If the dividend is not covered by earnings for two consecutive years, the company is disqualified.

8I. If Value Line suggests a dividend cut is possible, the company is disqualified.

MY 10 FAVORITE PAD-C STOCKS

The stocks listed below are all covered by the *Value Line Investment Survey*, and have at least occasionally satisfied all of the rules set out in this chapter. All have either been in my portfolio or have been recommended in the *PAD System Report*. (As evidence of the potential for diversification, each of these stocks is in a different industry group.) Nonetheless, this list, like the list at the end of Chapter 2, can in no way substitute for the application of the PAD-C rules to current VLIS reports.

Automatic Data Processing

ADP is the world leader in payroll processing services. ADP has also successfully diversified into brokerage services and has spent heavily on automation, which keeps its cost down. Even though payroll processing is a relatively mature industry, the company has one of the longest streaks in corporate America: more than 120 straight quarters of double-digit earnings growth.

Becton, Dickinson

This company is a relatively low-profile provider of medical supplies. Although health-care policy uncertainty has dimmed the prospects of many companies in a variety of industries, Becton's products, such as needles, syringes, and catheters, are not expensive frills. No government program can prevent the steady aging of the American population, with a concomitant increase in the demand for the medical supplies which are Becton's profitable niche markets.

Circuit City

Circuit City is a consumer electronics retailer that has survived and prospered in a fiercely competitive market. Although the stock is periodically beaten down by earnings reversals, these have always proved temporary and have been good buying opportunities. Price growth persistence is still a high "95."

Equifax

This company has established an enviable growth record (price growth persistence of "90") providing computerized information services to insurance companies and credit reports to lenders. The company continually expands and improves its services, even though it does not spend on R&D per se.

Fifth Third Bank

Fifth Third is one of the best managed regional banks in America. The stock is a conservative long-term investor's dream: earnings and dividends go up every year, the balance sheet is rock-solid, and the stock fluctuates much less than the average.

Merck

Merck plans to develop, or is already marketing, new drugs to combat every major disease: heart disease, hypertension, cancer, and so on. This research-driven and long-term approach makes Merck a perfect PAD company. It is suitable for the most conservative investors: Merck has consistently earned high Value Line ratings for financial strength and safety. Uncertainty over the future of health-care policy has pushed Merck's dividend yield above that of the average stock, making Merck attractive to income-oriented investors, too.

Reuters

Reuters is a household name in financial news services. The demand for its products and services is driven in part by the trend toward globalization of world financial markets, and "round-the-clock" trading of stocks, bonds, currencies, and other financial instruments. The company maintains its leadership position in its markets by spending 5 percent of revenues on R&D, assuring a continuing stream of new and more powerful products.

Sigma-Aldrich

Sigma is the market leader in research chemicals. It stocks every research chemical imaginable, including my personal favorite: the venom of the Formosan "100-step" snake. The company's commitment to quality and service is legendary, resulting in an enviable record of growth.

Thermoelectron

Although Thermo is a little riskier than the other stocks on this list, potential gains are also greater. The company is involved in a number of high-growth areas for the 1990s: cogeneration of power, environmental monitoring, explosives detection, paper recycling equipment, and cardiac-assist devices. Thermo has an entrepreneurial culture and high R&D, which produces a steady stream of new subsidiaries that exploit new technologies.

Worthington Industries

Worthington is proof positive that steel-making can be profitable. This "mini-mill" has concentrated its energy on making competitive products, and it has set earnings records in 7 of the last 10 years. Price growth persistence is the maximum "100" and financial strength is a solid "A."

A SHORTCUT CALCULATION OF TOTAL RETURN

Once you have switched to the total return approach of Rule 1C, it is necessary to calculate the average annual total return on your own. (This calculation is done automatically by the PAD Stock Selector Program.) This is not a difficult task, and it can be performed quickly with a $10 pocket calculator. The steps are listed below.

---

1. **Calculate the yield component of the total return.** The yield component can be approximated by simply averaging the current yield, reported each week by Value Line, with the future average yield, which appears in the full-page report several columns below the future average earnings (see Figure 2.1, line B).

$$\text{yield component} = \frac{\text{current yield} + \text{future yield}}{2} \qquad (1)$$

---

2. **Calculate the appreciation component of the total return.** First we must calculate the appreciation percent to the low end of the three- to five-year price range. This percentage is just the ratio of the three- to five-year price (low end) divided by the current price:

$$\text{appreciation percent} = \frac{\text{three- to five-year price (low-end)}}{\text{current price}} \qquad (2a)$$

The equivalent annual percentage can be calculated easily if we assume that these gains occur over a four-year period, since we can then just take the fourth root, or two consecutive square roots, of the appreciation percent:

$$\text{appreciation component} + 1 = \sqrt{\text{square root of appreciation percent}} \qquad (2b)$$

$$\frac{\text{appreciation}}{\text{component}} = \text{answer in (2b)} - 1 \qquad\qquad (2c)$$

---

3. Determine the average annual total return. Since total return is the sum of the yield component and the appreciation component, simply add the results of Steps 1 and 2c.

$$\frac{\text{estimated annual}}{\text{total return}} = \frac{\text{yield}}{\text{component}} + \frac{\text{appreciation}}{\text{component}} \qquad (3)$$

For those investors not of the mathematical persuasion, I offer an example. Suppose stock X has a current yield of 2.6 percent and an estimated future yield of 2.0 percent. If we add these two numbers together and divide the total by 2, we get 2.3 percent for the yield component (Step 1). If the low end of the three- to five-year price range is 20, and the current stock price is $12\frac{1}{4}$, the appreciation percent is $20/12\frac{1}{4}$, or 1.63 (Step 2a). The square root of this number is 1.28, and the square root of 1.28 is 1.13 (Step 2b). Subtracting 1 from this number leaves .13, which is 13 percent (Step 2c). We then add 13 percent to 2.3 percent to get 15.3 percent as the estimated average annual total return based on the current price (Step 3). Stock X would thus not satisfy Rule lC. Since this is a rough approximation, though, the 19 percent rule for this chapter need not be applied too rigorously. For example, a stock that manages 18.3 percent should probably be allowed to "make the grade." As an exercise, the reader may wish to determine how far stock X would have to fall to satisfy Rule 1C. (For those investors who *are* of the mathematical persuasion, there is no "closed-form" solution for this exercise. Iteration is the only way.)

CHAPTER 4
BUYING AND SELLING STOCKS

In 1989, *The Wall Street Journal* published the results of an in-depth survey of American buying habits. According to the survey, nearly half of all American adults do not have any "basic training" in buying and selling shares of publicly traded stocks. If you are in this category, I recommend reading first the Appendix to this chapter entitled "Getting Started." After graduating from "boot camp," you can use the rules of this chapter to improve your survival chances in the two great investment battles of stock selection and long-term market timing. Decorated veterans of the Wall Street Wars may still find the rules set out in this chapter illuminating and helpful. Buying Rule 1 alone can save investors thousands of dollars every year, if they only have the courage to apply it. Buying Rule 3 can protect investors from bear-market disasters.

HOW TO BUY STOCK

RULE 1: Use a discount broker exclusively.

There is no point in paying a full-service broker for services such as research and advice when you are not going to use them. A discount broker will provide the basic service you need, and at a much lower commission cost. It is simple to open an account with a discount broker, and finding one is not hard either. Many advertise regularly in financial publications such as *The Wall Street Journal.* One element you sacrifice when you deal with some of the least expensive, or "deep," discount brokers is the personal touch. You are often dealing with just a voice on the telephone, and usually a different one every time. But you can buy 100 shares of stock for a small fraction of the full-service charge. It's worth it: I have saved many thousands of dollars since I began following this rule in the 1970s. I would not deal with a firm that did not have its clients protected by the Securities Investor Protection Corporation (SIPC), but discount firms large and small have this protection. This, of course, does not mean that discount brokers cannot fail any more than FDIC insurance means that banks cannot fail. Bevill, Bressler, and Schulman failed in 1985, and their discount brokerage subsidiary was sold to another discount brokerage firm. While clients did not lose any money, and most were probably not inconvenienced at all, it is still a sobering reminder.

There is still another reason to use a discount broker. While most full-service brokers are well-trained and honest, there is a distinct minority lacking such traits. Even among those that are well-trained and honest, the pressure to get customers to buy or sell is strong: Almost all full-service brokers receive a substantial amount of their compensation (if not all of it) from commissions earned when their customers trade. There is also pressure to "move" financial products that are profitable for the brokerage firm. This can only work against a PAD investor, who must be as free as possible from the pressure to buy or sell or run with the herd.

After the crash of 1987, *The Wall Street Journal* reported the sad stories of investors who were wiped out in the crash because they were writing "naked puts" (see Chapter 10) on the advice of their brokers. It seems that the downside risks of such a strategy were never fully explained. This was bad advice indeed. It is a safe but sad prediction that future issues of *The Wall Street Journal* will contain horror stories of bad advice, bad products, and bad brokers.

PAD investors unfamiliar with discount brokerage are urged to study the Appendix A to this chapter. It contains information and advice on choosing a discount broker. If you already have an account at a full-service firm with cash and/or stock in it, it is relatively easy to transfer your account to a discount broker. Ask your discount broker for the form necessary to transfer an account. After you fill it out and return it to the discount broker, their personnel will be more than happy to carry out the transfer for you. The process should take from three to six weeks. Some discount brokers may even offer you a free first trade as a reward for an account transfer.

RULE 2: Buy stocks on your Buy List at fixed intervals.

When you have assembled your Buy List of PAD stocks using the rules of Chapters 2 and 3, and the long-term market timing indicator of Chapter 6 signals "buy," it is time to take your "shopping list" to the "store." Since no one can call the turns in the market precisely, especially the short-term fluctuations, which, if not completely inexplicable, are certainly unpredictable, a good strategy for purchasing stocks is to buy at fixed intervals. This is an important form of market discipline. If I am going to make a series of new investments, I restrict myself to one purchase a week or one purchase for every 3 percent decline in the Dow-Jones Industrial Average from its level at the time of the previous purchase, whichever comes first. So if the market is not declining, you are restricted to one purchase per week. During the final phase of a bear market, stocks often decline at a rapid rate, and thus your purchases will be accelerated, which will generally work in your favor. I also recheck each stock on my Buy List just before I buy it to make sure the stock is still a "buy" according to the PAD rules.

RULE 3: Do not buy on margin.

It is very tempting to consider enlarging your potential gains by purchasing stock on margin, which with a 50 percent requirement, increases your leverage by a factor of two, doubling your potential gains and losses. I recommend strongly against margin purchases for a patient investor with a three- to five-year time horizon. The biggest drawback to margin buying is the "margin call," a request by your broker to put up additional cash or securities to replenish your equity as your stocks decline. These calls force the investor's hand, and may result in forced liquidation of some or all of your portfolio if you cannot meet the margin call. PAD stocks may decline substantially before starting the long trek upward, and the investor who purchases them on margin just makes it more difficult to survive the hard times. Stocks are generally volatile enough to provide for sufficient excitement.

A simple hypothetical example illustrates the thrills and chills of margin investing. Margin requirements have been 50 percent for many years now. Thus, you can purchase $10,000 worth of stock for $5,000 of your own money, because the broker will lend you the rest. Brokers are delighted to lend you the money, because they charge you interest, often several points over the "broker call loan" rate, and the loan is collateralized, or secured, by the securities you purchase. When you buy 100 shares of X at $100 per share and send the broker just $5,000, you have leveraged your investment. Let's look at what can happen. Suppose the stock rises to $150 a share. You own the 100 shares, and they are now worth $15,000. You owe the broker the $5,000 he or she lent you, so your equity, or what's left over after deducting the amount you owe, is $10,000. Your stake, which started at $5,000, has doubled (before interest costs), while the stock has only risen 50 percent, all due to the magic of leverage. This is two-way magic, however. For suppose that the stock falls 50 percent instead, to $50 a share. Then your shares are worth $5,000, exactly equal to what you owe the broker. Thus, your equity is now zero. A 50 percent decline in the stock price has wiped out your investment completely. Now of course the broker will not let this happen, because if the stock continued to drop, it would be worth less than the amount of the loan, and the broker could suffer a loss if you refused to honor your loan commitment. So he will warn you to take action before his capital is in jeopardy. By the time the stock has fallen to $75, your broker will ask you to either put up more cash or sell the stock. If you do not put up more cash, the brokerage house will sell the stock for you, to protect itself against a loss.

This "margin call," which many sage Wall Streeters say not to meet, can never occur if you never buy on margin, of course. A 25 percent decline in a stock is not unusual, and there is no reason for a PAD investor to panic. A margined investor will panic, however, when the broker begins hounding him for more money. It is quite common at the end of bear markets for many margin customers to have their accounts liquidated by brokers because they have insufficient equity. This wholesale dumping of stocks can feed on itself for a while, as prices continue to fall, forcing more margined stocks to be dumped. This is invariably an excellent time to be purchasing stocks for the long term, and not on margin.

For decades, the Federal Reserve System has determined the margin rate for eligible securities. Although it has been at 50 percent for many years, there has been serious discussion of leaving the setting of margin requirements to the exchanges themselves, as a form of financial deregulation. Without a doubt, the exchanges will set lower requirements to compete for business. A rate of 30–35 percent would not be surprising. Before the Great Crash of 1929, margin requirements were 10 percent, and many investors were wiped out in the ensuing debacle.

History repeated itself in the crash of 1962, and again in the crash of 1987, which was even larger in percentage terms than the previous two. In every case, many small investors were wiped out as their margin accounts were liquidated just when stocks were at bargain-basement prices. It is sobering to note that the 1987 crash occurred while margin requirements were set at 50 percent.

RULE 4: Use market orders only.

Everyone loves a bargain. No one wants to pay list price. This holds true in the stock market, too. If you are ready to buy stock A at 22, and it drops to $21\frac{3}{4}$ and then returns to 22, it is a normal failing to think that you would rather pay $21\frac{3}{4}$ than 22. You may even be tempted to put in a "limit" order to purchase the stock when it reaches $21\frac{3}{4}$. I do not recommend this approach. When we take the long view, in which we expect the stock to rise to at least 44 (the 100 percent rule), it really does not make any difference whether we make the extra quarter point. It is also possible that the stock will not return to $21\frac{3}{4}$, and a large part of the upward movement could be sacrificed to gain a quarter of a point. I have made this mistake myself and am now sufficiently disciplined to use only "market" orders, to be executed at the market, and if this means paying $22\frac{1}{4}$, so be it. Make up your mind, call your broker, execute your order, and hang up. Don't decide while you are on the telephone and the market is moving; it is only another short-run distraction.

Richard Ney, one of the modern muckrakers of Wall Street, has written an expose of Wall Street's little-known exchange market-makers, the specialists. I have no independent evidence that his accusations are true, but I have had my suspicions for a long time. The main thrust of his argument is that most specialists are interested first in making money for themselves, and only secondarily in making an orderly market in exchange-listed stocks, which is what they are supposed to do. One way they can profit at the expense of the public is through the entries in the specialist's "book," where all buy and sell orders, other than market orders, are entered. All of these limit or stop orders provide valuable information to the specialist, and uncommon opportunities. The details are in Ney's book, which is listed in the Sources section at the end of this chapter. The exchanges piously deny any wrongdoing, which is of course self-serving. Don't make it any easier for the "big boys" to nail you.

SELLING: THE TOUGH DECISION

"If there is anything in speculation which requires courage and power of will, it is selling stocks at high prices."
—R. W. McNeel, *Beating the Stock Market* (1922)

It is much easier to buy a stock than to sell it. In part, this reflects the basic optimism that infuses most of the investing public most of the time. In part, it also reflects the common mistake, which we have all made, of "falling in love" with a stock, thus losing the objectivity that is crucial to investment success. Selling decisions must be considered in an absolutely cold-blooded manner.

The two basic reasons for selling an individual stock, as opposed to a general selling program as described in Chapter 6, are (1) to realize profits on a stock that has appreciated substantially, and (2) to eliminate stocks that have not performed up to expectations. Sales under (2) may result in either profits or losses. In the sections below I present the key rules to help you make the right selling decisions.

Selling a Stock That Has Performed Well

RULE 1: Sell between one-fourth and one-half of your holding when it has tripled, and then sell additional fractions at higher multiples of your cost. Use stock splits to ease the pain of parting.

It is quite painful, and for some investors, impossible, to sell a stock that has been performing well. No one wants to miss the top, and mere mortals feel foolish when a stock continues to rise after it has been sold. Unfortunately, many stocks decline with the same vigor that accompanied a previous rise. The simplest solution to this dilemma is to establish rules for selling, and sell part of your position each time. Admittedly, no one can stick to all the rules all the time, but if you do not discipline yourself, you will be forfeiting a crucial PAD edge. I sell part of my holdings when a stock has tripled in price, and then sell additional fractions when it has quadrupled, quintupled, and so on. I find it particularly easy to follow Selling Rule 1 when a stock has just split and I am in possession of some additional shares. This helps overcome the inertia and the sneaking suspicion that, in this one case, your tree will grow to the sky. It won't.

Selling Rule 1 is also designed to prevent premature selling, which can destroy the PAD System. There will be losers, and perhaps big ones, but the winners, if allowed to develop, will more than offset the losers. Although the PAD investor invests for the long term, this is appreciably shorter than forever. I cannot stress too much the twin dangers of selling after a stock has gone up a few points ("You can't go broke taking a profit") or refusing ever to sell until the big gains have all melted away. An intelligent but rarely followed adage is to cut your losses and let your profits run. Many investors do just the opposite, and pay dearly. (This type of investor behavior appears in many risky situations; see Chapter 9 for further details.) Obey the rules!

At some point it may be appropriate to liquidate all of your holdings in a particular stock. When a stock meets the criteria for a general selling program, as outlined in Chapter 6, you may wish to sell all rather than part of your investment. I do not state this as a hard-and-fast rule, given that a stock you own could always be the next Wal-mart and thus worth holding for a very long time even by PAD standards.

If your initial sale after a tripling is followed by a decline in price, you will feel very smart, unless you are still expecting perfection and are thus upset that you did not sell it all. But you must steel yourself for the possibility that the stock will continue to rise even though you have correctly lightened your position. You must remind yourself that you have realized a very large profit, that you still own some of the stock, and that you do not need to buy at the bottom and sell at the top to get rich. What the rule really does is keep your greed under control. If you can do this successfully, and keep your fear under control, too, your investment record will be enviable.

Selling a Stock That Has Not Performed Well

RULE 2: If a stock has declined 50 percent from purchase price, or has performed significantly worse than the market for six months, or has dropped to a "5" for short-term performance, it must be reevaluated carefully.

Mistakes are inevitable. Earnings fail to grow as anticipated, or the market places a lower value on those rising earnings. In either case, a stock, or perhaps several, becomes the black sheep in the family of investments, or to paraphrase Garrison Keillor, a dim bulb in your investment marquee. If you have called the market turn correctly and bought near the bottom, you may discover that some of your stocks do not rise as fast as the market; if your timing is somewhat less satisfactory, a market decline sends some of your stocks down at a precipitous rate. The question is when to get out and replace the dim bulbs. First, if you are a PAD investor, a price decline is a normal phase in the often inexplicable gyrations of the market and individual stocks. One should fully expect that a stock will decline after it is purchased, and it is a good rule to sit on a stock until it has declined 50 percent in price, or has had at least two quarters of disappointing

CASE HISTORY: General Instrument (GRL)

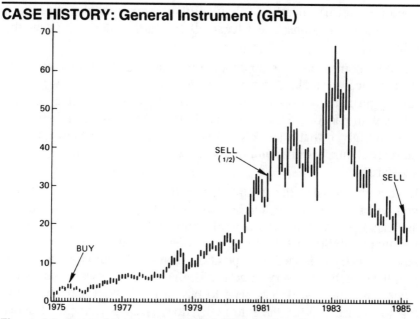

Figure 4.1: General Instrument (NYSE-GRL) 1975–1985
I purchased General Instrument (GRL) in 1975 at 4¼ per share (adjusted for a subsequent 3-for-1 stock split) and sold half of my position at 32 around split time. I was probably a little too patient in waiting for a stock split, since the price had already more than tripled long before. The stock then rose to a high of around 66, which should have triggered several sales, but I ignored my own rule. I sold the remainder in 1985 at 21¼, after GRL had underperformed the market for some time. This still resulted in a gain of 400 percent in 10 years.

price action relative to the market, before considering selling. I must emphasize that in neither case am I recommending a sale, just a thorough reexamination of the rationale for the purchase and the performance of the company since initial purchase. In addition, this rule does not have to be applied rigidly to stocks that have been in your portfolio for some time, but I recommend it, if only to prevent "falling in love" with a stock. This love is also blind, and will destroy the discipline of the PAD System.

One other event must trigger an immediate reevaluation of a stock: a drop in the Value Line short-term performance ranking to "5." This is a serious warning signal of hard times ahead, and they may be more than temporary.

Many investors and investment advisors argue strongly that stocks that decline in price by 10, 20, or 30 percent should be automatically eliminated from a portfolio. This is much too soon to bail out if you are a PAD investor, and these rules are among the most dubious of what passes for wisdom on Wall Street. Once your time horizon is measured in years, rather than weeks, a short-term decline can be suffered with equanimity. It may even present a better buying opportunity. On the other hand, these 10–30 percent rules overlook those stocks that do not do well during an extended rally. These laggards need to be reevaluated, for fear they will collapse during the next market decline.

RULE 3: If a stock reviewed under Rule 2 survives a reevaluation, cash reserves can be committed to it. If the price has fallen, this will enable you to "average down." This rule should be invoked only once for any stock and does not apply to a short-term "5."

If the basic rationale for purchasing the stock still holds, and all that has happened is that the market has been weak, the price decline is an excellent opportunity to "average down," that is, buy some additional stock at a lower price. This is of course possible only if you still have some cash reserves. It is also a policy I would invoke only once, to avoid the risk of tying up too much capital in a stock that is not performing well, even if there is no apparent reason for the poor performance. Some stocks do go to zero, or close to it. You must avoid the paralyzing panic which prevents you from cutting your losses, and the easy and false rationalization, "It can't go any lower." It can. A $1 stock can still drop 100 percent.

Averaging down is not an option for a stock with a short-term performance ranking of "5." The only choice here is hold or sell. My decision in these kinds of cases is often influenced by the length of my Buy List. The longer it is, the more likely I am to try a "switch" (see the section below titled "Switching").

RULE 4: Do not use stop-loss orders.

If you follow these rules, you obviously cannot use stop-loss orders as they are generally prescribed on Wall Street. Stop-loss orders set at 10–20 percent below purchase price (resulting in automatic sales) are inconsistent with a long-term strategy of investing in stocks that are fairly volatile. General Instrument is just one example of many: it declined to $2\frac{1}{2}$ before starting its dramatic rise to 66. Those without patience and discipline walked out of the first act of a hit show.

CASE HISTORY: Cray Research

Figure 4.2: Cray Research (NYSE-CYR) 1981–1989
The bittersweet story of Cray Research serves as an excellent illustration of the workings of the PAD System, with special emphasis on Selling Rules 1 and 2. I first discovered Cray, the world leader in supercomputers, in 1981, which was not long after Value Line began covering the stock. I built a position by purchasing shares on three occasions during the period 1981–1982, when the stock satisfied all the rules of Chapter 2 (Part 1) and the long-term market-timing rules of Chapter 6 allowed me to buy stock. My average cost was $15 per share, after adjusting for a subsequent 2-for-1 stock split. I then waited patiently for the stock to triple (Selling Rule 1). In 1985, the stock reached 45, and I sold one-sixth of my holding. (At the time I had not formalized the selling fraction at one-quarter to one-half.) I sold additional fractions in later years at prices as high as 134. Unfortunately, the remaining one-sixth (50 shares) was never sold. My feeling at the time was that I had banked enormous profits in the stock (via Selling Rule 1), so what damage could be done by holding a few shares "for old times' sake"? Cray proceeded to illustrate the damage by falling from 135 to 35 while the stock market was on its way to all-time highs. I received a $5,000 lesson in the dangers of sentiment and the risks of ignoring Selling Rule 2!

RULE 5: Use market orders only.

When the decision has been made to sell all or part of your holding in a particular stock, call up your discount broker and sell at the market.

CASE HISTORY: Novell

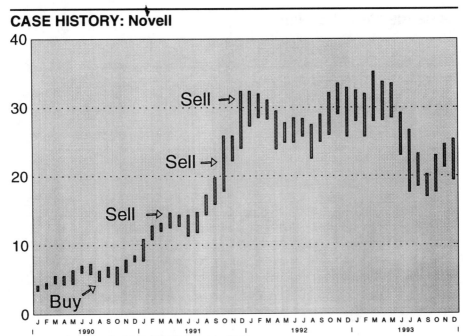

Figure 4.3: Novell (NDQ-NOVL) 1990–1993
Novell is a more recent example of the PAD System, and in particular, Selling Rule 1, in action. The *PAD System Report* bought Novell at 5 in August 1990, when long-term market timing was favorable and this computer networking powerhouse satisfied all of the rules of Chapter 2, Part 1. The stock began an immediate and dramatic upward ascent, which did not stop until the beginning of 1992. The *PAD System Report* sold shares at triple, quadruple, and eventually six times cost (see graph). Showing no sentiment at all, our final shares were sold at 31 when the stock was well above the low end of its three- to five-year appreciation potential. The shares stayed in a trading range for a year, and then tumbled to below 20 when earnings growth temporarily stopped. At this point, the stock satisfied all of the rules for purchase again (it was featured in the November 1993 issue of the *PAD System Report*), but long-term market timing was unfavorable. (All prices adjusted for 2-for-1 splits in 1990, 1991, and 1992.)

This is parallel advice to that given in the buying part of this chapter. It is not worth the time, effort, or risk to fight for quarters or eighths of a point.

RULE 6: Sell when a merger or buyout is announced.

In some happy circumstances, the market will help you decide when to sell. When another firm attempts a buyout or takeover of some kind, almost invariably at a price for your stock well above recent market prices, you have a golden opportunity to take your profits or

CASE HISTORY: Novellus

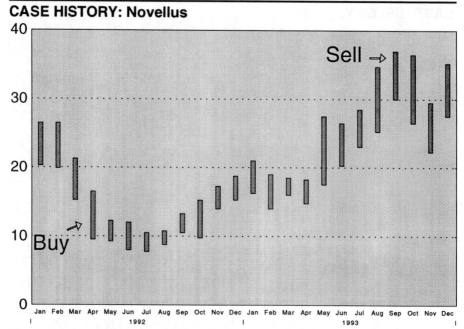

Figure 4.4: Novellus (NDQ-NVLS) 1992–1993

I first purchased Novellus, a semiconductor equipment maker, in April 1992 at 12¼ (see graph). This PAD-A stock had one of the highest betas in the Value Line universe and had just been pounded by a bad earnings report. I felt all was well with the company, and with low-end three- to five-year appreciation potential of 25, it looked like a steal. True to its beta, the stock made several heart-stopping moves after purchase. Decision time came when earnings took another nosedive and Value Line reduced the timeliness ranking to the dreaded "5." I reevaluated the stock carefully in accord with Selling Rule 2, and decided that Novellus had tremendous growth potential, especially in the Japanese market. I held on, and was rewarded in September 1993 when I sold my shares for a triple (Selling Rule 1), after the stock reached the low-end of its three- to five-year appreciation potential.

cut your losses at a suddenly more favorable rate. Most growth stocks that you will own will be taken over by companies in other industries, with less promising growth prospects. Fairchild Camera and Instrument and Silicon Systems, discussed in Chapter 2, are perfect examples.

My advice is to sell out and not even wait to receive the cash or stock from the deal. Some of the deals fall through, and since you don't want to own the stock of the acquiring company, don't wait. A possible exception to this rule could be made if the acquiring company is also a well-ranked PAD company. It may be worthwhile to continue to hold stock in the combined company.

Reinvesting and Repurchasing

It is very difficult to get off a winning horse, although my rules listed above should help. But what to do with the proceeds of a sale? If long-term market-timing analysis (Chapter 6) suggests that stocks are cheap, I would pick one or more stocks from my Buy List for reinvesting. If you already own the maximum number of stocks recommended for your portfolio size in Table 2.1, consider an additional investment in a stock you already own, which still meets the PAD requirements. Otherwise hold cash reserves and wait for a better opportunity to buy.

Sometimes a previous winner that you have taken profits on, in accordance with the above rules, or completely liquidated, will again become attractive under the buying rules of Chapter 2. Do not hesitate to purchase it again. Similarly, a loser that was deleted from your portfolio should be considered in the future. Its management may change, or some R&D could begin to pay off, or a host of other factors could change. You may have just bought the stock a little too soon. The fact that you have been "burned" once is not a reason in itself to avoid a stock forever after.

RULE 7: Review every stock in your portfolio at least once every three months.

All of your current holdings and prospective holdings should be reviewed regularly. I recommend at least once every quarter, which you can time with the regular reviews in the VLIS. As your portfolio gets larger, you may want to increase your time spent in review, but keep in mind that this is still just a serious hobby. You should guard against becoming too involved with either the market or your individual stocks. You must not lose your perspective.

The Sell List

RULE 8: Sell stocks on your Sell List at fixed intervals.

The rules previously presented in this chapter will produce a group of stocks which, for better or worse, are ready to be sold. Once a stock has been moved to this Sell List, do not wait for long-term market-timing indicators to signal "*sell.*" The stocks should be sold promptly, but I would recommend selling at fixed intervals if there is more than one stock on the Sell List, again to average out the unpredictable short-term fluctuations of the market. Selling one stock on your Sell List per week is a useful guideline.

If there are several stocks on your Sell List when Chapter 6's long-term market-timing indicator signals *"sell,"* you can begin selling promptly. If your Sell List does not contain any stocks at that time, however, it is necessary to build a Sell List from your current holdings. The easiest way to start this list is to review your entire portfolio for stocks that are far removed from qualifying for purchase. My favorite candidates are stocks whose Value Line three- to five-year appreciation potential, to the low end of the range, is zero or negative. Any stock rated "5" for short-term performance, which should already be under a cloud in your reviews, is also a good candidate for building a Sell List. I also look for stocks in my portfolio that have an appreciation potential to the high end of the range of less than 100 percent. Any stock that has dropped below minimum acceptable R&D spending, or minimum financial strength or safety ratings, is also a prime candidate for the Sell List. This set of criteria will almost surely be enough to generate a sizable Sell List. Since long-term market-timing indicators are signaling falling prices, all of the proceeds should be placed in cash reserves after a general selling program. While I have established no maximum level of cash reserves, I believe a PAD investor should be willing to keep as much as 50 percent of a portfolio in cash. This should ease the pain of any decline, provide the funds to capitalize on a decline, and yet allow participation in an unexpected continuation of a bull market. (Certain options strategies can provide further insurance against market declines, and these are discussed in Chapter 10.)

Switching

It is not at all unusual for some stocks to be added to your Buy List at the same time that other stocks in your portfolio are being added to your Sell List. If the long-term market timing indicator is either neutral or bullish, you can execute a switch, in which you sell a Sell List stock and immediately reinvest the proceeds in a Buy List stock. This kind of portfolio upgrading can be overdone, of course, and just result in high commissions and loss of patience and discipline. But when stocks have appeared on both your lists, and you have no reason not to be fully invested, make the switches. It is probably less difficult to sell a stock, particularly one you have held a long time, if you have a replacement waiting in the wings. Also, I am more willing to move

CASE HISTORY: Advanced Micro Devices (AMD)

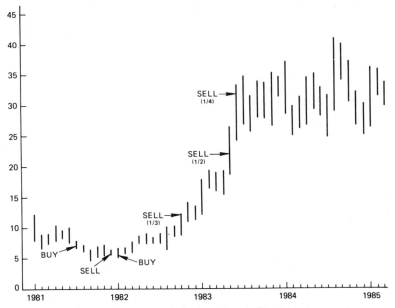

Figure 4.5: Advanced Micro (NYSE-AMD) 1981–1985
I first bought AMD in 1981 at 7½. It performed poorly for some time after my purchase, and I sold it and took a tax loss in 1981 at 5⅞. I then repurchased the stock 31 days later at 5¾. The stock eventually rose above $40 a share. The graph shows my subsequent partial liquidations, all for handsome PAD profits. All of the selling was timed in accordance with the PAD rules; in particular, selling when additional stock is received. This tree did not grow to the sky either: AMD subsequently retraced all of its gain. (All prices adjusted for 3-for-2 and 2-for-1 stock splits.)

those stocks that have fallen to "5" for short-term performance to the Sell List if I have stocks on the Buy List ready to substitute for them.

SUMMARY OF RULES FOR THIS CHAPTER

Buying

1. Use a discount broker exclusively.

2. Buy stocks on your Buy List at fixed intervals.

3. Do not buy on margin.

4. Use market orders only.

CASE HISTORIES: Xerox and Digital Equipment

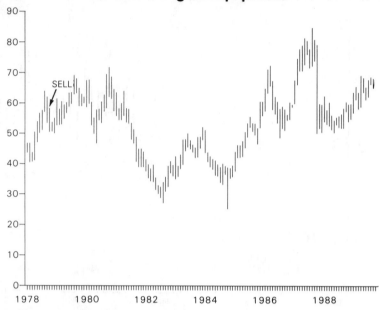

Figure 4.6: Xerox (NYSE-XRX) 1978–1989

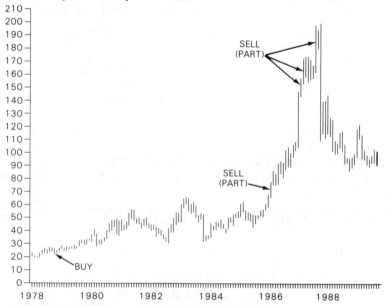

Figure 4.7: Digital Equipment (NYSE-DEC) 1978–1989

The most successful switch I ever made was accomplished in 1978. I owned 50 shares of Xerox, then selling at 58, which had been purchased a year earlier at 64 for no good reason. (I still had a lot to learn.) The company and stock had gone nowhere for a year, during which time I discovered Digital Equipment, then a relatively obscure computer company ($1.5 billion in sales). Digital was ranked higher for year-ahead performance, had a higher three- to five-year appreciation potential, spent much more on R&D, and was not inferior by any other comparison. I sold my Xerox at 58 and put the proceeds into Digital at 24¾ (adjusted for 2-for-1 split in 1986). By the end of the 1980s, even with two years of poor performance, Digital had quadrupled, while Xerox had managed to pull itself back up to 64. True, Xerox paid dividends during the interim, but by following Selling Rule 1, I sold parts of my Digital holding at prices as high as seven times my cost. (By 1994, however, the worm had turned: Xerox reached 100, while Digital was back to 24¾.)

Selling

1. Sell between one-fourth and one-half of your holding when it has tripled, and then sell additional fractions at higher multiples of your cost. Use stock splits to ease the pain of parting.

2. If a stock has declined 50 percent from purchase price, or has performed significantly worse than the market for six months, or has dropped to a "5" for short-term performance, it must be reevaluated carefully.

3. If a stock reviewed under Rule 2 survives a reevaluation, cash reserves can be committed to it. If the price has fallen, this will enable you to "average down." This rule should be invoked only once for any stock and does not apply to a short-term "5."

4. Do not use stop-loss orders.

5. Use market orders only.

6. Sell when a merger or buyout is announced.

7. Review every stock in your portfolio at least once every three months.

8. Sell stocks on your Sell List at fixed intervals.

SOURCES FOR THE PAD INVESTOR

McNeel, R.W., *Beating the Stock Market*. Wells, VT: Fraser Publishing, 1963. This little gem was first published in 1922. It contains advice about buying, selling, and brokers that still rings true today.

Ney, Richard, *The Wall Street Jungle*. New York: Grove Press, 1970. If you want to believe the wheel is crooked, this is the book for you. At the very least, Ney should convince you not to use limit orders of any kind.

APPENDIX 4A
DISCOUNT BROKERS: WHAT TO LOOK FOR

As a PAD investor, you will do your own research and make your own decisions about stock purchases and sales. Thus, there is no need to pay a full-service broker for research and advice that you do not and should not use. Discount brokers provide brokerage services without the research and advice and pass the cost savings on to their customers. Table 4A.1, located at the end of this appendix, contains a sampling of discounters large and small.

I use three criteria for selecting a discount broker: *cost, service,* and *safety.* Each of these is discussed below.

Cost

The main reason to use a discount broker is to save money on commissions. These savings are substantial, even with the relatively infrequent trades of a PAD investor. For example, purchase of 300 shares of a $50 stock may easily cost $200 or more at a full-service brokerage firm, while even the most expensive discounters will charge less than $100, and the least expensive discounters, called "deep" discounters, may charge as little as $25. It seems almost sinful that PAD investors can save hundreds or even thousands of dollars a year without giving up anything!

Unfortunately, it is not possible to rate discounters by cost. Each firm has its own system for calculating commissions, and these commission schedules can change at any time. Some firms charge by value of transaction, some by number of shares, some by both, and some have flat fees. All have minimum charges that may apply to a transaction. Thus, some orders will be cheapest to execute at one firm, and others will be cheapest at another firm. While you could set up accounts at many firms and execute each of your orders at the cheapest possible price, it will be much less time-consuming to pick one firm that is cheap for you: examine your recent transactions and then compare what your total commissions would be at several of the discounters listed in Table 4A.1, or any other firms you wish to consider. Several will no doubt come out below the others. You may want to choose among the leaders on the basis of service, or safety (see corresponding sections below). If you are dissatisfied with your first choice, you can switch to another fairly painlessly. I have switched several times in search of the optimal combination of low rates and good service. I like to shop around every few years just to make sure I cannot do better elsewhere.

All discounters should be willing to provide you with commission schedules to do your calculations. One toll-free telephone call will also get you account forms, lists of other services, and a recent financial statement. PAD investors following Selling Rule 1 of Chapter 4 will sometimes be selling round lots combined with odd lots. It is worth checking the commission schedules carefully to determine just how expensive a combination trade is. Some firms may charge as much for the odd lot as for the round lot, while others may add on only a nominal amount to the round-lot charge, or make no additional charge at all.

Service

Low commissions will not be a bargain if you cannot get through to your broker quickly, get rapid executions of your orders, and get prompt confirmations of your trades. Discounters vary in the quality of this basic and most important service. If you have trusted friends with discount brokerage accounts, they should be able to tell you just how good the basic service is at their discounter. Otherwise, you must find out through a process of trial and error. Remember, though, that you need not put up with unsatisfactory service. Complain. If that fails, open an account with another discounter. There are plenty of fish in the sea.

Several other aspects of service may be important to you. For example, I will not tolerate brusqueness on the telephone. I also expect to get monthly statements that are easy to understand, complete, and correct. I also look for interest paid on balances awaiting reinvestment, prompt payment of balances, and delivery of securities. You may wish to add other criteria to this list. Search until you find them.

Many "full-service" discounters offer services formerly available only at full-service brokerage firms: personal brokers, cash-management accounts, debit cards, no-fee trading of no-load mutual funds, IRAs and Keoghs, and more. If these services are important to you, and it simplifies your life to have all your financial dealings with one firm, go ahead and use them. These services are not necessarily free, however, and some of their costs may be included in commission rates. Some of these services are now provided by "deep" discounters, too.

Full-service discounters have large networks of offices throughout the United States. I consider this to be a dubious advantage. There is no reason for a PAD investor to visit a discount brokerage office. It is safer to deal only over the telephone and use the mail. This approach reduces the risk of getting too close to Wall Street.

I do not limit my searches to the "best" discount firm. I will also search for a satisfactory branch office. Many investors do not realize that you can choose to deal with a branch other than the one initially assigned to you when you open an account. In my case, I was dissatisfied with the telephone manners of the New York office of my favorite discount brokerage firm. I began routing my trades through the Chicago office of the same firm, and explained to them why I switched. End of problem.

Safety

The failure of Brevill, Bressler, and Schulman in the 1980s was an important reminder of the fragility of our financial intermediaries. No discount brokerage customers lost any money in this failure, however. The firm's accounts were taken over by another brokerage firm soon after the failure. Yet this failure was no doubt a jolt to customers of discount brokers everywhere. How can we be sure our assets are safe?

Our main protection is the Securities Investor Protection Corporation (SIPC), which insures most brokerage accounts up to $500,000. Some discount brokers have additional protection up to $2.5 million or more. Even with SIPC protection, investors still may have their capital or securities tied up for some time in the unlikely event of a failure. The best way to reduce this risk is to take delivery of your securities, and keep your cash balances in a money-market mutual fund. Examining a financial statement may provide some additional confidence, and dealing with one of the larger discounters may also help.

TABLE 4.A.1 A Sampling of Discount Brokers

Brown and Company
20 Winthrop Square
Boston, MA 02110
Telephone: 1-800-822-2829 #255

A deep discounter with ties to Chemical Bank. Minimum commission: $28. Motto: "Your experience is a small price to pay." $10,000 minimum account size, volume discounts, 7 regional offices.

Burke, Christensen & Lewis
303 W. Madison
Chicago, IL 60606
Telephone: 1-800-621-0392

A regional discounter with offices in the Midwest. Minimum commission: $34.

Fidelity Brokerage Services
161 Devonshire
Boston, MA 02110
Telephone: 1-800-544-8666

FBS is part of the Fidelity network, which includes Fidelity mutual funds. Minimum commission is $54. Not one of the lowest priced, but is a large "full-service" discounter, with no-fee mutual fund trading.

National Discount Brokers
Telephone: 1-800-4-1-PRICE

A new deep discounter with a flat $25 charge for any NASDAQ trade.

Olde Discount
Telephone: 1-800-USA-OLDE

If you have $500,000, you can "trade stocks free." Those of more modest means pay deep discount commissions.

Public Brokerage Services
5757 Wilshire Boulevard
Los Angeles, CA 90036
Telephone: 1-800-421-8395

PBS charges 5 cents a share up to 1,000 shares with a $29 minimum. One of the least expensive in the 100–500 share range.

Quick & Reilly
120 Wall Street
New York, NY 10005
Telephone: 1-800-926-0600

One of the large "full-service" discounters with a nationwide network of offices. Minimum commission is $49.

Charles Schwab
101 Montgomery Street
San Francisco, CA 94104
Telephone: 1-800-435-4000

Another large "full-service" discounter with a nationwide network of offices. Has automated quotes and no-fee mutual fund trading. Minimum commission: $55.

Note: All information was collected from sources believed to be reliable, but it cannot be guaranteed. Discount brokers may change their rate schedules frequently, and also change headquarters locations and telephone numbers. *The Wall Street Journal* and the *New York Times* are good places to look for up-to-date advertisements of discounters.

SUMMARY

Find the discount brokerage that meets your own requirements best, and then use them and save. When you discover that another firm can do a better job, switch. The competition among discount brokers is fierce, and PAD investors should get top value for their commission dollars.

SOURCE FOR THE PAD INVESTOR

Coler, Mark, *Investing at a Discount: Saving on Commissions, Management Fees, and Costs.* New York: New York Institute of Finance, 1990. An updated version of his *70% Off!* Solid, but already somewhat dated.

APPENDIX 4B
GETTING STARTED

This section is designed to provide "basic training" for the raw recruit. It provides instruction in three areas: (1) opening an account, (2) making trades, and (3) keeping records. If your confidence level is still not high enough to charge into battle after reading these sections, I have listed several "starter" books and one videotape at the end of this appendix.

Opening an Account

The first step in getting started is to open an account with a discount broker. Your choice is not limited to the firms listed in Appendix 4A. Any discount broker that satisfies the three criteria of cost, service, and safety should be satisfactory. Call the broker's toll-free number and say that you want to open an account. You will be turned over to someone who will be delighted to take your name and address and send you a "new account" package.

A typical set of forms will include: a new account application form, and one or more forms you do *not* want to fill out or sign: a margin agreement, which would let you trade on margin, and an options agreement, which would let you trade options. These forms are normally accompanied by "risk disclosure" statements. Since margin trading would violate Rule 3 of this chapter, and options are not for the beginner, it is best to avoid even opening a margin or options account. The account you will open is called a "cash" account. You cannot buy or sell on credit in this account. The brokerage firm will also include a commission schedule, which will show you how much will be charged for making a trade, and a brochure describing what additional services may be available, such as "round-the-clock" order entry, free Standard & Poor's stock reports, etc. Make sure you request delivery of stock certificates.[1]

Once you have filled out the appropriate forms and mailed them in, you must wait for confirmation that your account has been "opened." You will then receive an account number, which you will use to identify yourself when you trade, and one or more "800" numbers, which you can call to make your trades. Normally you will have to deposit cash in your account before you can buy stock. Send the check with a letter to the brokerage firm stating that "I wish to deposit the enclosed check in my account, number 12345." I would write my account number on my check too, just to be safe.

Making Trades

Once your account is open, you are ready to trade. (The next step, however, should be to read this entire book so that you will know what stocks to buy and sell, and when to buy and sell them!) If you are now ready to purchase a stock that meets all of the requirements of Chapters 2 or 3, and the market is "OK to Buy" as specified in Chapter 6, you can call your broker to make a trade.

I normally start my conversations this way: "Hello. May I have a broker please?" (In some cases the telephone is not answered by an individual authorized to handle trades.) I then ask for a quote on the stock(s) I am planning to buy: "Could you give me the 'last' and the 'bid' and 'ask' on XYZ?" The broker will then give you the price at which the last trade was made, and the current offer to buy (bid) and sell (ask): "Last is 46, currently $\frac{7}{8}$ to an $\frac{1}{8}$." This is short for: "The most recent trade was at 46, there is a bid (offer to buy) at $45\frac{7}{8}$, and an ask (offer to sell) at $46\frac{1}{8}$."

It can save time if you tell the broker the ticker symbol for XYZ (these are listed in *The Wall Street Journal* daily stock tables). If the price of XYZ has not moved sharply since the previous day's close, you are ready to say, "Buy 100 shares *at the market* for account 12345." Of course you may be buying 1,000 or 20, but 100 is the smallest "round lot," or normal trading unit, for most stocks. Smaller amounts are called "odd lots" and the commission charges are normally a bit higher. I emphasize "at the market" because a PAD investor will not be using any other kind of order. In general, a market order means you will be paying the ask price to buy (and receiving the bid price when you sell) but these eighths and quarters do not

---

1.   Some firms have begun charging hefty fees for issuance of stock certificates. Beware!

matter for long-term investors. However, the spread between the bid and ask is an important source of revenue to market-makers in the stock.

In some cases the broker can put you on "hold" for a minute while the transaction is being carried out; in other cases you may need to wait for a call back, or make a call later yourself to get confirmation of the trade. Unless trading is unusually hectic or disorderly, you will have your trade confirmed in a matter of minutes: "You bought 100 shares of XYZ at $46\frac{1}{8}$." The procedure for selling is analogous, except that you will normally receive the bid price when you sell at the market.

If the stock has moved sharply higher, but is still below the maximum price you can pay for it under the PAD rules, you can still buy it. With several stocks on your Buy List, however, a sharp upward move in one stock should make the others look that much more attractive. A sharp decline is more problematic. You can ask your broker if there is any news on the stock; most stock quote systems will flag the stocks of companies that have made announcements during the trading day. If there is a news item, such as "XYZ announces earnings will be below previous forecasts," you should defer action on the stock until Value Line has had a chance to update its report on the stock. It may no longer satisfy all the PAD rules. If your broker cannot or will not check on news items for you, you need to find another broker.

Figure 4B.1: A Typical Confirmation Statement of a Trade

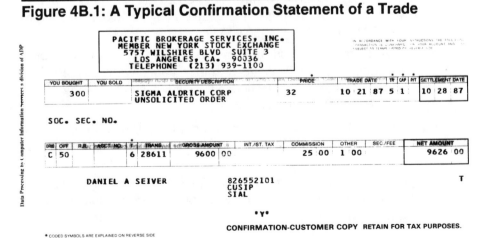

Keeping Track

Your broker will mail you a written confirmation of your trade. Figure 4B.1 is an example of a typical confirmation statement. The most important items on the statement are the date of the trade, the price, the number of shares, and name of the stock. These should all match exactly what was stated on the telephone. If there is a discrepancy, call your broker immediately and get it corrected.

A brokerage commission is either added to the total purchase cost or subtracted from the total sale proceeds. The brokerage firm will automatically deduct the total purchase cost from the cash you deposited in your account. The transaction is actually "settled" five business days after the trade.[2] By the settlement date you must have either provided the cash for the purchase or the stock certificates for the sale. New accounts will generally have to have the cash or stock in the account before a purchase or sale is permitted, but eventually the firm will trust you to make good by the settlement date. Keep all of your confirmations in a safe place. When your stock certificates arrive, put them in your safe-deposit box. Every month you will also receive a monthly statement of activity in your account, which you should check carefully for accuracy, and also keep on file. You will need these records for tax purposes. Details of recordkeeping and taxes are discussed in Chapter 12.

SOURCES FOR THE BEGINNING PAD INVESTOR

Abrams, R. A. & Associates, *The Stock Market*. A two-hour videotape that covers the basics of investing. Cost is $39.95 plus shipping. Write to: R. A. Abrams, 152 Maple Heights Road, Pittsburgh, PA 19232, or call 1-800-304-5552.

New York Institute of Finance, *Guide to Investing*. New York: Simon and Schuster, 1987. A good starter book, with chapters like "What is a stock?," "Opening an account," and "Entering an order." Has a nice glossary, too.

New York Institute of Finance, *How the Stock Market Works*. New York: Simon and Schuster, 1988. Covers some more advanced topics.

Teweles, R. J. and E. S. Bradley, *The Stock Market*. 5th edition. New York: Wiley, 1987. This is a big book with all you will ever want to know.

2.   The SEC is planning to reduce the number of days to "settlement" to three.

CHAPTER 5
MUTUAL FUND SELECTION USING THE PAD SYSTEM (PAD-M)

"Funds have become the little guy's way of tapping into the securities markets. But simply dumping some bucks into a few mutual funds isn't enough."

—Jonathan Clements, *Funding Your Future* (1993)

Many investors, including some PAD investors, prefer to bypass the process of individual stock selection and portfolio management and leave this time-consuming work to professional money managers. The good news is that mutual funds provide professional money management and instant diversification for the ordinary investor, especially one who is just starting out, or one who has a relatively small supply of risk capital. The bad news is that there are more mutual funds than stocks listed on the New York and American Stock Exchanges combined. The process of selecting one or more of the bewildering array of mutual funds can be turned over to still another professional, such as a stockbroker or financial planner. You will pay for this help, however, and it is only fair to point out that stockbrokers earn commissions from the mutual funds they sell to you. The purpose of this chapter is to show you how you can "do it yourself," that is, build and manage a portfolio of mutual funds on your own in your spare time. This portfolio can substitute for, or complement, a portfolio of PAD stocks selected with the rules of Chapters 2–4.

I have set out below the rules you must follow to build a solid, "all-weather" portfolio of equity mutual funds.[1] These rules are applied to data published in *Morningstar Mutual Funds*, a comprehensive source of information on mutual funds that can serve as a research base for the PAD mutual fund investor, much as the *Value Line Investment Survey* serves as a research base for the PAD stock investor. I would not buy any mutual fund without reading the Morningstar report first.

Morningstar Mutual Funds arrives biweekly in two parts: one section (Figure 5.1) contains full-page reports on approximately 120 mutual funds; a "Summary" section (Figure 5.2) lists key data, including most of the data the PAD mutual fund investor needs, for all funds. (The potential for "information overload" is so great that Morningstar includes a 50-page "User's Guide" and a videotape with all trial and annual subscriptions.) Before you can apply the rules of this chapter, it is necessary to build a basic understanding of the most important numbers and ratings reported by Morningstar.

Three of the most important ratings appear in the "Historical Profile" box within the price graph (see Figure 5.1, Line A). These ratings are also included in the Summary section for all funds (see Figure 5.2, Line A). The first rating measures the fund's load-adjusted total return[2] (income plus capital gains, with sales and other charges deducted) *relative* to all the equity funds in the Morningstar universe. The second rating measures the risk, as calculated by Morningstar, *relative* to all equity funds followed by Morningstar. Funds scoring in the top 10 percent for risk or for return are rated "High"; the next 22.5 percent are rated "Above Average," the next 35 percent are rated "Average," the next 22.5 percent are rated "Below Average," with the lowest 10 percent rated "Low." (Morgan Growth rates an "Average" for both categories.) The actual relative return and relative risk numbers, for three-year, five-year, and 10-year periods, are marked as Box "B" in Figure 5.1. (Morgan's numbers are all close to 1 for both relative return and relative risk.) Morningstar then divides the relative return by the relative risk to get a risk-adjusted rating. Again, these ratings are grouped into the five same categories as relative return and

---

1.   While Morningstar covers every flavor of mutual fund, from small-company growth to tax-free municipals, I have built the system for equity funds. Mutual fund investors principally concerned with taxable or tax-free income should consult the special section on income at the end of this chapter.

2.   In early 1994, *Morningstar Mutual Funds* switched the basis for its ranking system from total relative return to excess relative return. This change is an improvement, and it does not necessitate any changes in the PAD mutual fund selection rules.

risk: the top 10 percent of the return/risk ratios are rated as "Highest" (earning five stars), the next 22.5 percent are "Above Average" (four stars), the next 35 percent are rated "Neutral" (earning three stars like Morgan), the next 22.5 percent are rated "Below Average" (two stars), and the bottom 10 percent are rated "Lowest" (one star).[3]

While some investors buy only "five-star" funds, I believe this is a mistake, much as buying only Value Line stocks rated "1" for year-ahead performance is a mistake. Morningstar ratings do change (notice the arrows marking changed ratings in Figure 5.2), and the fact that a fund has dropped from five to four stars, for example, does not mean it is not an excellent long-term holding. In fact, I believe that the relative return and relative risk measures are at least as important as the overall rating, and that the Average Historical Rating ("C" in Figures 5.1 and 5.2) is also vital. I have used these measures to build the rules set out below. First, however, a little digression on risk.

Morningstar's measure of risk is somewhat controversial. No less a mutual-fund eminence than John Bogle[4] has found fault with it. More standard risk measures, such as the standard deviation of the mean return and beta, measure volatility. Morningstar prefers to separate upside volatility (good) from downside volatility (bad) by looking only at return shortfalls, that is, how many months did the fund return less than the risk-free T-bill rate, and how big were these shortfalls on average? This average shortfall is the only measure of a fund's risk, which is then compared to all equity funds to determine relative risk. My own position is that since the Morningstar risk rating is fairly closely correlated with the standard deviation of mean returns, there is little harm in using it. In particular, most of the divergences between Morningstar relative risk and the standard deviation can be traced to especially good or bad performances by a fund in the fourth quarter of 1987 and/or the third quarter of 1990, both periods of sharply falling stock prices. I think it is a good idea to give extra weight, as Morningstar does, to these investor nightmares, since they will certainly be repeated in some form in the future.

John Bogle and others also find fault with the "star" system, which is based simply on the ratio of relative return to relative risk. They have a point: why should return and risk be weighted equally? My solution, as noted above, is to put less emphasis on the fund's current

3. Funds with less than a three-year history are too young to receive a rating, and also too young for the PAD mutual fund advisor to purchase.
4. John C. Bogle, *Bogle on Mutual Funds* (New York: Irwin, 1994). See Sources section at the end of this chapter.

Figure 5.1: Vanguard/Morgan Growth

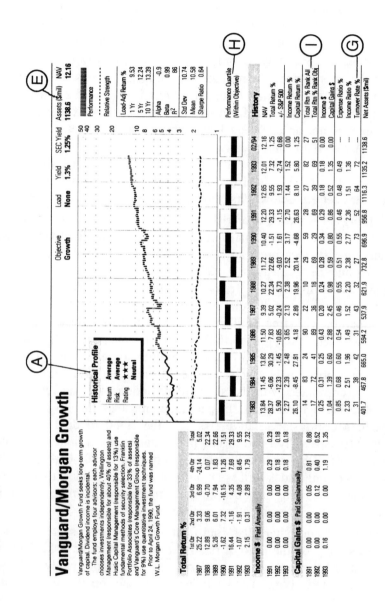

Vanguard/Morgan Growth

Vanguard/Morgan Growth Fund seeks long-term growth of capital. Dividend income is incidental.

The fund employs four advisors; each advisor chooses investments independently. Wellington Management (responsible for about 40% of assets) and Husic Capital Management (responsible for 13%) use fundamental methods of security selection. Franklin Portfolio Associates (responsible for 33% of assets) and Vanguard's Core Management Group (responsible for 9%) use quantitative investment techniques.

Prior to April 24, 1990, the fund was named W.L. Morgan Growth Fund.

Total Return %

	1st Qtr	2nd Qtr	3rd Qtr	4th Qtr	Total
1987	25.22	3.33	6.99	-24.14	5.02
1988	12.89	9.06	-0.70	0.07	22.34
1989	5.26	6.01	7.94	1.83	22.66
1990	-1.62	7.32	-16.15	11.26	-1.51
1991	16.44	-1.16	4.35	7.69	29.33
1992	-1.07	-1.91	4.08	8.45	9.55
1993	2.15	0.31	2.89	1.79	7.32

Income $ Paid Annually

	1st Qtr	2nd Qtr	3rd Qtr	4th Qtr	Total
1991	0.00	0.00	0.00	0.29	0.29
1992	0.00	0.00	0.00	0.18	0.18
1993	0.00	0.00	0.00	0.18	0.18

Capital Gains $ Paid Semiannually

	1st Qtr	2nd Qtr	3rd Qtr	4th Qtr	Total
1991	0.00	0.00	0.05	0.81	0.86
1992	0.00	0.00	0.12	0.40	0.52
1993	0.16	0.00	0.00	1.19	1.35

Historical Profile

Return	Average
Risk	Average
Rating	★★★
	Neutral

Objective	Load	Yield	SEC Yield	Assets ($mil)	NAV
Growth	None	1.3%	1.25%	1138.6	12.16

Relative Strength

Load-Adj Return %	
1 Yr	9.53
5 Yr	12.24
10 Yr	13.39

Alpha	-0.9
Beta	0.99
R²	86

Std Dev	10.74
Mean	10.58
Sharpe Ratio	0.64

Performance Quartile
(Within Objective)

History

	1983	1984	1985	1986	1987	1988	1989	1990	1991	1992	1993	02/94
NAV	13.84	11.45	13.82	11.50	9.39	10.27	11.72	10.40	12.20	12.65	12.01	12.16
Total Return %	28.37	-6.06	30.29	7.83	5.02	22.34	22.66	-1.51	29.33	9.55	7.32	1.25
+/- S&P 500	5.90	-12.33	-1.45	-10.85	-0.24	5.73	-9.03	1.61	-1.15	1.93	-2.74	0.66
Income Return %	2.27	2.39	2.48	3.65	2.13	2.38	2.52	3.17	2.70	1.44	1.52	0.00
Capital Return %	26.10	-8.45	27.81	4.18	2.89	19.96	20.14	-4.68	26.63	8.10	5.80	1.25
Total Rtn % Rank All	14	83	24	90	22	10	29	59	28	27	82	27
Total Rtn % Rank Obj	17	72	41	89	36	16	69	29	69	39	69	51
Income $	0.25	0.31	0.25	0.43	0.20	0.24	0.28	0.34	0.29	0.18	0.18	0.00
Capital Gains $	1.04	1.39	0.60	2.88	2.45	0.98	0.59	0.80	0.86	0.52	1.35	0.00
Expense Ratio %	0.85	0.68	0.60	0.54	0.46	0.55	0.51	0.55	0.46	0.48	0.49	--
Income Ratio %	2.33	2.51	1.96	1.49	1.52	2.20	2.38	2.77	2.36	1.51	1.36	--
Turnover Rate %	31	38	42	31	43	32	27	73	52	64	72	--
Net Assets ($mil)	401.7	467.8	665.0	594.2	537.9	621.9	732.8	696.9	956.8	1116.3	1135.2	1138.6

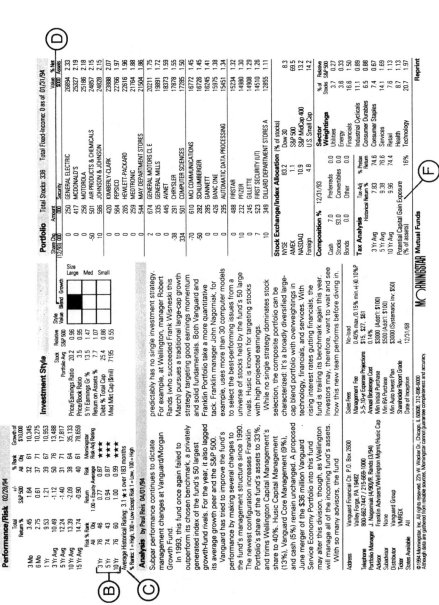

Source: *Morningstar Mutual Funds.* Morningstar, Inc. 225 West Wacker Drive, Chicago, IL 60606. 312-696-6000

Figure 5.2: Morningstar Index

Index

Bost – Dean

Page	Fund	Obj	Month End NAV*	TR% YTD 12/31/93	3Mo	6Mo	1Yr	3Yr	5Yr	10Yr	Perfor-mance	Risk	Mstar Rating	Avg Rating	Mos Rated	Yield%	Sales Chg%
120	Boston Company Special Growth Retail	G	17.97	20.01	-6.31	4.62	20.01	25.08	17.22	12.81	+Avg	+Avg	★★★	2.6	104	0.0	None
121	Brandywine	G	24.97	22.59	-0.58	13.88	22.59	28.37	23.11		High	+Avg	★★★★★	3.8	61	0.0	None
731	Brinson Global	AA	10.79	11.15	1.23	3.66	11.15							—	0	2.5	None
568	Bull & Bear Gold Investors	SP	18.52	87.63	23.64	9.73	87.63	15.39	7.37	5.25	-Avg	High	★	1.8	181	0.0	None
333	Burnham A	GI	21.86	9.35	-0.87	3.53	9.35	11.59	10.88	13.19	Avg	Low	★★★★	3.5	181	3.9	3.00
765	Calvert Social Investment Mgd. Growth	B	30.42	5.95	0.17	3.38	5.95	10.28	10.13	11.67	+Avg	-Avg	★★★	3.4	99	3.1	4.75
1159	Calvert T/F Reserves Limited-Term	MN	10.72	4.02	0.88	1.96	4.02	5.18	5.83	6.35	Low	Low	★★★★★	4.4	118	3.6	2.00
510	Calvert World Values Global Equity	WW	17.47	22.52	7.31	14.97	22.52							—	0	0.4	4.75
122	Calvert-Ariel Appreciation	G	22.89	7.95	7.60	12.87	7.95	17.64			Avg	Avg	★★★	2.8	13	0.2	4.75
645	Calvert-Ariel Growth	SC	30.19	8.75	6.18	12.15	8.75	17.27	11.11		-Avg	Avg	★★	3.2	52	0.9	Closed
73	Capital Income Builder	EI	34.30	15.29	3.15	9.22	15.29	16.82	14.71		Avg	Low	★★★★	4.1	42	4.6	5.75
1094	Capital World Bond	WB	16.33	16.73	2.84	6.79	16.73	16.70	9.63		-Avg	-Avg	★★★	3.1	42	6.0	4.75
732	Capital World Growth & Income	AA	18.07		10.95	19.75								—	0	—	5.75
334	Cardinal	GI	12.85	5.88	2.23	5.14	5.88	15.45	12.00	13.35	Avg	-Avg	★★★★	3.4	174	2.1	6.00
1053	Cardinal Government Obligations	GM	8.54	4.37	0.89	1.40	4.37	7.85	9.30		-Avg	-Avg	★★★★★	3.6	59	8.3	4.50
448	Centerland Kleinwort Benson Intl Eq B	WF	15.07	28.48	8.60	16.85	28.48	11.54	7.78	14.50	Avg	+Avg	★★★	3.0	181	0.0	4.50
539	Century Shares	SF	24.04	-0.36	-8.60	-2.97	-0.36	18.50	16.78	15.42	+Avg	Avg	★★★★	3.0	181	1.8	None
123	CGM Capital Development	G	27.71	28.66	9.03	17.48	28.66	44.37	29.16	21.88	High	+Avg	★★★★★	4.3	181	0.2	Closed
766	CGM Mutual	B	28.88	21.83	0.25	6.68	21.83	22.11	17.50	16.74	High	+Avg	★★★★★	3.4	181	2.8	None
335	Clipper	GI	50.05	11.26	5.65	7.20	11.26	19.57	14.05		Avg	Avg	★★★	3.8	83	1.3	None
627	Cohen & Steers Realty	S	31.92	18.75	-6.86	2.50	18.75				—	—		—	0	4.5	None
1132	Colonial CA Tax-Exempt A	MC	7.62	10.54	1.28	4.24	10.54	9.84	8.92		-Avg	-Avg	★★★	3.1	55	5.8	4.75
993	Colonial Federal Securities A	GG	11.25	12.15	-0.43	2.26	12.15	11.12	10.68		+Avg	+Avg	★★	1.8	82	7.3	4.75
336	Colonial A	GI	8.20	14.46	1.47	5.92	14.46	17.70	12.57	13.88	Avg	-Avg	★★★★★	3.4	181	1.8	5.75
124	Colonial Growth Shares A	G	13.83	9.99	1.48	6.91	9.99	17.85	13.61	13.64	Avg	Avg	★★★	2.8	181	0.6	5.75

No.	Fund	Cat																Load
846	Colonial High-Yield Securities A	CY	6.95	19.69	5.12	7.07	19.69	27.78	12.20	12.47	Avg	Low	★★★★	3.0	181	9.5	4.75
890	Colonial Income A	CG	6.72	12.06	0.04	3.55	12.06	13.15	9.86	10.61	↑-Avg	Avg	★★★	2.8	181	7.5	4.75
806	Colonial Strategic Income A	I	7.39	14.96	3.39	5.65	14.96	17.39	10.61	10.18	-Avg	-Avg	★★★★	2.8	164	8.6	4.75
1160	Colonial Tax-Exempt A	MN	14.10	10.73	1.11	4.40	10.73	10.24	9.03	10.72	↑Avg	-Avg	↑★★★★★	3.9	76	6.0	4.75
1161	Colonial Tax-Exempt Insured A	MN	8.54	10.96	0.95	3.97	10.96	10.02	9.11	—	-Avg	Avg	★★★	2.4	62	5.3	4.75
994	Colonial U.S. Government A	GG	6.77	5.66	0.33	1.60	5.66	7.23	8.38	—	Low	-Avg	★★★	3.3	39	7.1	4.75
604	Colonial Utilities A	SU	13.77	9.28	-4.43	-1.13	9.28	18.31	13.13	10.91	Avg	Low	★★★★	3.4	113	5.0	4.75
767	Columbia Balanced	B	17.91	13.62	0.76	4.80	13.62	—	—	—	—	—	—	—	0	3.1	None
926	Columbia Fixed-Income Securities	CO	13.44	10.47	-0.55	2.47	10.47	11.71	11.54	11.06	+Avg	Avg	★★★	3.3	95	6.1	None
125	Columbia Growth	G	26.38	12.99	2.32	8.19	12.99	19.26	16.18	13.62	+Avg	Avg	★★★	3.7	181	0.6	None
1273	Columbia Municipal Bond	MS	12.71	10.73	0.89	3.90	10.73	9.62	8.93	—	↑Avg	↑Avg	↑★★★★	3.3	78	5.2	None
646	Columbia Special	SC	19.51	21.55	3.44	12.07	21.55	27.64	19.17	—	↑+Avg	+Avg	★★★★★	4.2	62	0.0	None
337	Common Sense Growth & Income	GI	15.95	9.40	1.03	4.76	9.40	15.52	13.71	—	Avg	-Avg	★★★	2.9	45	1.6	8.50
126	Common Sense Growth	G	15.26	9.37	1.52	4.66	9.37	17.54	14.95	—	Avg	Avg	★★★	2.8	45	0.7	8.50
74	Compass Capital Equity-Income	EI	12.48	17.10	5.57	9.42	17.10	16.47	—	—	Avg	-Avg	↑★★★★	3.9	20	3.1	3.75
768	Composite Bond & Stock	B	11.99	9.27	1.41	4.45	9.27	13.47	10.43	10.37	-Avg	-Avg	★★★	2.9	181	3.7	4.50
338	Composite Growth	GI	12.20	6.80	4.21	4.62	6.80	14.71	9.73	11.21	-Avg	-Avg	★★★★	3.0	181	1.5	4.50
891	Composite Income	CG	9.33	10.86	-0.38	3.30	10.86	11.77	10.06	10.69	Avg	Avg	★★★★	2.4	180	6.6	4.00
127	Composite Northwest 50	G	14.39	2.42	6.68	4.34	2.42	15.15	15.82	↑	Avg	+Avg	★★★	4.1	50	0.5	4.50
1162	Composite Tax-Exempt Bond	MN	8.04	12.60	0.90	4.59	12.60	10.98	9.53	10.47	Avg	Avg	★★★	2.3	168	4.9	4.00
995	Composite U.S. Government Securities	GG	10.79	8.12	-0.05	1.93	8.12	9.59	10.30	10.12	-Avg	Avg	★★★	3.0	97	6.4	4.00
996	Comstock Partners Strategy O	GG	9.92	20.47	1.40	11.55	20.47	10.28	11.31	—	↑+Avg	High	★	1.2	32	7.4	Closed
128	Connecticut Mutual Growth	G	15.14	20.91	0.91	8.20	20.91	22.82	18.12	—	+Avg	-Avg	★★★	3.2	64	1.8	5.00
733	Connecticut Mutual Total Return	AA	14.54	15.89	0.91	5.88	15.89	17.74	14.84	—	+Avg	-Avg	★★★★	3.4	64	3.1	5.00
75	Cowen Income+Growth	EI	11.63	9.25	0.16	3.01	9.25	15.76	11.64	—	-Avg	Low	★★★	3.2	52	3.9	4.85
734	Crabbe Huson Asset Allocation	AA	13.07	18.21	5.38	8.57	18.21	17.15	—	—	+Avg	-Avg	★★★★★	3.8	24	1.6	None
129	Crabbe Huson Equity	G	15.84	25.97	8.83	12.42	25.97	25.58	—	—	+Avg	Low	★★★★★	4.5	24	0.4	None
130	Dean Witter American Value	G	23.10	18.70	-4.34	6.88	18.70	24.54	19.14	14.19	+Avg	Avg	★★★★	2.9	129	0.0	5.00d
1133	Dean Witter CA Tax-Free Income	MC	13.31	10.47	0.20	3.46	10.47	9.49	8.73	—	+Avg	+Avg	★★	1.9	78	4.5	5.00d
131	Dean Witter Capital Growth Securities	G	12.23	-9.01	5.14	5.06	-9.01	10.25	—	—	-Avg	Avg	★★	2.0	8	0.0	5.00d

*NAVs are through 12/31/93

MORNINGSTAR *Mutual Funds*   Reprint

Source: *Morningstar Mutual Funds*. Morningstar, Inc. 225 West Wacker Drive, Chicago, IL 60606. 312-696-6000

number of stars, and more emphasis on relative return, relative risk, and the Average Historical Rating.

Rule 1M: Morningstar's (relative) return must be at least Above Average.

Relative return is the most fundamental measure of performance. No matter how many stars the fund earns, if returns are not at least above average, there is no reason to commit your funds. Although the past does not necessarily foretell the future, there are enough funds earning consistently above-average returns to choose from.[5]

Rule 2M: Morningstar's (relative) risk must be no higher than Average.

Some funds earn above-average returns by taking above-average risks. I prefer funds that earn above-average, although perhaps not spectacular, returns without taking a lot of risk, as measured by Morningstar. During long bull markets, the high-risk funds may generate top returns, only to get clobbered when the market finally suffers a major setback. Funds satisfying rule 2M should not be hurt so badly. In fact, I search for funds that have Below Average risk to accompany their Above Average rule 1M returns. Funds with this near-ideal combination are doing more with less, which is just what a careful PAD investor should be searching for in a professional manager.

Rule 3M: Morningstar's star rating must be at least four stars.

This rule allows me to further winnow down the list of funds I want to consider. Normally, funds that satisfy rules 1M and 2M will also satisfy rule 3M, but it is possible that a fund will just barely sneak into the Above Average category for return and the Average category for risk, and a three-star overall rating will often result. While this three-star fund is certainly not a bad choice, four- and five-star funds passing rules 1M and 2M are still better choices. Since a PAD investor only needs a handful of funds for diversification, it makes sense to be very picky.

Rule 4M: Average Historical Rating must be at least 3.0 stars.

Some funds with a current *Morningstar* rating of four or five stars, which also pass rules 1M and 2M, may have a long-term record that is inferior to the average fund. This is possible because the current

---

5. There is some academic evidence that past returns may in fact predict the future. See the "Hot Hands" paper listed in the Readings section at the end of this chapter.

star rating is a blend of star ratings for the most recent three-year, five-year, and 10-year periods; some funds without long rating histories have their current rating based on three-year and five-year ratings, or even just the three-year rating. Thus one or two years of outstanding performance could hide a long-term record of mediocrity or worse. The Average Historical Rating (AHR) (see "C" in Figures 5.1 and 5.2) will reveal this, and a fund that has not even managed a three-star average rating over its rated life should be excluded from consideration. While it is true that a low AHR fund with five current stars may not be just a "flash in the pan," some will indeed revert to mediocrity. For the fund that is truly "born again" with a new manager, or new philosophy, or just better luck, continued above-average performance will eventually raise the AHR to 3.0, thus enabling the fund to pass rule 4M.

Rule 5M: The fund should be a "no-load" fund.

"...[T]here is absolutely no evidence that the returns on stock funds that charge a load are sufficient to overcome the drag of their sales charges." So says John Bogle.[6] I agree. Certainly there are "load" funds that have generated superior risk-adjusted returns, but there are plenty of no-load funds that have also done so. As a PAD investor, you will be doing your own research to build a mutual fund portfolio. Why handicap your performance by paying an extra commission, which usually goes to a salesperson? Of course, the load hurts most if you switch out of a mutual fund soon after purchase. But how can you be sure that won't be the best decision? A "back-end" load, which is assessed when you exit the fund, ties your hands in the same way. While I fully expect to hold my mutual funds for many years (I have held some for 20 years), I want the flexibility to change my portfolio without paying unnecessary fees or charges.[7]

Although the average level of mutual fund loads has been dropping in recent years, a new and less obvious fee, called a 12b-1 fee, has partly replaced the standard load. This fee has also been adopted by some "no-load" funds; thus a "pure no-load" fund is one that has no front- or back-end load or 12b-1 fee. This 12b-1 fee, which can be as high as 1 percent of assets, is ostensibly for the benefit of the fund, since it usually goes to defray advertising and marketing/distribution expenses. As John Bogle points out, however, there is no evidence

6. Bogle, p. 196.
7. Some Fidelity funds will waive the "load" for IRA investors, thus making them acceptable under rule 5M for IRA investors.

that shareholders of the fund benefit in any way from this fee.[8] I would be inclined to sharply limit in my portfolio the number of funds with these fees.

Rule 6M: Diversify (especially internationally).

Diversification should be easy with mutual funds, since each fund owns many stocks. Yet there are several ways a mutual fund investor can fail to get the full risk-reducing benefits of diversification. First, a number of specialty mutual funds, also called "sector" funds, invest in just one or a few industries, such as biotechnology, communications, real estate, etc. (Fidelity alone has about 20 of these funds.) Filling your portfolio with these funds means you are betting on very narrow sectors of the market with little diversification. I would limit a mutual fund portfolio to one of these funds at most. Second, an investor purchasing five funds, which are all oriented toward "large-cap" growth stocks, will discover that the funds are holding shares of many of the same companies in their portfolios. Again, the degree of diversification will be less than meets the eye. Morningstar is quite helpful here. The "style box" (see "D" in Figure 5.1) shows which of nine "styles" best describes a fund's holdings. These styles range from large-cap to medium-cap to small-cap, and from straight value to a value/growth blend to straight growth. If all of your chosen funds have exactly the same style of the nine possible, then you haven't fully diversified. Of course it is not necessary to cover all bases, but your set of funds should cover at least two style boxes.

Further diversification can be achieved with "asset allocation" and "balanced" funds, which hold a varying mix of stocks, bonds, and cash. (Several of my favorites in these categories are listed at the end of this chapter.) Still more, and crucial, diversification can and should be achieved by investing in "international" funds, which invest primarily or exclusively outside the U.S. market. It is now commonplace to hear that the American stock market has become a smaller and smaller part of the total world equity market. So even a well-diversified U.S. portfolio is not truly diversified. Adding foreign stocks to a U.S. portfolio can further reduce risk without any reduction in expected returns. Mastering foreign markets is just too complex a task for the individual PAD investor, so the international mutual fund is a tailor-made solution to the international diversification problem.

These six rules are sufficient for a PAD mutual fund investor to build a well-diversified portfolio. A list of funds that have regularly satis-

---

8.   Bogle, pp. 198-200.

CASE HISTORY: Vanguard International Growth Fund

I have owned shares of Vanguard International Growth Fund since its inception in 1985. I had originally purchased Vanguard's Ivest Fund beginning in the mid 1970s, and this fund was split into Vanguard World-U.S. and Vanguard World-International (now called International Growth) in 1985. I kept all of my shares of the international fund, since this gave me an effortless way to maintain international diversification. (Ivest did have some international holdings, but had no mandate to hold any foreign stocks.) As Table 5.1 illustrates, returns have been good enough to match the U.S. market over the 10-year period ending in December 1993, but what is more important, the pattern of the fund's *annual* total returns does not match up with the returns on the S&P 500. What this means, in nontechnical terms, is that if I own the S&P 500 (the U.S. market) and Vanguard International, I will do as well as someone holding either one, but with less risk: subpar years for the S&P, such as 1987, could be offset by a good year for Vanguard International, and vice versa (1991).

TABLE 5.1 Vanguard International Growth Fund

TOTAL RETURNS:		VANGUARD INTL	S&P 500	DIFFERENCE
YEAR	1985	56.96%	31.74%	25.22
	1986	56.71	18.68	38.03
	1987	12.48	5.26	7.22
	1988	11.61	16.61	−5.00
	1989	24.76	31.68	−6.92
	1990	−12.05	−4.98	−8.93
	1991	4.74	30.49	−25.75
	1992	−5.79	7.62	13.40
	1993	44.74	10.06	34.68
Ten Years (12/31/93)		16.96%	14.93	2.03

fied these rules appears in the appendix to this chapter. A number of these funds have been purchased for the mutual fund portfolio of the *PAD System Report*. Yet the optimal time to hold a mutual fund is not forever. A fund can change managers or philosophy or both and then proceed to underperform the market for a long period of time. A simple rule should help a PAD investor decide when to jump ship.

Rule 7M: If Morningstar's star rating drops to two stars, or the Average Historical Rating drops below three stars, or risk rises to "Above Average," or return drops to "Below Average," sell at least half of your fund holding.

This rule may seem a bit harsh, but a fund that has passed all of the first five or six rules to get in your portfolio in the first place will not qualify for sale under rule 7M unless it has a substantial period of relative underperformance, or a significant change in philosophy. If you really believe that the fund has just suffered a long run of bad luck, you can hold on to the other half of your investment and give the fund another six months or a year to shape up. If it doesn't, ship it out.

If you use this rule, I think it is unnecessary to worry about changes in managers. Fidelity Magellan is, of course, the most famous example: the fund has done quite well since the departure of "Saint" Peter Lynch and has maintained superb Morningstar ratings under a succession of mere mortals. By the same token, however, I would not purchase or hold a fund solely because it has a new "hot" manager. If the manager really is the next Peter Lynch, there will be plenty of time to buy the fund after it qualifies under rules 1M–5M.

Many PAD mutual fund investors will be perfectly happy to remain fully invested through bull and bear markets, switching out of a fund and into a new one only when the above rules dictate such a change. This approach minimizes the time and effort that must be devoted to the market without sacrificing much potential return. For busy investors, this is an unbeatable combination. For PAD mutual fund investors who would like to take a more active role in managing their fund holdings, it is possible to practice some simple long-term market timing using the VL MAP rule (Value Line Median Appreciation Potential) of Chapter 6.

Rule 8M (OPTIONAL): When the VL MAP reaches the SELL range (65 percent), begin selling shares in your mutual funds and raising cash reserves. Continue raising cash reserves as long as the VL MAP stays in the SELL range, with an upper limit of 50 percent cash reserves.

Rule 9M (OPTIONAL): When the VL MAP returns to the BUY range (100 percent), begin reducing cash reserves, and if the VL MAP stays in the BUY range, reduce them to zero.

If the VL MAP continues to be a good indicator of periods of market over- and undervaluation, this pair of rules can add significantly to your long-run investment performance by reducing your losses during major market declines, and then returning you to a fully invested position in plenty of time for the next bull market.

It is quite likely that 10 or even 20 no-load funds rated by Morningstar will meet all of the PAD requirements for purchase. Since 5 to 10 funds should be sufficient for full diversification, it will be necessary

CASE HISTORY: Vanguard Morgan Growth Fund

I first purchased shares of Morgan Growth in 1976, as part of a "403(b)" tax-de-ferred annuity program available to employees of educational institutions. After I completed my accumulation phase, I loyally held all my shares of what would turn out to be a thoroughly middling stock fund (see Figure 5.1). (Of course, there was no Morningstar for me to consult for most of this time.) Although the VL MAP was firmly in the SELL range all through 1987, and I did liquidate much of my stock portfolio, I was unaware that I could shift my 403(b) funds from Morgan to a Van-guard money-market fund, since my account had a life insurance company as cus-todian. Too bad I didn't check on this. After the crash, I decided I should find out if I could shift the funds directly. In 1989, I did so, and made two partial switches into one of Vanguard's money-market funds. I switched the rest of my money out of Morgan by May 1990, and then switched back into Morgan in August and Septem-ber 1990, after the market had declined substantially and the VL MAP had returned to the BUY range. The upshot of this flurry of activity was that in September 1990 I had 19 percent more shares than I would have if I had stayed fully invested. Not all switches will be timed this well, though. Although Morgan had a lackluster year in 1993, gaining only 8 percent, my Morgan money was already back in the money-market fund, earning only 3 percent.

to winnow your group of prospects. One approach I have used is to "raise the bar" by requiring, in particular, that all funds have "Below Average" risk rather than just "Average" risk. The advantage here is that the fund could go up a notch in risk without triggering a potential sell signal. A second and possibly complementary approach to the winnowing process is to examine other data in the full-page Morning-star report on a fund. I discuss a number of these items, and guide-lines for their use, in the paragraphs below.

One obvious practical consideration is the minimum initial investment required, which appears in small print near the bottom center of the fund page. Morgan, for example, has a $3,000 minimum initial in-vestment. If a PAD investor has just $5,000 to put in mutual funds, this minimum will make it very difficult to achieve the necessary di-versification. (In many cases, including Morgan, the minimums are much smaller for IRAs.) You may even stumble across "institutional" funds, with minimums of $100,000 or more, which are suitable only for the very largest portfolios.

I also consider the size of the fund, as measured by net assets (see "E" in Figure 5.1). Morningstar does drop coverage of a few funds in almost every biweekly issue, and the most common reason is a low or dwindling asset base. Any fund with less than $50 million in assets should be avoided simply because there is a good chance Morningstar will cease coverage. If Morningstar does drop a fund you own, begin looking for a replacement right away.

Many mutual funds make large year-end distributions to their shareholders. They are required to pay out almost all of their income and realized capital gains every year to maintain their tax-exempt status. These distributions are, of course, taxable to the shareholder unless the account is tax-sheltered. A mutual fund investor purchasing a fund in December may receive a rude jolt when a $10.00 net asset value (NAV) fund becomes a $9.00 NAV fund after the payment of a $1.00 per share capital gains distribution. This distribution is fully taxable as far as the IRS is concerned, even though the shareholder has really just received a return of capital. This unpleasant situation can be avoided by checking the "potential capital gains exposure" of the fund (see "F" in Figure 5.1). This is Morningstar's estimate of the amount of realized and unrealized capital gains as a percent of the fund's assets. The higher the percentage, the greater the chance for that rude jolt. A high percentage is, of course, no reason to avoid a fund, since any fund that has done well will have capital gains, and for some investors capital gains may be taxed at a lower rate than ordinary income. A call to the fund (see the lower left portion of the report) should provide the information on the size and date of any year-end distribution. If it is going to be a "biggie," just buy the fund on the day after it is made.

The frequency with which "unrealized" gains become "realized" depends in part on the rate of turnover[9] of the fund, which I also like to check on (see "G" in Figure 5.1). Turnover rates well in excess of 100 percent make me a little uneasy, because they suggest that the manager is trading rather than investing for the long term.

Another good tiebreaker is the Morningstar measure of the fund's performance versus its peer group. For example, I list several no-load international funds at the end of this chapter. Assuming all still pass all the rules when you are ready for your dose of international diversification, how would you pick just one? Try comparing the performance quartile graphic for the last five years (see "H" in Figure 5.1). Has one fund stayed out of the bottom quartile all of those years? Has one stayed above the midline all of those years? If visual inspection

9.   The simplest way to think of the turnover rate is as follows: if a fund with a constant $100 million in assets buys $100 million in securities during the year, and also sells $100 million in securities during the year, its turnover rate is 100 percent. In effect it has "turned over," or replaced, its entire $100 million portfolio exactly once during the year.

does not reveal a winner, you can examine the precise performance ranking relative to all funds with the same objective (see "I" in Figure 5.1). Still another potential tiebreaker is the series of annual performance statistics for the fund. Does one fund beat the S&P or other appropriate benchmark more often than another? At this point, however, the returns from additional investigation are likely to be slim. This could be the only situation where I might compare the length of tenure of the current manager(s), which I normally ignore in favor of performance data.

I also look at a fund's expense ratio. There is normally no reason for this ratio to exceed 1 percent, and low-cost funds like John Bogle's Vanguard Group cluster around 0.5 percent. All else equal, that extra bite will come out of future returns, year after year.

THE VALUE LINE ALTERNATIVE

In late 1993, Value Line launched its own *Value Line Mutual Fund Survey*. There is no doubt that more competition in the mutual fund rating field will be good for investors. While I have examined this service, I am not ready to throw over Morningstar for the "upstart" yet, especially since it is quite possible that the market will not support two comprehensive mutual fund rating services.[10]

INVESTING FOR INCOME

A mutual fund investor seeking income can certainly apply rules 1M–6M to those funds that seek income as well as capital gains. I have included balanced funds and an asset allocation fund among my favorite funds listed below, although it is certainly true that these funds have profited greatly from a long bull market in bonds, which apparently ended in 1994. Investors placing even higher emphasis on income can apply rules 1M–6M to the various types of bond funds covered by Morningstar, although I should point out that I have not done this myself.

INDEX FUNDS

Many mutual fund investors have further simplified the mutual fund choice problem by buying "index funds," mutual funds that are pas-

---

10. Readers can check on my current thoughts on the Value Line versus Morningstar battle by writing to me at P.O. Box 554, Oxford, OH 45056.

sively managed to match the returns of an index like the Standard and Poor's 500 Index. This is certainly an acceptable strategy, since the evidence suggests that, on average, U.S. stock funds fail to match the returns earned by the unmanaged S&P 500. Although the PAD mutual fund investor's portfolio is designed to be above average, it is quite likely that a low-expense, no-load index fund like Vanguard Index 500 will pass rules 1M–5M, and thus be a suitable PAD holding. The logic for this is both simple and revealing: If the average stock fund is trailing the S&P 500, then an index fund matching the S&P 500 will have above-average returns as measured by Morningstar (rule 1M). Since the Morningstar relative risk of a portfolio holding the whole S&P 500 should be no higher than average, and probably below the typical stock fund (which on average holds more volatile issues), Vanguard Index 500 should also pass rule 2M, and this risk/reward combination will frequently earn four stars (rule 3M). If Vanguard Index 500 earns either three or four stars all of the time, its Average Historical Rating will also be at least three stars (rule 4M). Thus it is quite likely that one or more index funds (new ones are being created all the time) will pass all the rules of this chapter.[11] Vanguard Index 500, the oldest and lowest-cost of index funds, is in fact included in my "Favorites" list in the appendix to this chapter.

THE "SINGLE-FAMILY" APPROACH

Many mutual fund investors may be tempted to further simplify their lives by restricting their mutual fund portfolios to funds that are part of a single "family" of funds, like Fidelity or Vanguard. While this certainly does reduce the paper flow, simplify recordkeeping, and make fund switching easy, the hidden and perhaps substantial cost is loss of choice. The best example of this cost is probably the Vanguard Group of funds, which is one of the largest fund groups and one of my favorites. And yet many Vanguard funds, like Morgan Growth, have turned in quite mediocre performance records over long periods of time. I am not willing to restrict my mutual fund portfolio to just one fund group, and my list of favorite funds at the end of this chapter includes mutual funds from 15 different fund groups.

---

11. Further reflection should convince the reader that if Vanguard Index 500 consistently earns four stars, with above-average returns and below-average risk, the average stock mutual fund must be consistently earning lower returns than the S&P 500, while taking more Morningstar risk. A cautionary thought indeed.

FIDELITY FUNDSNETWORK® AND SCHWAB ONESOURCE™

Mutual fund investors can have choice and convenience with new no-fee mutual fund services offered by industry giant Fidelity Investments and discounter Charles Schwab. These services allow you to own and trade as many as 350 different no-load mutual funds from a variety of fund families, with no transaction fees, and a single statement. While these services are probably ideal for IRA investors and others with tax-deferred investments, there are drawbacks. First, fees for this service could be reinstated at any time. Second, there is still some loss of choice, since, for example, Fidelity funds are not available through Schwab, and Vanguard funds are not available through either Schwab or Fidelity. Nonetheless, PAD mutual fund investors should weigh carefully the merits of these services, and others like them that will no doubt appear in the future, since it may now be possible to have your cake and eat it too.

SUMMARY OF RULES FOR CHAPTER 5

1M. Morningstar's (relative) return must be at least Above Average.

2M. Morningstar's (relative) risk must be no higher than Average.

3M. Morningstar's star rating must be at least four stars.

4M. Average Historical Rating must be at least 3.0 stars.

5M. The fund should be a "no-load" fund.

6M. Diversify (especially internationally).

7M. If Morningstar's star rating drops to two stars, or the Average Historical Rating drops below three stars, or risk rises to "Above Average," or return drops to "Below Average," sell at least half of your fund holding.

8M. (Optional) When the VL MAP reaches the SELL range (65 percent), begin selling shares in your mutual funds and raising cash reserves. Continue raising cash reserves as long as the VL MAP stays in the SELL range, with an upper limit of 50 percent cash reserves.

9M. (Optional) When the VL MAP returns to the BUY range (100 percent), begin reducing cash reserves, and if the VL MAP stays in the BUY range, reduce them to zero.

APPENDIX 5
MY FAVORITE MORNINGSTAR EQUITY MUTUAL FUNDS

All of the funds listed below have regularly passed rules 1M–5M, many with flying colors. They represent a good "starter list" for a mutual fund investor, although the latest Morningstar reports should of course be consulted before investing, and a PAD investor can certainly find excellent funds that are not on this list. A useful time-saving technique I employ is to go through the "Summary" section (see Figure 5.2) of Morningstar first, since it contains most of the ratings information necessary to find funds which pass rules 1M–5M.

Any of these "no-load" funds could, and may already have, adopted 12b-1 fees. It is also possible that one or more of these funds could be temporarily or permanently "closed" to new investors. This can be easily checked by examining the "Sales Charge" column in the Morningstar Summary section (see Figure 5.2). I have marked with an asterisk those funds that also provide good current income.

Crabbe Huson Equity

Dodge and Cox Balanced*

Fidelity Asset Manager*

Fidelity Balanced*

Fidelity Disciplined Equity

Founders Balanced

Gabelli Asset

Gabelli Growth

Janus

Laurel Stock

Lindner

Lindner Dividend*

Mutual Beacon*

Neuberger and Berman Partners

Nicholas

T. R. Price International

Scudder Growth and Income

Scudder International

Stein Roe Prime Equities

Vanguard Index 500

Vanguard International Growth

Vanguard Quantitative

Vanguard Wellesley Income*

READINGS FOR THE PAD MUTUAL FUND INVESTOR

Bogle, John C., *Bogle on Mutual Funds.* New York: Irwin Professional Publishing, 1994. Thorough, no-nonsense guide to mutual funds of all types. Bogle is at his best when discussing the industry's fee structure and its other shortcomings.

Clements, Jonathan, *Funding Your Future: The Only Investment Guide to Mutual Funds You'll Ever Need.* New York: Warner Books, 1993. A good book for the beginner, filled with good advice, including "Discipline" and "Patience."

Dickson, Joel M. and John B. Shoven, "Ranking Mutual Funds on an After-Tax Basis," National Bureau of Economic Research Working Paper #4393, July 1993. Taxes do matter for mutual fund investors, and low turnover may be beneficial for many growth fund investors.

Hendricks, Darryl, et al., "Hot Hands in Mutual Funds: Short-Run Persistence of Relative Performance, 1974–1988," *Journal of Finance,* March 1993. The results (pending further academic scrutiny) provide additional support for the PAD approach.

Morningstar Mutual Funds. Published by Morningstar, Inc., 225 West Wacker Drive, Chicago, IL 60606. The champion.

Value Line Mutual Fund Survey. Published by Value Line, Inc., 220 E. 42nd Street, New York, NY 10017-5891. The challenger.

CHAPTER 6
LONG-TERM MARKET TIMING

"There is a tide in the affairs of men, which, taken at the flood, leads on to fortune; omitted, all the voyage of their life is bound in shallows and miseries."

—Shakespeare, *Julius Caesar*

"How's the market today?" This question must be asked millions of times each day between the hours of 9:30 a.m. and 4 p.m. Eastern time. Yet no one owns the market. As a stockbroker I once knew used to say, "It's a market of stocks, not a stock market." But this idea is dangerously misleading, because when the market goes down, so will most of your stocks, most of the time, even if there is no reason. Wall Street commentators are paid regular salaries to tell audiences why the market went up or down on a particular day, but I am firmly convinced that no one knows, and that it does not matter. The fluctuations do matter, however, as great PAD stocks bought at the beginning of a bear market will fall—probably a lot—even if their long-term prospects are still bright. A disciplined investor can avoid buying at market tops and can concentrate purchases during periods of undervaluation and sales during periods of overvaluation. This rare ability, which I call long-term market timing, can be cultivated with a combination of fundamental, technical, and psychological indicators of the market's likely overall direction. The long-term market-timing rule explained below, in combination with the stock selection rules of Chapters 2 and 3, are the two beacons that will guide the PAD investor to financial success.

THE FUNDAMENTAL APPROACH

RULE 1: The market is OK to buy if *Value Line Investment Survey* Median Appreciation Potential (VL MAP) equals or exceeds 100 percent. Selling should be undertaken when this potential is below 70 percent. From 70 to 95 percent is a neutral area.

The most important question to be asked about the market, in a fundamental sense, is how fairly it is valued compared to historical norms. The valuation that is crucial, however, is not price relative to current earnings, but price relative to future earnings capitalized at historical norms. The best single measure of overvaluation or undervaluation is published by Value Line: The median estimated appreciation potential (MAP) for all 1,700 stocks followed by the service (see Figure 6.1, line A). This median has fluctuated between 234 percent at the bottom of the 1974 bear market, perhaps the worst postwar market debacle, and 18 percent at the market peak in 1968, one of the most severe periods of overvaluation in modern times. My rule of thumb is that if this median is at least 100 percent, the market is not overvalued and it is OK to buy. Once this indicator falls below 100 percent, it is time to be cautious. I consider 70–95 percent to be a neutral range: delay any new investments until the MAP is more favorable (switching is still OK). When the MAP falls below 70 percent, begin to build cash reserves by selling stocks.[1]

Chapters 2–4 will guide you in making up your Sell List. Although I first formulated Rule 1 in my own mind in the early 1980s, and have used it since then to successfully time purchases and sales of stock, I never performed a detailed "backcast" to see how the rule would have worked before the early 1980s. Once the data became available, however, I compiled a record of "buy" and "sell" signals (see Table 6.1) for VL MAPs going back to January 1968. It turns out that the VL MAP indicator has an excellent long-term record of signaling whether the market is cheap or dear: Rule 1 does a very good job of getting investors out of a bull market before it collapses, and getting them back in the market while stocks are still on the bargain counter.

To make the backcast as simple as possible, I ignore the neutral range of Rule 1 and define a buy signal as the first VL MAP reading of 100

---

1.   In the second edition of this book, a VL MAP reading of 70 percent was considered to be part of the sell range. I pointed out, however, that since Value Line rounds its MAP to the nearest 5 percent, 70 percent was an ambiguous reading, and a VL MAP of 65 percent was the clear signal to begin raising cash. I have now formally adopted this 65 percent rule, and have put 70 percent in the neutral range.

Figure 6.1: The Value Line Investment Survey

THE **VALUE LINE**
Investment Survey

Part 1
Summary
&
Index

File at the front of the
Ratings & Reports
binder. Last week's
Summary & Index
should be removed.

March 18, 1994

TABLE OF SUMMARY-INDEX CONTENTS	Summary-Index Page Number
Industries, in alphabetical order	1
Stocks—complete list with latest prices, Timeliness and Safety Ranks, Betas, estimated earnings, estimated dividends, and option exchanges; also references to pages in Ratings & Reports carrying latest full-page reports	2-23
Noteworthy Rank Changes	24

SCREENS

Industries, in order of Timeliness Rank	24	Low P/E stocks	35
Timely stocks in Timely industries	25-26	High P/E stocks	35
Timely stocks (1 & 2 for Performance)	27-29	High total return stocks	36
Conservative stocks (1 & 2 for Safety)	30-31	High 3- to 5-year dividend returns	36
High Yielding stocks	32	Companies with high return on capital	37
High 3- to 5-year appreciation	32	Bargain Basement stocks	37
Cash generating companies	33	Untimely stocks (5 for Performance)	38
Best Performing stocks last 13 weeks	33	High yielding non-utility stocks	38
Poorest Performing stocks last 13 weeks	33	High growth stocks	39
Stocks below book value	34	Stock market averages	40

The Median of Estimated **PRICE-EARNINGS RATIOS** of all stocks with earnings	The Median of **ESTIMATED YIELDS** (next 12 months) of all dividend paying stocks under review	The Estimated Median **APPRECIATION POTENTIAL** of all 1700 stocks in the hypothesized economic environment 3 to 5 years hence
16.3	**2.5%**	**60%** (A)
26 Weeks Ago* / Market Low 12-23-74* / Market High 9-4-87*	26 Weeks Ago* / Market Low 12-23-74* / Market High 9-4-87*	26 Weeks Ago* / Market Low 12-23-74* / Market High 9-4-87*
15.9 / 4.8 / 16.9	2.5% / 7.8% / 2.3%	60% / 234% / 40%

*Estimated medians as published in *The Value Line Investment Survey* on the dates shown.

ANALYSES OF INDUSTRIES IN ALPHABETICAL ORDER WITH PAGE NUMBER
Numeral in parenthesis after the industry is rank for probable performance (next 12 months).

	PAGE		PAGE		PAGE		PAGE
Advertising (23)	1825	Diversified Co. (31)	1356	Insurance (Life) (43)	1198	Railroad (13)	282
Aerospace/Defense (30)	551	Drug (37)	1259	Insurance(Prop/Casualty) (81)	621	R.E.I.T. (73)	1170
Air Transport (27)	251	Drugstore (18)	796	Investment Co.(Domestic) (51)	2091	Recreation (16)	1751
Aluminum (90)	1231	Electrical Equipment (76)	1001	Investment Co.(Foreign) (4)	363	Restaurant (6)	292
Apparel (66)	1601	Electric Util. (Central) (95)	701	Investment Co. (Income) (61)	972	Retail Building Supply (7)	885
*Auto & Truck (17)	101	*Electric Utility (East) (96)	159	Machinery (47)	1301	Retail (Special Lines) (40)	1665
*Auto & Truck (Foreign) (85)	108	Electric Utility (West) (93)	1720	Machinery (Const&Mining) (34)	1343	Retail Store (46)	1626
Auto Parts (OEM) (70)	807	Electronics (21)	1020	Machine Tool (75)	1335	Securities Brokerage (9)	1184
*Auto Parts (Replacement) (19)	114	Environmental (80)	347	Manuf. Housing/Rec Veh (1)	1540	Semiconductor (2)	1057
Bank (35)	2001	European Diversified (72)	829	Maritime (52)	276	Shoe (78)	1655
Bank (Canadian) (55)	1564	Financial Services (14)	2044	Medical Services (3)	665	Steel (General) (69)	604
Bank (Midwest) (48)	641	Food Processing (56)	1451	*Medical Supplies (26)	195	Steel (Integrated) (5)	1405
Beverage (Alcoholic) (89)	1526	Food Wholesalers (39)	1515	Metal Fabricating (62)	591	Telecom. Equipment (8)	774
Beverage (Soft Drink) (11)	1533	Foreign Electron/Entertn (64)	1549	Metals & Mining (Div.) (24)	1231	Telecom. Services (86)	746
Broadcasting/Cable TV (22)	1904, 379	Foreign Telecom. (29)	781	Natural Gas (Distrib.) (94)	470	Textile (79)	1614
Building Materials (38)	851	Furn./Home Furnishings (50)	902	Natural Gas(Diversified) (77)	449	Thrift (60)	1151
Canadian Energy (82)	432	Gold/Diamond (S.A.) (—)	1213	Newspaper (28)	1808	*Tire & Rubber (53)	123
Cement & Aggregates (15)	892	Gold/Silver Mining (42)	1219	Office Equip & Supplies (41)	1116	Tobacco (91)	312, 1571
Chemical (Basic) (49)	1249	Grocery (74)	1495	Oilfield Services/Equip. (68)	1851	Toiletries/Cosmetics (84)	818
Chemical (Diversified) (84)	1876	*Home Appliance (65)	128	Packaging & Container (36)	945	Toys (54)	1895
Chemical (Specialty) (57)	498	Homebuilding (32)	873	Paper & Forest Products (67)	913	Trucking/Transp. Leasing (10)	264
Coal/Alternate Energy (83)	1870	Hotel/Gaming (45)	1772	Petroleum (Integrated) (87)	401	Water Utility (88)	1415
Computer & Peripherals (44)	1075	Household Products (20)	959	Petroleum (Producing) (92)	1833	
Computer Software & Svcs (12)	2103	Industrial Services (25)	321	*Precision Instrument (33)	136	
Copper (71)	1232	Insurance (Diversified) (63)	2074	Publishing (59)	1789	*Reviewed in this week's edition.

In three parts: This is Part 1, the Summary & Index. Part 2 is Selection & Opinion. Part 3 is Ratings & Reports. Volume XLIX, No. 27.
Published weekly by VALUE LINE PUBLISHING, INC. 220 East 42nd Street, New York, N.Y. 10017-5891
For the confidential use of subscribers. Reprint by permission only. Copyright 1994 by Value Line Publishing, Inc. ® Reg. TM — Value Line, inc.

percent or higher recorded when a sell signal is in effect. By the same logic, a sell signal is the first reading of 65 percent[2] or lower occurring when a buy signal is in effect. Within this simplified framework, only 15 buy and sell signals were recorded in the 25-year period 1968–1993, so adherence to the rule certainly does not induce frequent trading. Since my data series begins in January 1968, when the VL MAP was already in the sell range, I consider the first signal to be a sell signal given at that moment. This was an "early" signal, in that the market did not hit its peak until December 1968. I prefer early signals to late ones, however, since a PAD investor should have at least several months to raise cash in a cautious and thoughtful manner. This leisurely selling is much easier to accomplish when the market is still rising. In addition, since I am willing to stop liquidating stocks when my cash position reaches 50 percent (see Chapter 4, Selling Rule 8), my remaining stocks normally participate in the final stages of the bull market. This increase in the value of my remaining portfolio will force my cash position below 50 percent, so that additional sales, at even higher prices, will be undertaken late in the bull market. Example: Suppose I am holding $30,000 cash and $30,000 stock late in a bull market. In spite of my best efforts to force it down, the market continues to rise, so that my stocks are now worth $40,000. My $70,000 portfolio is now less than 50 percent in cash, so I sell an additional $5,000 of stock so that I have about $35,000 of cash and $35,000 of stock. If the market stubbornly continues to rise, I will be forced to raise cash repeatedly. Of course, the bears will finally have their say. Even if a sudden decline forces my cash position above 50 percent, however, I cannot reduce it to 50 percent by buying stock until Rule 1 has given the signal that stocks are "OK to Buy."[3]

Looking again at Table 6.1, the Rule 1 sell signal in effect through 1968 would have forced a PAD investor to remain heavily in cash until the 1969–1970 bear market was almost over. The summer of 1970 was indeed an excellent time to buy stock. While a PAD investor would have been forced to begin selling stocks again by the end of 1970, another great buying opportunity arrived in 1973–1974,

2. To be fair, I have used a VL MAP of 70 percent as a sell signal for the period 1968-1990. Since 1990, I have used 65 percent as a sell signal, because the second (1990) edition of this book suggested that 65 percent was actually the "true" sell signal.
3. Note that the VL MAP may have an unusually large change in the March-April or July-August period, simply because Value Line extends its three- to five-year forecasts for individual stocks by one calendar year at one of these times.

TABLE 6.1   Buy and Sell Signals for VL MAP, 1968–1993

DATE	SIGNAL
1/5/68	SELL
5/29/70	BUY
12/18/70	SELL
6/1/73	BUY
6/16/78	SELL
11/3/78	BUY
6/5/81	SELL
7/10/81	BUY
4/22/83	SELL
2/17/84	BUY
12/6/85	SELL
11/6/87	BUY
3/2/88	SELL
8/31/90	BUY
11/22/91	SELL

when stocks became grossly undervalued. The VL MAP gave a buy signal in the summer of 1973 and remained in the "OK to Buy" range for more than a year. A PAD investor would have had ample time to become fully invested and would have remained that way until the summer of 1983 (10 years) with only two short bouts of liquidation in 1978 and 1981. Both of these sell signals were followed by periods of market weakness. A new round of buying in 1984 was followed by (early) selling at the end of 1985. By 1987, this 1985 sell signal appeared to have been wrong rather than early, but the crash of 1987 wiped out much of the gain that had been foregone, and afforded a new opportunity to buy stocks cheaply (see Figure 6.2).

The post-crash buy signal was followed by a March 1988 sell signal, which, with hindsight, was again too early. Nonetheless, the informal 50 percent cash rule allowed me to profit handsomely from the post-crash bull market, while sleeping more soundly at night. Additional sell signals were given in 1990, before the market again took a drubbing and pushed the VL MAP back over 100 percent (see Figure 6.3). The VL MAP remained above 100 percent until early 1991, and then, after spending most of 1991 in the neutral range, gave the first of many sell signals in November 1991. I began raising cash at this time, and reached the 50 percent cash level in 1993. These recent sell signals were again very early, since the market continued to gain

Figure 6.2: Value Line Map 1987

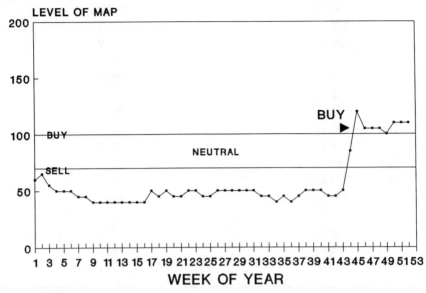

Source: Value Line

Figure 6.3: Value Line Map 1990

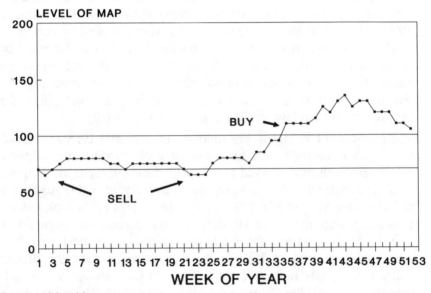

Source: Value Line

ground, without even a 10 percent correction, for more than two more years.[4] Although the VL MAP indicator forced me to hold "too much" in cash reserves during 1992 and 1993, the 25-year performance record of Rule 1 has been excellent.

This excellent performance has not gone unnoticed. The "cat" was officially let "out of the bag" in the summer of 1993, when two Baylor University finance professors reported in the *Journal of Portfolio Management* that the VL MAP was useful for forecasting future movements of the stock market. High levels of VL MAP tended to be followed by high returns for stocks, while low values of VL MAP tended to be followed by low returns for stocks.[5] Value Line reported in September 1993 that its own studies confirmed those reported by the Baylor professors.[6] Mark Hulbert, in a *Forbes* column in October 1993, reported these results and those of other studies, which came to the same conclusion.[7]

While this academic support is gratifying, the fact that the VL MAP secret is now widely known is a concern. Will it be true now that, to paraphrase the words of Shakespeare's Prospero, "all my magic is now o'erthrown?" I think not. There was no massive selling of stocks in late 1993 in response to the publicity, even though the VL MAP was within 10 percentage points of its low recorded before the crash of 1987. I still believe that Rule 1 is as valuable as any other rule in this book. It provides a fairly objective indication of the state of the market compared to historical norms, a priceless long-term perspective.

This perspective is not cheap, however: a PAD investor must have the patience and discipline to wait months, and sometimes years, before committing cash reserves to the market. In the last stages of a bull market, when stocks are rising to dizzying heights on wave after wave of optimism, this is admittedly very difficult. But of course that is why so many investors fail to outperform Wall Street.

THE TECHNICAL APPROACH

Stock exchange trading generates an enormous supply of data every day. All of the prices, volumes, and the like can be analyzed in an

4. The 10 percent correction finally arrived in early 1994.
5. William Reichenstein and Steven Rich, "The Market Risk Premium and Long-Term Stock Returns." *Journal of Portfolio Management* (Summer 1993).
6. Value Line, "Selection and Opinion." Value Line, Inc., 220 East 42nd Street, New York, NY 10017-8991.
7. Mark Hulbert, ". . . And the News Isn't Good." *Forbes* (Oct. 25, 1993).

almost infinite variety of ways in an attempt to foresee market trends. Those who study the data are called market technicians, and what they create are technical indicators whose levels or changes give advance warning of market rallies and declines. Some are, of course, more reliable than others, yet I do not consider any one indicator sufficiently reliable to let it determine my investment posture. I have listed below a number of individual technical indicators that can signal market bottoms and tops with some degree of reliability. My favorites are marked (F).[8] (A PAD investor with limited time can simply monitor Rule 1.)

Technical Indicators of Market Bottoms

New Lows (F)

Every day all major newspapers report in their financial sections the number of NYSE stocks that traded, on the previous day, at their lowest price in the past 52 weeks. These are called new lows. When the number of new lows exceeds 400 in a day, it is usually a sign that the market is nearing an important bottom and will begin rising soon. It takes a large amount of general selling pressure to drive 400 stocks to new 52-week lows in one day, and this is usually a sign of, and also a cause of, great pessimism on Wall Street. Many margin accounts are also damaged in this kind of selling, which can bring on further liquidation. Markets can bottom without new lows ever reaching 400 (1982 and 1984), but in 1987 new lows reached the 1,000 level after the crash. In 1990, the number of new lows peaked at 700.

Oddlot Sales-to-Purchases Ratio

Oddlotters, those who trade fewer than 100 shares (a round lot) at a time, have a time-honored reputation for being wrong at critical market turning points. This reputation is rather self-serving, for the Wall Street community in general is often wrong about the market. Nonetheless, the intensity of oddlot selling compared to buying tends to pick up at market bottoms. A good rule of thumb here is that when this ratio of shares sold to shares bought reaches 3.0, the "little guy,"

---

8. The "Wall Street Week" Technical Market Index (WSW TMI) was my all-time favorite technical indicator, and had its own "Rule" in earlier editions of this book. However, Robert Nurock, former "Chief Elf" of Wall Street Week, took himself and his elves off the show in the fall of 1989, and the TMI is no longer available. Louis Rukeyser, host of "Wall Street Week," now reports on a new set of elves (actually 10 Wall Street "technicians") every week, but this indicator is still too new to have a convincing track record.

as he is condescendingly known on Wall Street, is getting panicky and the market is approaching a bottom.

Investors must be careful when calculating the oddlot sales-to-purchases ratio, since it can be distorted by "program trading." Some variations of these computerized strategies entail "short" sales of stocks in the Standard and Poor's 500 Index in oddlot amounts of less than 100 shares. These program trades are, of course, completely unrelated to the activities of the little guy. Fortunately, short sales are listed separately from "other" sales in newspaper reports of oddlot trading. I calculate the ratio by dividing "other" sales by purchases, leaving out the distorting effect of short sales.

The sale/purchase indicator often shows the effects of forced liquidation of stock from margin accounts in the final stages of a bear market. The patient investor can profit from the bargain-basement prices if he avoids buying on margin and can keep from being swept along with the lemmings marching to the sea. This is, of course, very difficult to do. The herd instinct is very strong, and the managers of billions of dollars are subject to the same human frailties as ordinary investors. (The importance of psychology in market timing is discussed in "The Psychological Approach" section below.)

During the summer of 1984, the sale/purchase ratio exceeded 3.0, which is an unusually high level. In the summer of 1985, with the Dow-Jones Industrial Average 250 points above its 1984 low, the sale/purchase ratio fell to a neutral range between 2 and 2.5, but again returned to 3 before the market rallied sharply in 1985.

In 1987, the ratio reached the 1.0 level, suggesting that the small investor was too optimistic. Although I do not consider a low ratio of sales to purchases to be a first-rate indicator of market tops, I consider a reading of 1.0 (sales equal to purchases) to be a caution flag. Immediately after the 1987 crash, however, the ratio did fall below 1.0, but this was an anomaly: many investors who wanted to sell were unable to reach their brokers or were unable to get their sell orders executed.

In the early 1990s, this indicator fell below 1.0 and stayed there for many months at a time. The caution flag kept flying as the market kept rising, again suggesting that this indicator is not a particularly good forecaster of market tops.

CBOE Put-Volume/Call-Volume Ratio (F)

Chapter 10 is devoted entirely to the explanation of options trading and options strategies for the PAD investor. I include here only the briefest summary explanation of one kind of option, to make this technical indicator a little less abstruse.

A call option gives the buyer the right to buy a stock from the option writer at a specified price for a certain period of time. A put option gives the buyer the right to sell a stock to the option writer at a speci-fied price for a certain period of time. A put buyer is betting on or hedging against a decline in a particular stock, while a call buyer is betting on or hedging against a rise in a particular stock. Thus, put buyers are bearish and call buyers bullish. Some options traders buy or sell combinations of puts and/or calls, but their activity will have a smaller effect on the volume ratio.

Trading in these options has mushroomed in the past decade, with the creation of organized exchanges to trade options on many stocks. The oldest and largest is the Chicago Board Options Exchange (CBOE). *The Wall Street Journal,* the *New York Times,* and various financial publications carry complete listings of daily options trading. The number of puts and calls purchased each day varies fairly regularly with the market's short-term trend. Normally, call volume exceeds put volume by a significant amount, as option buyers tend to be (over?) optimistic. When the CBOE put-volume to call-volume ratio exceeds .9, it is quite likely the market is making a short-term bottom. The higher the ratio, the more powerful the ensuing rally should be. The buyers of puts and calls are supposed to be, in the aggregate, rela-tively uninformed investors who run with the herd that the PAD in-vestor is trying to avoid. Although this ratio falls significantly during a bull market, and can stay as low as .3, it does not signal tops as reliably as bottoms. I would consider persistent readings below .4 to be grounds for caution, however.

The put-volume/call-volume ratio does have an excellent short-term forecasting record. I cannot overemphasize the importance of "short-term." In the midst of a major bear market, this ratio will give buy signals (as in early September 1987), which may signal no more than a brief "dead-cat bounce." I use the ratio to determine my intraweek timing of purchases after Rule 1 of this chapter has flashed an "OK to Buy" signal. If I haven't already made my weekly purchase when the put/call ratio gives a buy signal, I will make a purchase the next morning, which almost always results in a well-timed purchase. Conversely, if I am in the midst of a selling program, I will postpone a sale for several days if the put/call ratio gives a buy signal.

The put/call ratio was featured in a *Wall Street Journal* article in early 1994. This wide publicity may reduce the usefulness of the put/call ratio for a period of time, especially since the the indicator's buy signals in early 1994 were not followed by a significant market rally. Readers should review this indicator's recent performance carefully before giving it "favorite" status.

Volume and the Selling Climax

Often, in the last stage of a bear market, there is a final precipitous drop of stock prices accompanied by very high volume. This collapse is usually followed immediately, even in the same day, by an upsurge of equal or even greater violence. You have not earned your investing stripes until you have survived one of these "selling climaxes." Unfortunately, not all bear markets end this way. Many die with a whimper rather than a bang: the 1981–82 bear market is a case in point. The last day of decline in August, before one of the greatest rallies in postwar history, saw the Dow-Jones Average fall by a minuscule 0.08 points. Complete exhaustion, but no climax. An investor waiting for a selling climax would have missed the entire 1982–83 bull market. In general, I think volume is a dubious indicator of any market trend, either up or down.

Mutual Fund Cash Percentage

The "big guy" can be wrong, too. Mutual fund managers often accumulate cash reserves as the market declines, and these reserves reach a peak at market bottoms. At market tops, cash reserves are often extremely small. Let this pattern be a caution to those who will trust all their money to mutual fund managers. Let it also be an indicator for the PAD investor: When the cash percentage is 15 percent or greater, stocks are probably ready for a significant rally. The statistic is regularly mentioned on the market commentary page of *The Wall Street Journal,* which is how I keep current on it. The major drawback of this indicator is that there is some controversy about the correct measurement of the cash percentage. The problem is that some mutual fund managers may stash their cash in Treasury notes, for example. These are highly liquid and can be sold in an instant to buy stocks, but they may not be counted as cash. You can follow the controversy on the market commentary page of *The Wall Street Journal.*

Investor's Intelligence™ Sentiment Index

Investor's Intelligence is an investment advisory letter that compiles an index of the sentiment of over 100 market letters, and its success as a contrary indicator should give pause to anyone who subscribes to a large number of market letters. Advisory letters tend to be bullish most of the time, probably reflecting the tendency of their readers to be bullish most of the time. When a large minority, or a majority, of letters are bearish, this usually signifies enough pessimism for a market bottom. Extremes of optimism, in which very few letters are bearish relative to historical norms, usually signal a market top. Rating the letters for bullish or bearish is as much an art as a science, though. This index is proprietary, and therefore not free, but it has a good track record as a contrary indicator.[9]

You can keep the cost of monitoring the index down to a minimum by occasionally purchasing a copy of *Investor's Business Daily,* the newspaper that lists the latest reading of the index in a box on the page entitled "General Market Indicators."

Indicators Old and New

Two other well-known indicators are the GM indicator and the Dow Theory. I feel these both have limited usefulness, although their proponents obviously think otherwise. *Caveat emptor:* The GM indicator stakes everything on the movement of the price of GM stock. In general, when GM stock is in an uptrend, that is good for the market, and when it is in a downtrend, that is bad for the market. GM usually moves with the market, but in those instances where it does not, I cannot see any reason why it can predict a change of direction for the entire market. When GM is at its peak (or nadir), so is the market much of the time. Indeed, there has even been controversy here, with proponents of this indicator disagreeing, in *The Wall Street Journal,* on the timing of true buy and sell signals.[10]

The Dow Theory, another old indicator, uses the Dow-Jones Transportation Average to confirm any signals given by the Dow-Jones Industrial Average, such as a decline below a previous major low (bearish), or a rise above a previous major peak (bullish). When the Transports fail to perform in the same manner, the original signal is not "confirmed." It seems to me that by the time the signal finally is confirmed, the bear or bull market could be closer to its end than its

9.   For a contrary opinion, see John Dorfman, "Professors Bring Bad News for the Pessimism Theory," *The Wall Street Journal,* January 26, 1989, p. C1.
10. See *The Wall Street Journal,* October 18, 1984.

beginning. It certainly tells us nothing about market turning points, which is the primary goal of market timing of any type.

Others Yet Unborn

There are many other technical indicators of the market's current condition and future health. As we have seen, *The Wall Street Journal,* especially the market commentary page, is a good source of information on new indicators. New indicators are probably being created at least as fast as old ones are being retired from the Wall Street battlefield. A good reference source, which should give any reader sufficient amounts of technical analysis to last a lifetime, is contained in a Chartcraft, Inc., publication called the *Encyclopedia of Stock Market Techniques.* It even has supplements, which will keep you up to date on the creation of new indicators. If you find an indicator that works, use it. But if there is no basis for its accuracy, I would be quite cautious. It is well known that the numbers of strikeouts of the old Washington Senators baseball team tracked the market very well for a number of years. And then there is the Superbowl indicator. While I can't deny that this indicator has a good predictive record, and was right on target from the late 1960s to the early 1990s, do we really want to bet our investment dollars on the outcome of a football game? I do not, but I must admit that it seems that many others do. The rally on the Monday after the 1985 Superbowl was quite impressive, and there was no other news to account for it. If enough Wall Streeters rely on this indicator, it could work for some time just because it is believed to work. This is of course a self-fulfilling prophecy, and a dangerous one.

If you are intrigued by this indicator, it should be noted that the Superbowl "theory" is silent on the effects on the market of a victory by an expansion team that was neither in the old AFL (bearish for the market for that year) or the old NFL (bullish for the market for that year). Note also that there are four old NFL teams in the AFC, so it is possible to have a Superbowl contest between two old NFL teams. In this case, if enough investors believe the indicator, the market should rally before the Superbowl is even played!

Technical Indicators of Market Tops

The preceding indicators are generally better at signaling market bottoms rather than tops. The following ones may be of some help in pinpointing market tops. Again, my favorites are marked (F).

New Highs

Although the number of 52-week new highs is not as reliable as the number of new lows, massive numbers of new highs, say 400 or more, are a signal for caution. The optimism generated by this pleasant turn of events will feed on itself for a time, but eventually we return to earth.

Bad Breadth

Many technicians study the number of stocks advancing each day relative to the number declining, called market breadth, and add or subtract the difference to a cumulative total, which, when plotted on graph paper, is called the advance-decline (A/D) line. While I would not put too much faith in the squiggles of the A/D line, there is a fundamental truth here: When the market is advancing, it frequently happens that it will get tired, that is, fewer and fewer stocks will participate in the uptrend by closing higher for the day. Breadth gets bad. This period of "brutal selectivity" often characterizes the last stage of a bull market. When only a few more stocks rise than fall on an up day, or even worse, when more stocks fall than rise even though the Dow and other indexes are rising, it is often a short-term sign that the market is getting tired. Unfortunately, it can happen that the market can "catch its breadth" and start rising again. A PAD investor needs more than breadth to be moved to buy or sell stock.

A/D technicians also use the term "divergence" to mean that the A/D line is not moving in tandem with the popular market averages. When the A/D line lags behind the averages in a rally, this is negative divergence and should indicate that the rally will not continue. Divergence in the opposite direction may signal the end of a market decline. Again, the main value of this indicator is as a check on the popular averages.

The value of the standard A/D line for the NYSE has been reduced in recent years by the listing on that exchange of large numbers of non-operating companies, such as closed-end mutual funds. A report in the *New York Times* Sunday Business Section (August 1, 1993) suggested that there was a growing divergence between the overall A/D line and an A/D line based solely on price movements of operating companies. Unfortunately, this "new-and-improved" A/D line is not readily available.

Another form of divergence occurs when the popular averages do not move in tandem to new highs in a bull market. This divergence is also supposed to be unhealthy for the market. An unusual example of this form of divergence occurred in 1985, when the rise in General Foods stock caused the Dow-Jones Average to make new highs when the rest of the market averages did not. The market then proceeded to rally strongly. Remember this example the next time you are told about the evils of divergence.

The *Time* Magazine Indicator (F)

This used to be my favorite indicator, in part because they never published my letters, and in part because I thought no one else knew about it. There is very little new under the sun on Wall Street, however: This indicator has been mentioned in *The Wall Street Journal.*

Time has a record for predicting the stock market and the fortunes of individual companies that is second to just about everyone. A favorable story about a company should be treated the same as the *Sports Illustrated* cover story jinx (same publishing company!). When *Time* runs an upbeat story on the market, it's time to build cash reserves. When *Time* features a stock of yours that has had a major run-up, it is time to sell. I know. It first happened to me in 1975, which is when I discovered this indicator. I held Fairchild Camera and Instrument, which in the beginning of 1975 had a meteoric rise mentioned in the July 7 issue of *Time*. This was, of course, its peak price for several years. The price chart of Fairchild in Chapter 2 shows the approximate date of the *Time* story and the price level at that time. After Fairchild's price collapse, I did some further research. I remembered that *Time* had featured McDonald's on its cover in September 1973. Sure enough, the stock fell by more than 70 percent in 14 months, as shown in Figure 6.4.

I have resisted purchasing IBM stock, even when it meets all of the criteria of Chapter 2, because *Time* ran a cover story on "Big Blue" in July 1983. This was sufficient to convince me that everyone's favorite would be a dog for some time to come. Hard times did arrive, and the stock performed poorly for more than a decade after the cover story (Figure 6.5).

In the summer of 1985, *Time* devoted a full-page story to the improving fortunes of Cray Research, one of the few high-technology stocks that doubled in 1985. I sold some of my holdings even though the stock had not quite tripled from my purchase price, just to be on the safe side. (Eventually the *Time* jinx did them in. See Figure 4.2.)

The *Time* magazine indicator is not like the Superbowl indicator at all. *Time* is rarely a first source for news of any kind. Most of the stories are already old news by the time they are reported. If a com-

Figure 6.4: McDonald's (NYSE-MCD) 1973–1975

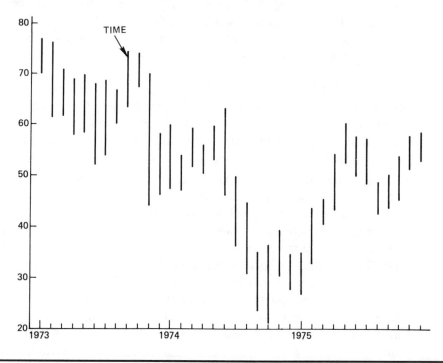

pany has built up a growth record enviable enough to be reported in detail in *Time*, it is probably ripe for a fall from grace. When the market has advanced or declined strongly enough to be chronicled in *Time*, the movement is probably over. I would consider a cover story on a raging bull market to be a major sell signal. Likewise, a cover story on a raging bear market would be a major buy signal. (This indicator is not perfect, however. I found a January 1955 cover story on a bull market that did not appear at the peak.)

Speculative Excesses in New Issues (IPOs) (F)

Often in the final phase of a bull market, relatively unseasoned speculative stocks, especially initial public offerings (IPOs) or new issues, outperform the general market by a wide margin. This is one indication of a frenzy that is invariably followed by disappointment. A large volume of new issues is sufficient cause for alarm, although I have no quantitative measure for it. A rapid rise in the NASDAQ index, which consists of many speculative issues, is another warning sign. The most dangerous sign of impending doom can often be found in the

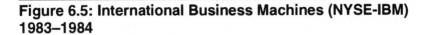

Figure 6.5: International Business Machines (NYSE-IBM) 1983–1984

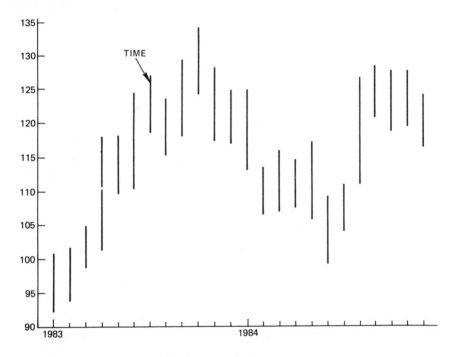

pages of *The Wall Street Journal.* In February 1983, when the stock of Diasonics went public, it was reported that a number of buyers of the stock had not the slightest idea of their business, other than that it was "hot." These "investors" pushed the price from $22 a share on the offering to $29 before the roof fell in. The stock subsequently fell as low as $2, and recovered to just $4 while the Dow was soaring to new highs. The entire OTC market began a severe decline shortly after Diasonics reached its peak price. There will be new-issue crazes in the future, as there are always new lambs for the slaughter. The PAD investor would be wise to avoid these stocks, and when all others are buying them, it is time to judiciously increase cash reserves. While the absence of a significant number of new issues is a positive sign for the market, the IPO market will dry up long before the general market has hit bottom. This boom-bust cycle repeated itself in 1987, when a boom in IPOs was cut off by the October crash. The IPO market then slowly revived, and by 1993 was red-hot again. The classic example was an IPO of Boston Chicken, a rotisserie-chicken restaurant chain that went public in the fall of 1993 at 20, and soared as high as 51 on its first day of trading. At that price, the stock was selling for about 100 times projected 1994 earnings. Within three months, the stock market began its first significant correction in more than three years.

NYSE Specialist Short-Sale Ratio (F)

New York Stock Exchange (NYSE) specialists are charged with making an orderly market in individual NYSE stocks. These specialists are permitted to sell short their assigned stocks as one way to maintain orderly markets. But, as noted in Chapter 4, specialists have more information than other investors, and are in business to make money. Some academic research[11] has suggested that in fact the specialists often intensify their short selling near market peaks, and reduce it to low levels near market bottoms.

The specialist short-sale ratio can be computed from data reported every Monday in the "Money & Investing" section of *The Wall Street Journal*, under the heading "Odd-Lot Trading." Divide the number of shares reported as short sales by NYSE specialists by the total number of shares sold short on the NYSE for the week. The result is the specialist short-sale ratio, which normally fluctuates between 35 percent and 50 percent. Although the specialists are sometimes wrong, my rule of thumb is that when the specialists' share of total NYSE short sales reaches 50 percent, the market is poised for a tumble. (The specialist short-sale ratio reached this level in 1987 before the crash.)

THE PSYCHOLOGICAL APPROACH

A number of the technical indicators listed above are really attempts to measure market psychology. Most experienced Wall Streeters will admit that the market is subject to bouts of excessive greed, which push stocks to unsustainably high levels, and periods of excessive fear and pessimism, which have the opposite effect. (Many academic economists deny that this is an accurate description of the market; their arguments are discussed in Chapter 9.) It is very difficult to observe this fear-greed cycle from the outside and not be caught up in it yourself. Panic spreads in human beings much the same as in animals in the forest, except that modern communications can spread it faster and farther. Paroxysms of greed are slightly more subtle, but

11. See Barbara Donnelly, "Short Sales: Do the Specialists Know the Most?" *The Wall Street Journal,* June 30, 1987.

the famous Dutch tulip craze and later speculative "bubbles" are not that far back in human history.

One valid, albeit difficult, technique to measure market psychology is the much-maligned use of introspection. If you are good at introspection, at analyzing your own emotions, you can feel the onset of fear as the market plummets downward toward a bottom. A certain queasiness spreads throughout your psyche as you begin to doubt your abilities and to second-guess yourself for jumping into the market too soon. Then comes the creeping fear that most of your assets will be lost in the market collapse and the sense of resignation that it may take years to recover to the position you were in a few short months before when all was well. If you are married, you may feel that vague sense of irritation that your spouse will not understand when you explain that the family is getting clobbered in the stock market decline, which you did not foresee. In difficult situations like these, which occur too often for my taste, you must constantly fight off the twin demons of fear and pessimism, hold on, and commit cash reserves if you have them. This is the time for patience and discipline. I would recommend reading this section over whenever the demons are on the attack, much as the missionaries read the Bible while in the stew pot. The difference is that if you hold on, you will not get cooked! One key rule we have discussed is: *Do not buy on margin.* This rule gives you extra protection when the market is collapsing toward a bottom: You are not forced to sell.

If you are also adept at analyzing others, you may notice the excesses of fear and greed in your friends, relatives, and acquaintances. Again, you have to resist the temptation to run with the crowd, which is easier said than done. Two ways to make this easier are as follows:

1. Do not discuss the market with Wall Street professionals, including brokers. They are all subject to this herd instinct, being surrounded by the ebb and flow of the market every day. In fact, it is probably wise not to discuss the market with anyone until you have reached the stage where you can do it in a coldly objective manner. This is all much easier if you live far away from the "action," in a small town somewhere in the Midwest or South. Splendid isolation is the best defense.

2. When all else fails, you must keep your sense of humor. You must remind yourself that it is only money, only a game. You should be able to laugh at the cartoon in *The New Yorker* (Figure 6.6) with the caption, "What do you suppose happens when the stock market goes down to zero?" A special reason to laugh is that *New Yorker*

Figure 6.6

"What do you suppose happens when the stock market goes down to zero?"
Drawing by Dana Fradon. © 1974, *The New Yorker* Magazine, Inc.

cartoons are a good contrary indicator. This particular cartoon appeared in September 1974, very close to a major market bottom. *The New Yorker* "indicator" also gave an uncannily accurate "sell" signal with the cartoon captioned "3,000 or bust, Higby!" which appeared in the August 30, 1987, issue of the magazine (Figure 6.7).

Some of the most dramatic panic selling takes place when there is a major national or international crisis. When President Kennedy was assassinated in 1963, I ran to the telephone to call my broker to tell him to sell all my stock immediately. Fortunately for me, the market was closed early, just to prevent this kind of irrational selling. The following Monday the market recovered all its losses. Investors who sold Friday were sadder and wiser on Monday. In the 1950s, whenever Ike was rumored to have had a heart attack, the market would decline. The Cuban missile crisis of October 1962 was accompanied by a sharp market collapse, which was followed by the great bull market of the sixties. More recently, the market sold off sharply during the abortive Soviet coup in 1991. If it looks like the world is going to end, you might just as well buy stock, because if it does end, it will not make any difference anyway, and if it does not, you have bought cheap and can later sell dear.

The essence of the psychological approach is to gauge the mood of the crowd and then have the intestinal fortitude to move in the opposite direction. You should use any tools for this endeavor that you can

Figure 6.7

"3,000 or bust, Higby!"

Drawing by Stan Hunt; Copyright 1987, *The New Yorker* Magazine, Inc.

fashion. Some on Wall Street refer to the "cocktail party" indicator. When everyone at cocktail parties is discussing or listening to stories of killings made in the market, it is time to sell some stock. If you are not a partygoer, you can still monitor your friends, neighbors, and associates on the job for the same warning signals. Introspection works here, too: if you notice yourself bragging about your success or even tacitly patting yourself on the back for your Wall Street wisdom, beware. Those whom the gods would destroy…

SUMMARY

Use a combination of fundamental, technical, and psychological indicators to time your purchases and sales. If the technical jargon appeals to you, go to it with abandon. You can repent at leisure. If you can't abide either the technical approach or the psychological approach, use Rule 1 to guide your long-term market timing. This rule alone, if followed religiously, can protect you from many of the errors of optimism and pessimism of the average investor.

SUMMARY OF RULES FOR THIS CHAPTER

1.   The market is O.K. to buy if Value Line Investment Survey Median Appreciation Potential (VL MAP) equals or exceeds 100 percent. Selling should be undertaken when this potential is below 70 percent. From 70 to 95 percent is a neutral area.

SOURCES FOR THE PAD INVESTOR

Encyclopedia of Stock Market Techniques. Published by Chartcraft/Investor's Intelligence, 30 Church Street, P.O. Box 2046, New Rochelle, NY 10801. Contains articles by 48 famous authors. They also do seminars.

Hulbert, Mark, "...And the News Isn't Good," *Forbes* (Oct. 25, 1993). A nontechnical report on the value of VL MAP.

Mackay, Charles, *Memoirs of Extraordinary Popular Delusions.* London: Richard Bentley, 1841. Reprinted by the Noonday Press, New York, 1974. Also available in a Modern Library edition. All of the great speculative "bubbles" in modern history are discussed in fascinating detail.

Reichenstein, William and Steven Rich, "The Market Risk Premium and Long-Term Stock Returns," *Journal of Portfolio Management* (Summer 1993). Academic support for the VL MAP indicator.

Time Magazine. Published by Time Warner, Inc., 10880 Wilshire Boulevard, Los Angeles, CA 90024. Any story about a company or the stock market is worth reading, for the reasons stated in the text.

Value Line Investment Survey. Published by Value Line, Inc., 220 East 42nd Street, New York, NY 10017-5891. The PAD investor's bible.

The Wall Street Journal. Published by Dow-Jones and Co., 200 Liberty Street, New York, NY 10281. All the facts are here.

CHAPTER 7
THE ECONOMY AND
THE STOCK MARKET

"If all the economists were laid end-to-end, they would not reach a conclusion."

—attributed to George Bernard Shaw

INTRODUCTION

Our faith in carefully selected growth stocks and mutual funds, purchased at reasonable prices and held for long-term investment, is in part based on the rosy scenario for the U.S. economy for the next several decades, which is spelled out in Chapter 8. But it is highly unlikely that the economy will grow steadily in future decades. We have not learned how to prevent recessions, during which business activity, corporate profits, and the stock market all fall. We have eliminated double-digit inflation, but there is no guarantee that it will not return. Double-digit inflation is invariably accompanied by high interest rates, which make bonds, for example, strong competition for stocks, often resulting in low valuations of corporate earnings (falling P/E ratios). In addition, rapid inflation is usually brought under control through a wrenching recession, which damages corporate profits and the stock market directly. All of this unpleasantness suggests the value of understanding a little of how the economy works and what makes business cycles happen. This branch of economics is known as macroeconomics.

A little macroeconomic knowledge can help the PAD investor understand major trends in the economy that will influence stock prices. This understanding could improve long-term market timing, and also help you to avoid being panicked by some of the macroeconomic nonsense that passes for wisdom.

At the end of the chapter, I summarize the basic economic data with which the PAD investor should be familiar in order to protect his or her portfolio. But one chapter can provide only the briefest introduction to the subject. A college introductory textbook, such as the one listed at the end of this chapter, will provide more depth and breadth for the interested reader.

Before proceeding with a most difficult task, I must point out that much of macroeconomics is embroiled in controversy. The views I present are mostly "middle-of-the-road." I do present alternative viewpoints in the appropriate places, however.

THE GOVERNMENT BUDGET AND THE DEFICIT

Once upon a time, and not so very long ago, a $250 billion annual federal budget deficit would have been unthinkable. Our experience in the 1980s and 1990s made it commonplace. Nonetheless, optimists point out that prosperity has continued in spite of dire warnings of calamity. Pessimists counter that the deficits are larger than reported, thanks to accounting tricks, and that, as Yogi Berra said, "It ain't over 'til it's over." I tend to lean toward the pessimistic side, but it is certainly true that the pessimists have cried "wolf" too often and too soon. Nonetheless, if the pessimists do turn out to be right, our current and future deficits will have a significant impact on the economy and the stock market. In this section, I will explain why we have a persistent deficit and what should be done about it, what probably will be done about it, and what it all means for the stock market.

For the last 25 years, the U.S. government has spent (outlays) more than it has taken in (revenues) every year. There are three basic reasons why eliminating these budget deficits is so difficult. First, federal outlays are extremely difficult to cut. Second, taxes, the main source of revenue, are extremely difficult to raise. Third, "tax expenditures" are almost impossible to eliminate. I will discuss each of these points in turn.

Every government spending program has its defenders either in Congress or the White House. In general, a relatively small number of beneficiaries of a program have much more to lose individually from a cut than the large number of taxpayers would individually gain. An excellent example of this problem is government protection of American farmers. The cost of agricultural support programs has often exceeded $20 billion a year. This is a little less than $100 for every American, but it represents many thousands of dollars to the farmers who share in the largesse. They fight very hard to keep the programs, because their way of life may depend on these payments, but taxpayers as a group do not fight very hard to reduce or eliminate the programs. There are thousands of spending programs like this one, large and small, each with its own powerful constituency mobilized to protect it from the budget-cutting ax. Most may even have made good sense when enacted, but it is well-known that old programs (almost) never die, or even fade away.

Some of the biggest items in the budget affect almost all of us. Spending on social security and medicare is determined by formula, but the formulas are determined more by political pressure than anything else. The recipients of these programs carry much influence in Washington, and it is a fact of life that members of the House of Representatives must run for reelection every two years. Our $300 billion defense budget was cut substantially after the "Evil Empire" melted away like the Wicked Witch of the West, but even if our troops are not committed to Somalia, Bosnia, or other trouble spots, we may have to rescue the former Soviet Union from economic chaos, or worse, deal with a resurgent expansionist Russia. Waiting in the wings is a necessary overhaul of our roads and bridges ($500 billion), cleanup of our nuclear weapons facilities ($200 billion), space exploration, the war on drugs, health care.... Every program costs far more than anticipated. There was once a time when the S&L "problem" was going to be fixed without any taxpayer funds!

In sum, we do not have the political will, with or without Gramm-Rudman or similar laws or agreements, to cut expenditures in a meaningful way that will shrink the budget deficit to zero.[1] The Gramm-Rudman law did contain a timetable for the elimination of the deficit. But this timetable was revised and extended whenever it began to bite. Worse still, the law's timetable created pressures to take expenditures "off budget," so they would not count against the timetable limits. Even this charade was upstaged by the Office of Management and Budget's (OMB) annual October 15 "estimate" of the

---

1. As I note later, not all budget deficits are unhealthy. It should also be noted that government accounting does not distinguish between current expenditures and capital expenditures. A portion of government spending purchases long-lived assets, such as roads, which provide benefits for many years. Yet the costs are all "expensed" when incurred. Although this makes the deficit less frightening, it does not reduce the borrowing needs of the Treasury!

prospective deficit. By law, if the OMB "estimate" exceeded the Gramm-Rudman target for the year, automatic "across-the-board" spending cuts would go into effect. Fear of this calamity was supposed to make Congress and the President agree to spend responsibly. But OMB made the rosiest possible assumptions about revenues and outlays, and then, once the deficit was projected on October 15 to be under the target, the actual budget deficit became irrelevant. In effect, all players had a free hand to increase spending for the rest of the fiscal year. In the early 1990s, the Clinton administration set out to tame the deficit monster with some tough talk, and some tough action, on spending. Yet the bulk of government spending is in areas that cannot (interest on the debt) or will not (social security, medicare, veterans' benefits, etc.) be cut.

If we cannot cut spending, we could always raise taxes to eliminate some or all of the budget deficit. Unfortunately, Ronald Reagan came down from the supply-side mountain and gave us the First (Political) Commandment: THOU SHALT NOT RAISE TAXES. Even though he sinned on this one a bit now and then, President Reagan seemed to have successfully passed the faith on to George Bush, but Americans adept at lip-reading noticed in 1990 that taxes were raised, and sure enough, George Bush was defeated in 1992. Bill Clinton raised taxes a bit (early in his term, when it is least risky), but Americans may yet exact a price for this apostasy. Higher taxes would probably be less unpopular if a president made a convincing case for them (as opposed to disguising them as "revenue enhancements" or "premiums"), and if the issue of "fairness" of the tax code could be resolved. Tax reform has made the system a little more fair, but every remaining "loophole" is staunchly defended by the special interests that have benefited greatly from it. And every loophole that is closed can always be opened again in the future (see Chapter 12 for a discussion of true tax reform and its prospects).

These "loopholes," which are "legitimate deductions" to their defenders, are called tax expenditures, because they increase the budget deficit by not collecting revenue on income that would otherwise be subject to tax. The effect is the same as a direct government expenditure. As with government spending programs, most were created with the best of intentions. We have used our tax code for "social engineering" for a long time. But every exemption and deduction, whether for blindness or intangible drilling expenses, reduces someone's taxable income and taxes paid, and makes the budget deficit larger. The Brookings Institution has estimated that tax expenditures for fiscal year 1988 totaled $361 billion. The 1986 tax reform, which was supposed to make the system fairer, proposed eliminating some of these tax expenditures in order to keep revenues constant while cutting tax rates. Yet every one of the potential changes was opposed, in many cases successfully, by groups that would lose out if their special tax expenditure were eliminated. Many of these groups are large and include "ordinary" Americans: the deduction for mortgage interest is a good example of a "sacred cow" tax expenditure. Again, the problem is basically political. Without very strong pressure from an aroused public, tax expenditures will continue, and a system perceived as unfair will lead to increased cheating by ordinary Americans. The Commissioner of the Internal Revenue Service has estimated that $90 billion of tax revenue is lost annually because of illegal tax evasion. This certainly makes the budget deficit significantly worse.

The Reagan administration deserves a good share of the blame for boosting defense spending at a rapid rate in the 1980s, while cutting everyone's taxes at the same time, and arguing that the deficits would magically go away. They did not, but we need to assess the actual damage done to the economy today and for the future. In fact, the severe recession of 1981–82 would have been worse without a large budget deficit, because deficit spending tends to stimulate the economy. So the damage of a deficit depends in part on the state of the economy. The damage also depends on the response of the Federal Reserve System. While this is discussed fully in the next section, we can say here that when the economy is not in recession, large deficits can force the monetary authority to either push the economy into recession (as in 1990) or allow inflationary pressures to build, and neither is desirable. (Both of these evils have been avoided in most years with the help of other countries; see the section entitled "The Dollar.")

Every annual deficit adds to the accumulated total of deficits, which is our national debt. Many commentators, authors of "doom" books, and political candidates are frightened by the level of the debt, which has passed $4 trillion. While this is indeed a large number, so is the gross domestic product (GDP), at $6 trillion. So is private debt, which is larger than government debt. Some government debt is offset by government assets, like roads, bridges, buildings, and the like. More important, though, is the fact that much of the government debt is held by American households, corporations, and the government itself. Only about 13 percent of the total is held by foreigners. The rest we owe to ourselves. Taxes levied to pay the interest on the debt are thus mostly paid out to American holders of our government bonds.

Thus, the debt itself, to the extent we owe it to ourselves, is not a major problem.[2] Attempting to prevent the debt from ever increasing in the future, through a constitutional requirement that the budget be balanced every year, is a major problem. Aside from the practical impossibility of implementing such an amendment, it would also prevent us from ever using fiscal policy to stimulate the economy in a recession, or cool it off during inflation. It would also be very difficult to cut a $250 billion deficit to zero in one year. While Gramm-Rudman was supposed to stretch the pain over several years, a target of an annually balanced budget at a mandated point in the future was, and still is, a wrongheaded way to make fiscal policy.

A more subtle drawback of large budget deficits is that worthy new programs, or existing programs worthy of expansion, are often starved for funds because they would increase the size of the deficit, or force cuts in established (but perhaps not so worthy) programs, or worse, require higher taxes. For example, increased spending on fighting crime may be very popular, but the funds must come from somewhere.

In summary, the projected budget deficits for the 1990s will make it more difficult to achieve economic growth without inflation. We do not seem to have the political will to close the gap, but any action we take in this direction will help the economy in the long run. We will thus attempt to muddle through, and we will, unless a crisis forces dramatic action on the budget. Since the budget deficits forecast for the 1990s may be hazardous to our economic health, they could put a damper on future bull markets unless and until they are dealt with in a sensible way.

MONEY AND INTEREST RATES

In recent years, Wall Street and Main Street have been both captivated and frightened by interest rates and their gyrations. Not only have interest rates fluctuated more violently than in much of our history, but Americans are affected directly by the changes in interest rates more than ever: in addition to installment credit, whose cost fluctuates with interest rates, many American families have variable-rate mortgages. This financial innovation shifts much of the risk of interest rate volatility onto (unsuspecting?) homeowners. And then

---

2.   If the debt continues to rise relative to the GDP, we could have a serious problem. Or, if foreigners acquire a significantly larger share of our debt or of our physical assets, we could also face difficulties.

there are bonds, which Americans once thought of as much less volatile than stocks. No longer. Most Americans know that Alan Greenspan, the Chairman of the Federal Reserve System (the Fed), has some control over interest rates, and that big federal budget deficits, discussed in the previous section, make matters worse. But to explain it all, we have to step back and lay the foundation. At the end of this section we can answer the questions that demand answers: Do high interest rates always choke off economic growth? Could inflation ever return to double digits? Does M2 really matter? We will also pinpoint important data for the PAD investor to watch. These numbers may foreshadow economic trouble in time for the PAD investor to raise cash reserves before an economic and stock market debacle.

Let's start with the Federal Reserve System. The Fed is generally controlled by the Chairman of the Board of Governors. (President Reagan appointed Alan Greenspan to this position, and George Bush reappointed him.) The Fed has a number of official duties, but the one that concerns us here is the conduct of monetary policy. Monetary policy involves the regulation of the quantity of money and credit existing in the U.S. economy. The purpose of monetary policy is to promote the growth of the economy without either rapid inflation or severe recession. This is a very difficult task, of course, which is further complicated by the fact that the President and Congress also have important effects on the economy through their spending and taxing decisions, which are collectively called fiscal policy.

The Fed may suffer from a dearth of information about what the economy is doing, and this so-called information lag is discussed later, but the Fed is overwhelmed with advice from the Congress, the executive branch, private and university economists, and former journalists. This advice is invariably conflicting, a sure sign that some of it is dealt by players who lack a full deck of economic knowledge. The following sections may add an ace or two to your deck.

How does the Fed conduct monetary policy? The main tool is called open-market operations, which are a little complex to describe, but worth the intellectual effort to comprehend. While the Fed can print money directly and control the amount of currency in circulation, currency is not the principal way we hold our money balances. Bank deposits, some of which pay interest, and all of which we can write checks against, are the main component of the stock or quantity of money that is in circulation at any time. In fact, currency held by the public and these checkable deposits, savings deposits, and deposits in money-market mutual funds, form the bulk of what is called M2. We will see that M2 can have an important impact on economic growth, inflation, and recession.

When the Fed conducts an open-market operation, it buys (say) government securities, which are not part of M2. But when the Fed pays for what it buys, it credits the bank accounts of the securities dealers it buys from. These extra deposits are money.[3]

Through a more complex process, which I will not describe here, this immediate increase in the money supply can often lead to a much larger increase later. The money supply shrinks in the opposite case, when the Fed decides to sell government securities. Dealers pay for these securities by drawing down their checking accounts, which reduces M2, in general by a multiple of the Fed sale. The Federal Reserve owns hundreds of billions of dollars of Treasury securities and buys and sells frequently, mainly to influence the growth rate of the money supply.

The Fed has a lot of control over the money supply, but not total control. Recall that M2 includes checkable deposits. When you borrow money from a bank, and it gives you a check or deposits money in your checking account, the level of M2 has increased. The bank has created money in accepting your IOU, which is not money, in return for a deposit, which is money. Thus, the Fed has some control over the amount of lending the banking system can do, but only indirectly, unless direct credit controls are imposed, as in 1980.

Lacking complete control over M2, the Federal Reserve sets target ranges for the growth rate of the money supply that are supposed to be consistent with noninflationary growth of the economy. The Fed then uses the open-market operations described above to try to achieve those targets. (The Fed can also vary reserve requirements and the discount rate, but these policy tools are not nearly as important as open-market operations.) The Fed does not, however, always manage to keep money growing within the target range. In the early 1990s, the growth rate of M2 fell persistently below the Fed's target range, despite efforts by the Fed to speed up monetary growth and alleviate the so-called "credit crunch."

This unusual pattern was particularly disconcerting to "monetarists," who watch the money numbers religiously as evidence of future trends of the economy. Their intellectual leader is Milton Friedman, a

---

3.   The Fed may also end up buying the securities from commercial banks. The following story is only slightly different in that case. The reader who wishes to pursue the matter further should consult one of the references at the end of this chapter.

Nobel Prize winner and former economics professor at the University of Chicago. Die-hard monetarists argue that the rate of growth of the money supply is the major determinant of economic activity and inflation, and that rapid growth of the money supply must lead to rapid inflation. By the same token, very slow growth in the money numbers should eliminate inflation. A slightly unfair simplification of their arguments is that any "extra" money the Fed creates will be spent on goods and services, and if the economy cannot churn out goods and services fast enough, the spending will just drive up prices. Imagine what would happen if everyone in the United States woke up Monday morning and discovered that the amount of money in their bank accounts had miraculously doubled over the weekend. An orgy of spending would probably occur, and as the goods disappeared from retailers' shelves, prices would no doubt start to rise. This is often described as "too much money chasing too few goods." As retailers try to rebuild stocks, factories producing consumer goods will increase their output and perhaps hire more workers, and the process will continue to feed on itself. As more workers are sought, they may be able to bargain for higher wages, which will also fuel the fires of inflation. Once rapid inflation is under way, it is certainly self-reinforcing: If everyone sees prices rising, everyone will try to buy to beat the next round of price increases, and further inflation is guaranteed. Whenever the rate of growth of the money stock exceeds what the monetarists consider to be a rate consistent with price stability, they proclaim that rapid inflation is just around the corner. Milton Friedman himself did just this in a September 1, 1983, op-ed article in *The Wall Street Journal,* in which he stated with near certainty that double-digit inflation would return before the end of 1984. He was wrong.

Our money fable can also illustrate the major weakness of the monetarist approach. Suppose that all Americans decided to let the magical extra money in their bank accounts just sit there. No law requires them to spend it. What then happens to the economy? Nothing. This nonmonetarist version of the fable is as extreme as the first version, but both make a point.[4] In the nonmonetarist version, if Americans slow the rate at which they spend and re-spend the money in circulation (in technical terms, the "velocity" of money falls), an increase in the amount of money in circulation may not have much of an impact on economic activity.

---

4. In the second version, the extra bank balances would probably lead to a fall in interest rates, which should stimulate economic activity. I have ignored these and other details for the sake of simplicity.

Many nonmonetarists argue that the emphasis on money growth is misplaced, especially since velocity can change suddenly and unpredictably. They argue that the Federal Reserve should pay more attention to interest rates, since they have a direct impact on household and corporate spending decisions and are a better indicator of whether money is easy or tight. Yet recent experience suggests that high interest rates cannot always slow down an overheated economy, nor do falling interest rates invariably stimulate the economy. It takes time, perhaps many months or even years, for the full effects of monetary policy, working either directly through changes in the growth of the money supply or indirectly through interest rates, to be felt by the economy. There are additional delays before the (sometimes conflicting) economic data are available, too. These lags make the Federal Reserve's task of guiding the economy between the perils of recession and inflation that much more difficult. A partial solution to this dilemma is to give more weight to the actual performance of the economy, that is, inflation and economic growth, since the level of interest rates and the growth rate of the money supply are not really important targets in and of themselves. If the economy is showing signs of overheating, that is, growing fast enough to fan the fires of inflation, the Federal Reserve will make money tight enough to prevent this calamity. If the economy is sinking into a deep recession, and inflation is not a threat, the Fed will follow an easy money policy, with rapid growth of the money supply and falling interest rates, to prevent a catastrophe.

The events of 1987 showed the Fed in both of its roles. Until October 19, 1987, the Fed was gradually tightening monetary policy in an attempt to cool off a surging economy. Interest rates were rising steadily. As soon as the stock market crashed, however, the Fed immediately began flooding the credit markets with liquidity, to prevent an economic crash. Interest rates tumbled, the stock market recovered, and a recession was averted. Once it was clear that the economy had been saved, the monetary authority returned to its inflation-fighting role. This role continued to create controversy in the early 1990s, as the economy suffered through a recession and several years of sluggish growth, which some commentators blamed on the Fed's attempting to slay an imaginary inflation monster.

When it does occur, however, rapid inflation is bad for the stock market, in part because the Fed will use tight money to slow down inflation, and tight money usually leads to a recession and a fall in corporate profits. High interest rates, which usually accompany tight money, also make bonds more attractive relative to stocks. While many readers may already have firsthand knowledge of the effects of tight money, let's use a money fable similar to the previous one to illustrate it. This time the American public wakes up to find that its money balances have been magically cut in half. Many will queue up to borrow, others will put off purchases they may have been planning, and economic activity should decline in the same way that it increased in the first version of the fable. As unemployment rises and goods pile up on retailers' shelves, price increases and wage increases will start to moderate, and the Fed will be on its way to victory over rapid inflation, although there will be, as always, heavy casualties. Almost every episode of tight money is accompanied by a stock market decline, so a PAD investor can profit from "Fed-watching."

Of course, the rate of growth of the economy, as measured by the growth of the real GDP,[5] is of even greater concern to the Fed; and just as important are measures of inflation, not just the Consumer and Producer Price Indexes (CPI and PPI, respectively), but also a much broader index called the GDP Deflator. The GDP Deflator, which is published at the same time as the GDP, measures inflation for all domestically produced goods and services. Wall Street has actually caught on to the importance of these numbers, and stock prices are often volatile after a surprise in the GDP numbers. All of these figures are reported in leading financial publications.

I also watch indexes of (1) commodity prices, since rising raw materials prices can translate into faster inflation, and (2) hourly compensation data, which can reveal wage inflation, which can also be a precursor of price inflation. These data are also published regularly in *The Wall Street Journal.*

Many nonmonetarist economists and other public policy makers have urged the Federal Reserve to pay more attention to the level of interest rates and less to money supply growth. I have pointed out the fallacy of strict monetarism, but the nonmonetarists must also face up to the fact that rapid money-supply growth, if it persists long enough, can create severe inflationary pressure. The Federal Reserve Board of Governors is determined to avoid a return to rapid inflation, and thus they are willing to let interest rates rise and in fact cause a recession, if necessary to prevent rapid inflation. If the Federal Reserve in the future attempted to keep interest rates down and ignore money

---

5. GDP measures the total output of goods and services produced in a country in a year. See the Mansfield text listed at the end of the chapter for technical details.

growth altogether, it could unleash severe inflation. I see no evidence, however, that the Federal Reserve is likely to let this happen. The only true threat to the Fed's inflation-fighting resolve comes from the U.S. Congress. Periodically, disgruntled members of Congress introduce bills designed to make the Federal Reserve more responsive to the wishes of the Congress or the White House or both. If the Fed ever did lose its cherished independence, I would expect monetary policy to be executed with the same deftness and wisdom as fiscal policy.

A fringe group of economists and former journalists who call themselves "supply-siders" would argue that my discussion so far misses the essential economic points, except for the fact that tight money can send the economy into a tailspin. The supply-siders argue that the focus of both fiscal and monetary policy should be on increasing the supply of goods and services, which will keep inflation down and the economy growing rapidly. All economists agree that this is desirable; the argument is joined over whether supply-side economics, as it is now preached, can actually do it. Most economists argue, quite correctly in my opinion, that there is little evidence that supply-side policies have any scientific support behind them, nor does the evidence of the 1980s and early 1990s change the picture. Two examples should suffice. First, in spite of tax reduction in the 1980s, particularly for high-income earners, and the creation of tax-deferred IRAs, Americans did not save any more of their income than they did before supply-side economics was introduced. The promised burst of private saving never arrived. Second, the personal tax cuts were also supposed to generate so much more tax revenue that the budget deficits would go away. They didn't.

Nonetheless, it is true that policies that stimulate the supply of goods and services or lower business costs can give us growth without inflation. These goals can be achieved by either conscious policy or favorable accidents, such as a drop in energy prices, which ripples through the economy much as the energy price increase did in the 1970s, only in reverse.

In spite of pressure from supply-siders, monetarists, Congress, and the executive branch, the Federal Reserve has remained on a middle course that has been called pragmatic monetarism. In short, whenever inflation threatens, money gets tighter, and when the economy weakens sufficiently, money is eased. This middle course is endangered by federal budget deficits of $200 billion per year. If the Federal Reserve does not buy up any of these new securities the Treasury must issue to cover the deficit, interest rates will rise, because the Treasury will compete very hard with private borrowers for whatever lendable funds are available. When interest rates are high enough, they can choke off economic growth, as consumers reduce purchases and firms cut back on expansion plans. If, to keep this from happening, the Fed buys up all of the new government securities, interest rates may not rise for a while, but the ensuing rapid growth of the money supply (remember, Fed purchases of securities increase the money supply) will lead to faster inflation, with all of its negative consequences for the economy. The Federal Reserve thus appears caught between a rock and a hard place. The clear solution to the dilemma is to remove the pressure created by the budget deficits. We have already discussed how difficult this has been, and it will continue to be difficult with our current spending and taxing system. Although a crisis might bring about action in Washington, foreigners have helped us avoid such a crisis so far by buying up a sizable portion of the Treasury's new securities. This inflow of dollars has kept interest rates lower than they would otherwise be, and thus the economy has continued to grow. If foreign investors suddenly refused to buy any more Treasury securities, a crisis would be upon us, and I suspect the Fed would allow interest rates to rise and the economy to sink before it would allow inflation to get out of control again.

We can now answer the questions posed at the beginning of this section. Will high interest rates choke off economic growth? Probably not. The economy grew for several years at a respectable rate with a prime rate in double digits. If, however, the budget deficits are not reduced significantly in the 1990s, we will continue to depend on foreigners to keep our economy growing. When foreigners stop buying our new debt, interest rates will probably rise enough to choke off economic growth.

Will inflation ever return to double digits? Probably not. The Federal Reserve's inflation-fighting resolve has not been weakened. Does M2 really matter? Not that much. The velocity of M2 seems to change in large and unpredictable ways, in part because financial deregulation has changed the way we hold and use our money balances.[6]

---

6. In fact, according to "Goodhart's Law," this is a direct result of the Fed's concentration on M2. According to this law, whenever a stable relationship (such as that between M2 and GDP) is used for policy making, it will break down. This happened in the 1980s with M1. Goodhart's Law is discussed on pages 392-3 of the Dornbusch and Fischer book listed at the end of this chapter.

With some luck, we can achieve new heights of prosperity and well-being over the next decades. If we fail, it will most likely be a result of poorly chosen fiscal and monetary policy. At the end of this chapter, I summarize the crucial information the PAD investor can review to be forewarned of such a policy failure.

THE DOLLAR

After World War II, the American dollar became the fixed star around which orbited the planets of the lesser currencies. The dollar did not, and in fact, could not change in value against all other currencies. In those simpler and happier times, known as the Bretton Woods era of "fixed" exchange rates, there were occasional crises in which one or more currencies would be "devalued" or "revalued" against the dollar. But these crises had little impact on Americans. We always exported more than we imported (a trade surplus), the Japanese sold few cars in the United States, and foreign trade had relatively little impact on our economy.

How the world has changed. The Bretton Woods system of fixed exchange rates, with the dollar as the linchpin, fell apart between 1969 and 1973. Since then the exchange rates among the major world currencies—the U.S. dollar, Japanese yen, and German mark—have been allowed to "float," that is, change in value against each other. This floating has unfortunately taken place on stormy seas: the dollar had a dramatic fall that lasted until 1979, when the currency began an equally dramatic rise, which did not stop until 1985. The rollercoaster pattern did not stop there, as the dollar then plunged until the end of 1987, when it began still another sharp rise, followed by still more gyrations against the currencies of our major trading partners. Americans discovered during the floating-rate era just how important the exchange value of the dollar could be: America's perennial trade surplus turned into an endless trade deficit, the Japanese sold many cars in the United States, and the impact of foreign trade on our economy was now painfully obvious to all Americans. Even worse, movements of the dollar, and pronouncements by central bankers about their plans for the dollar, sent shock waves through the currency, bond, and stock markets on a regular basis.

It is thus easy to understand the nostalgia, especially in this country, for the good old days of fixed exchange rates. Most central bankers would like to see exchange-rate movements reduced in size and frequency, and many economists and other policy analysts favor a return to some form of exchange-rate fixity. Could the U.S. dollar be fixed in value again? Should it be? What effect does a fixed or floating dollar really have on the economy and the stock market? I will attempt to answer these questions in the sections below. (The reader tempted to skip these sections should note that, in my opinion, the proximate cause of the stock market crash of 1987 was the attempt by the U.S. Federal Reserve to "defend" the international value of the dollar with high interest rates.)

When the dollar is strong, or increasing in value relative to other currencies, it is because foreigners very much want to hold dollars and are willing to bid them up in terms of their own currencies to get them. Foreigners use some of these dollars to buy U.S. debt obligations, such as Treasury bills. The yields on U.S. bills, notes, and long-term bonds have for years been very attractive relative to our inflation rate. This high real return is also coupled with political stability and economic growth. The rate of return is very attractive mainly because the Federal Reserve, to keep inflation under control, is unwilling to buy up all the new debt being issued by the Treasury, as we saw in the previous section.

Unfortunately, an increase in the value of the dollar has a devastating effect on our balance of trade with other countries. A simple example should make this clear. Suppose an American computer manufacturer is selling computers in France. Suppose also that he is selling them for $10,000, and that the value of the dollar in francs, or the exchange rate, is 8 francs to the dollar. The French selling price is then 80,000 francs (8 times 10,000). A French computer company may be able to sell a similar computer for 90,000 francs, reflecting our technological lead over the French. The American company garners much of the market and makes a tidy profit. Now we allow the value of the dollar to increase, as it did during the period between 1979 and 1985: Foreigners buying dollars as an investment drive up the exchange rate to 10 francs to the dollar. (This is identical to the statement that the franc has fallen from $12\frac{1}{2}$ cents to 10 cents.) Now, if the American computer manufacturer wants to take home $10,000 for each computer, he must raise his price to 100,000 francs from 80,000. He will then get the same number of dollars when he exchanges his francs. But he will now probably surrender a lot of market share to his French competitor, who can, at the new exchange rate, undersell him by 10,000 francs. If he tries to hold the line at 90,000 francs, his profit margin will shrink and perhaps disappear. This example was played out in real life by American firms in export markets all over the world. When the value of the dollar rises, either sales are lost or profit margins must shrink. The volume of U.S. exports rises slowly, if at all, and American firms, including PAD firms, lose profits.

The same forces were at work in the United States, leading to a surge in imports of goods from all our major trading partners. Suppose the American computer maker was selling the same computer in the United States for $10,000, and the French competitor was charging $11,000 (about the same as 90,000 francs at 8 francs/dollar.) Now when the dollar rises to 10 francs, the French firm can cut its dollar price in the United States to $9,000 and still take home 90,000 francs. Score one for the French. Our imports of French and other goods rise, and American firms lose sales and profits at home. Our imports rise far above our exports.

Normally, when a country cannot pay its own way in international trade, that is, it cannot earn enough foreign currency from exports to pay for its imports, the value of its currency will tend to decline. As in the case of the French, the fall in the value of the franc to 10 cents will stimulate its exports and cut its imports. In a world financial system where currencies are allowed to fluctuate freely, this decline in value, or depreciation, is the inevitable result. But the pressure of foreigners demanding dollars as an investment was so strong during the period from 1979 to 1985 that it drove up the dollar to levels that severely unbalanced our trade.

The strength of the dollar had some beneficial effects. The rate of inflation in the United States was held down by cheap imports, both directly and through the effects of competitive pricing on domestic producers. The purchases of our debt by foreigners allowed us the luxury of excessive deficit spending while putting off the "day of reckoning." By 1985, however, the dollar had risen so far, and U.S. international accounts were so far out of balance, that the world's central bankers decided they should try to push the dollar's value down. Whether central bankers can successfully manipulate currency values is still a subject of debate, yet the dollar certainly did fall. What is just as clear, though, is that a weaker dollar has never come close to eliminating our trade deficit.[7] The day of reckoning cannot

***

7.   Our "current account" deficit in 1993 was $110 billion. One reason for the persistence of the deficit is the "beachhead" effect: Foreign firms that established beachheads in the American market in the 1979-1985 period refused to leave when the dollar changed direction and fell. They accepted smaller profit margins rather than let the declining dollar force their prices up to uncompetitive levels. At the same time, American competitors tended to match any price increases the foreign firms were forced to make. For these and other reasons, our trade deficit has shown no sign of going away.

be put off forever, though. The other side of the trade imbalance is that we must issue new IOUs or sell our productive assets (Rockefeller Center) to foreigners to pay for the extra imports. In the 1980s, these new IOUs were large enough to turn the world's biggest creditor into the world's biggest debtor. At some point, foreigners may become less willing to let the debt continue to build. If the reduction of inflows is gradual, which is likely, the international value of the dollar should decline gradually. A further decline in the dollar might move us closer to balancing our international accounts, which we must do eventually.

The dollar cannot decline unless the United States allows it to float lower. If it is fixed in value, the Federal Reserve must defend an attack on the currency's value by either buying up excess dollars offered for sale (the size of these purchases would represent our balance-of-payments deficit) or keeping interest rates high enough (through tight money policies) so that potential sellers of dollars are willing to hold them. In late 1987, it appeared that the Federal Reserve was committed to keeping the dollar from falling below 140 yen. The Fed used the interest-rate weapon to keep the currency from falling until the financial markets "threw in the towel" on October 19. The Federal Reserve let interest rates drop to save the economy. Not surprisingly, the dollar proceeded to drop sharply, too.

This episode is instructive: We can fix the value of the dollar, if we are willing to suffer the domestic consequences. Since the dollar needs to be on a gently declining path until our international accounts are balanced, we will periodically be forced to suffer these consequences. This is not a difficult or bizarre prediction, since it was a common occurrence for countries like England under the Bretton Woods system of fixed rates.

The consequences of a fixed dollar will be that much worse if our continuing trade deficit spawns still more measures to restrict trade with other countries. This is the biggest danger to our long-term economic health: Congress and the President may once again respond to the intractable trade deficit (especially our bilateral deficit with Japan) by enacting protectionist measures that create still more barriers to the international flow of goods and services. The damage this would cause, in return for only short-run gains for us at best, is spelled out in detail in Chapter 8. The last time the world traveled too far down the protectionist road, we had a Great Depression.

To sum up the arguments of this section, the dollar should decline in the 1990s as the United States slowly gets its international payments back in balance. This will not be too painful a process unless we try to fix the value of the dollar to keep this adjustment from taking place. If we fix the dollar, we should expect a replay of October 1987.

SUMMARY: WHAT TO WATCH

Fiscal Policy and the Deficit

If the President and Congress can stick to a substantial deficit reduction program, the deficits projected into the 1990s and beyond can be reduced to a level consistent with noninflationary economic growth and stable or declining interest rates. If the budget deficits are not so reduced, they will act as a drag on economic activity, as high real interest rates keep a lid on growth. If the deficits are reduced in a meat-ax fashion à la Gramm-Rudman, we will be attempting to balance the budget whether it is good for the economy or not—a dangerous approach to fiscal policy. If the United States adopts a balanced-budget constitutional amendment, the economic consequences will be severe, and a PAD investor will want to invest in Treasury bills rather than stocks, at least until the madness has passed. We also should not expect foreigners to keep buying up our new debt at the same rates in the future.

Monetary Policy and the Fed

The Fed will continue to fight inflation first and nurture economic growth second. As long as inflation is not showing any new signs of life (as indicated by the CPI, PPI, commodity prices, and compensation per hour) and economic growth is not so fast that it threatens to rekindle inflation, money will not be too tight and will not cause a recession.

The Dollar

The dollar must fall in the 1990s if we are ever to balance our international accounts. A gradual fall should not cause too much economic pain. The real danger is that persistent trade deficits will spawn protectionist "solutions."

SOURCES FOR THE PAD INVESTOR

Dornbusch, Rudiger and Stanley Fischer, *Macroeconomics*. New York: McGraw-Hill, 1994. An excellent intermediate text for those willing to venture beyond the introductory level. Thorough and illuminating discussions of fiscal policy, monetary policy, and business cycles.

Friedman, Benjamin, *Day of Reckoning*. New York: Vintage Books, 1989. A sensible and nontechnical explanation of the insidious economic harm that budget deficits can cause.

Mansfield, Edwin, *Economics*. 7th edition. New York: Norton & Co., 1992. This is a readable introductory text on all branches of economics. I recommend the chapters on money and banking to the interested nonspecialist. All Americans should have some knowledge of economics. The economy is too important to be left to the economists.

Ritter, Lawrence and William Silber, *Money.* New York: Basic Books, 1984. 5th edition. Readable and witty. Parts I-IV add considerable depth to the discussion here.

CHAPTER 8
AMERICA AND THE WORLD
IN THE TWENTY-FIRST CENTURY

"Be an optimist—at least until they start moving animals in pairs to
Cape Canaveral."

—Current Comedy

Most Americans are not especially optimistic about the future. Every
day the morning newspaper reports that still another consumer product is hazardous to our health. Our crime rate and the drug problem
resist all solutions, and our educational system seems to be part of the
problem when it should be part of the solution. The air may not be
safe to breathe, our water may not be safe to drink, and our dispos-
able society is running out of places to dispose of our trash. The earth
itself may eventually heat up uncontrollably as a result of industrial
activity, and the ozone layer is thinning. America may have won the
Cold War, but countries like the Ukraine, Kazakhstan, and probably
North Korea, possess nuclear weapons. Saddam Hussein still controls
Iraq and thumbs his nose at the West. It is actually quite a trick to
avoid a state of continuous depression! Yet most of us manage to do
this most of the time. History is on our side. The human race, and the
American version in particular, has always managed to muddle
through somehow.

In the paragraphs that follow, I discuss the major and minor maladies
that have afflicted the U.S. economy over the last two decades, and I
make educated and sanguine guesses about their potential effects in
future decades. I then describe my view of the electronic and biologic
revolutions and their effects on our economy and everyday lives. I
believe that the long-run prospects for our economy are bright and

that PAD investors will be handsomely rewarded for taking stock in America and American technology.

DEMOGRAPHICS

Demography is the study of population, that is, fertility (births), mortality (deaths), population growth, mobility (migration), and labor force participation. Demographics is the application of demographic statistics and projections to business decisions and planning. For example, Gerber Products, which controls 65 percent of the baby food market, must be vitally concerned with fertility in the United States because the rate at which women have children will determine their customer base. Nursing home operators are equally concerned with the number of persons 65 and older, and in particular 85 and older, because these individuals comprise the customer base for their operations. Firms that operate in just one or a few regions of the country and depend on the local population for sales must consider migration trends.

The key demographic element in a long-run economic forecast for the United States, however, involves the aging of the U.S. population and, in particular, the graying of the Baby Boom generation. Although the Baby Boom and subsequent Birth Dearth are two of the most significant demographic events of this century, their causes are still not well understood by demographers. Economists, take heart.

The facts are these: The number of births in the United States began to climb rapidly after World War II and reached a peak in the early 1960s. There was a steady decline after this Baby Boom, which was not reversed until the mid-1970s. By the early 1990s, total annual births had risen about 30 percent above the low point of the 1970s, and once again reached the 1960s peak of about 4 million per year. What this means, then, is that whatever the ages of the baby boomers, they are larger in numbers than the age groups younger and older than they are, and are rivaled in size only by the very young. The demographic bulge of the Baby Boom has been slowly passing through the American age structure. When the Baby Boomers reached school ages, there was a demand for and unprecedented growth in the number of schools and teachers required to educate these large age groups, or cohorts, as the demographers call them. The college boom in the 1960s was created mainly by the arrival of the Baby Boomers into the 18–22 year age group. Many colleges and universities found it difficult to expand and then contract physical plants and faculties as the surge of Baby Boomers was followed by the reduced numbers of the Birth Dearth. Primary and secondary schools faced the same problem. By the end of the 1980s, increasing numbers of school-age children again put pressure on much-reduced primary and secondary facilities as the cycle began repeating itself. Colleges faced the worst of the Birth Dearth in the early 1990s, which will inevitably be followed by rising numbers of college-age students until at least the year 2010.

The next big step for the Baby Boomers was their entry into the labor force, which was completed by the mid-1980s. The very largest cohorts, born in 1961–1962, have long since finished college and entered the labor force, and many smaller cohorts are marching behind them. It was not an easy task for the economy to absorb these ever-rising numbers of new and untrained workers. In particular, those not absorbed were added to the unemployment rolls until they found jobs. Even when employed, these new workers had to be trained. Until sufficiently trained and experienced, the flood of new workers was not as productive as older workers. Labor productivity was depressed as a consequence. But the tough times are behind us, demographically, until the Baby Boomers reach retirement age, which will occur at about the same time the babies of the early 1990s begin pouring into the labor force. The retirement crisis will commence in about the year 2010, and it is unlikely that we will deal with it much before then, since our society is not well known for advance planning on these matters. Although the Social Security compromise of 1983 appeared to have "fixed" Social Security for good, a closer look at the projections reveals that sometime after the year 2010, the entire system will be bankrupted. The vast numbers of retiring Baby Boomers will exhaust all of the trust fund "surpluses" being built up in preparation for this event.

There will also be a severe strain on Medicare, since the aging Baby Boomers will absorb a growing share of medical resources, regardless of the health-care system in place at that time.[1] Unless fundamental changes are made in the Social Security and Medicare systems, the possibility of "generational warfare" in the 21st century cannot be ruled out. The tax burden on the working-age population, which will be necessary to fund Social Security and Medicare in the years after

1. For example, if we ration medical care and use price controls in order to "keep medical costs down," there will be "shortages" of medical care, which will appear as long waits for medical care of all types, and perhaps even a separate "private market" for medical care will spring up.

2010, may become intolerable, and lead to a political deadlock pitting young against old.

We could reduce the magnitude of this crisis, before it is upon us, with some overdue adjustments to our retirement and health-care systems. In particular, we must take account of the fact that Americans live significantly longer now on average than they did in the 1930s, when the Social Security system was established. If we just increased the age at which full benefits are paid to retirees to reflect this increased life expectancy, the strain on the Social Security system, and our political system, could be reduced considerably. At the same time, I believe that any reform of our health-care system ought to increase "patient responsibility," that is, we, as consumers of health care, need to be responsive to costs. At the same time, we should also more heavily subsidize *preventive* health care, which has a huge payoff in reducing curative health care.[2] These types of changes could help avoid a 21st century political deadlock, which could do serious long-term harm to the economy.

Between now and 2010, however, the Baby Boomers will be aging into the most productive years of their labor force attachment, while the numbers of new and untrained entrants to the labor force will remain relatively low (the Birth Dearth), at least until the early years of the new century. This will have a beneficial effect on the economy that could equal the detrimental effect of the past swelling of the labor force with Baby Boomers.

Another source of labor force growth in recent decades has been an unprecedented increase in the female labor force, especially women with preschool-age children. More than half of all married women with children under five are in the labor force now. As recently as 1960, this percentage was 20 percent. Even though these rates may rise a little further in the future (they could drop, also), they reflect a change in American lifestyles which is in large part accomplished. Thus, this source of labor force growth should also be attenuated in the future.

I conclude, then, that the American economy will not be so hard-pressed to create new jobs in the future and that the average level of experience of the labor force will rise for at least 20 years as Baby Boomers continue to gain experience. These two trends are very fa-

---

2.   The most egregious example of flat-out waste of our scarce resources is that we are not vaccinating all of our children against preventable (and often costly) childhood diseases.

vorable for the outlook for inflation, unemployment, and economic growth. If we can find the courage to prepare for the retirement of the Baby Boom generation, our demographics should not cloud this vision of a better tomorrow.

INFLATION, PRODUCTIVITY, AND REAL WAGES

The fundamental source of long-run economic growth, and rising living standards, is rising labor productivity. Consider a simple example. Suppose a chip maker can make chips at the rate of 10 per hour. If the chip maker is paid $10 an hour, the labor cost per chip is $1 ($10/10 chips). Now, suppose the chip maker learns how to make 13 chips per hour. If her pay is increased to $13 per hour, a 30 percent increase, will the chip firm's labor costs per unit rise? No. If the chip maker is 30 percent more productive, she can be paid 30 percent higher wages, without labor costs per unit rising ($13/13 chips = $1). The firm does not then need to raise prices to maintain its operating margin. This is the magic of productivity growth: higher output, higher wages, and higher income for all without higher prices. But if labor productivity does not rise, any increase in wages will cause an increase in unit labor costs. These increases are often passed on in the form of price increases, which fuel inflation. Demographic effects for the next two decades, however, will lead to a more experienced labor force and thus favor more rapid productivity growth. This is very good medicine for the U.S. economy.

The productivity of American workers depends not only on their training and experience (and motivation!), but also on the quantity and quality of the physical capital with which they work. The sheer numbers of tools, machines, and computers are important: More capital means more productive workers. But better capital also means more productive workers. For example, computers have replaced typewriters and calculators in the home and at the office. We are all made more productive with this new capital, and as computers become faster and more powerful, and eventually "user-friendly," we will become more productive still. New technology provides us with this new and better capital, and new technology springs from research and development (R&D). Large investments in R&D by U.S. firms and the government promise us a neverending flow of "productivity enhancers" that can stimulate economic growth without inflation. Industries providing these new tools should experience rapid growth in the long run.

This growth will not be affected greatly by changing tax incentives for R&D spending or capital spending. Both the R&D tax credit and accelerated depreciation schedules have powerful supporters who will fight hard to keep or restore them, and more importantly, these forms of spending are influenced by many factors besides tax policy. It is true, though, that we do not spend as much on nonmilitary R&D as we should. Military downsizing in the 1990s, however, should enable us to divert more of our research resources to civilian projects. It is also true that we often do not invest as much in new capital as we should, but by the early 1990s it appeared that American industry was finally making the capital investments necessary to prepare us for the next century.

If our chip maker productivity story is true, we should expect to see the wages of the average American worker rising faster than inflation in the long run as long as productivity is rising. This increase in "real" wages is what makes possible the American dream of a better tomorrow and better lives for our children. Until the 1970s, our best measure of real wages[3] did grow fairly steadily. Between the late 1970s and the early 1990s, however, real wages stagnated. It is no accident that in the same period productivity growth was much slower than it was in earlier decades. A pickup in productivity growth, brought about in part by the technological changes I discuss below, should help restore our real wage growth.

OIL AND ENERGY

American economic growth, and the economic growth of many other nations, has been periodically derailed by "energy crises." It is probably true that in the next several decades we will witness relatively steady energy prices and an absence of the energy shocks of the 1973–1980 period. The explosion of energy prices at that time hit the U.S. economy, and much of the world economy, with a double whammy. At the same time that prices of raw materials were rising dramatically, with obvious effects on inflation, the declines in workers' real incomes pushed the economy into recession. We had the worst of both worlds: inflation and stagnation at the same time, called, for lack of a better term, stagflation. The economics profession was rightly taken to task for having taught a generation of students that these twin evils would not occur simultaneously. But the new

---

3.   Real total compensation per hour in the non-farm business sector. See the *Economic Report of the President*, 1993 (Table B-44, p. 398).

lesson has been well learned, and has spawned the so-called "supply-side" movement, which, in spite of rhetorical excesses, helped us to refocus our attention on supply conditions and the long-run growth of the economy.

The rapid rise in the price of energy in the 1970s set in motion several crucial long-run trends in the American economy. First, we have learned how to economize on energy when we produce our GDP. Everything in America is more energy efficient than it was before OPEC. This trend toward higher energy efficiency has yet to run its course, but already we can see the benefits. The amount of energy needed to produce a dollar of our GDP has been falling steadily, with no end in sight. Thus, we can grow without requiring more energy, especially OPEC oil. At the same time, higher energy prices have stimulated the search for new deposits of hydrocarbons and the reworking of existing fields. The United States, which was supposedly on an irreversible downward trend in oil production, actually increased production in the 1980s. Much bigger increases in production occurred elsewhere, much to the chagrin of OPEC: increased output from Mexico, the North Sea, and other sources steadily reduced OPEC's share of world output and its influence on prices. Once-mighty OPEC has been frequently forced to cut the price of cartel oil, and it is unlikely that this price can be increased sharply in the foreseeable future.

The favorable trend in energy prices in the 1982–1990 period paid dividends in the form of noninflationary growth of the economy, and it was certainly not a coincidence that the Iraqi invasion of Kuwait and the subsequent, albeit temporary, surge in oil prices was followed by a recession in the United States. In fact, low oil prices before and after "the Iraqi thing" reduced drilling activity enough that oil production in the U.S. resumed its downward trend, while lower energy prices stimulated demand for energy products. The inevitable result is that the United States has become increasingly dependent on imported oil, but the diversity of our suppliers and our strategic oil reserve should keep future supply problems manageable. Nonetheless, unless we find a way to reduce our dependence on imported oil, we can expect that periodic instability in the oil-rich Middle East will adversely affect American economic growth in the short run.

On balance, though, demographics and energy should not interfere with long-run economic growth, which will enable long-term stock investors to continue to earn total returns at least equal to the historical average of 10–11 percent per year.

AMERICA IN A MULTIPOLAR WORLD

The growth that I foresee for the American economy in future years does not depend on America remaining "#1" in the world economy or polity. We should expect that our share of the world's GDP will continue to shrink as a united Europe, Japan, and newly capitalist countries like China grow more rapidly than we do. A multipolar world, in which the United States is merely first among equals and faces no monolithic political and economic antagonist, is perhaps ideal for the growth of a country that once believed that "the business of America is business." The whole world, with only a few minor exceptions, has now bought our credo as the surest road to prosperity and higher living standards. We stand to gain enormously as new markets are opened for our goods and services, at the same time that our consumers will benefit from a wider choice of goods and services available at reasonable prices. If, as I believe it will, prosperity eventually brings in its wake a movement toward popular government and away from dictatorship, the world will also become a safer place for all nations. Democracies rarely fight wars with democracies.

America can and will adjust to this new world order. We will no longer be able to go it alone as the world's policeman, as the Gulf War made clear: the Iraqis were no match for our arms, or our allies' wallets. We can no longer afford to commit troops to every trouble spot in the world, and we should look forward to a more equal sharing of the burdens of world leadership.

This new multipolar world will steadily become more integrated economically, and in some cases (Europe) politically. We could of course opt out of this inexorable movement toward worldwide economic integration, by turning inward and erecting barriers to trade with other countries. This appealing but misguided policy of "protectionism" is discussed in a separate section below. A second major threat to worldwide economic growth is worldwide environmental degradation, which is also discussed in a separate section below.

While this movement toward free markets and economic integration will be of great benefit to the "great powers" of the 21st century (North America, Europe, Japan, China, and perhaps Russia), it may take a century or more before the many "have-nots" of the world, from Afghanistan to Zambia, escape from grinding poverty. The growing gap between the world's rich and poor will be a source of continuing tension and acute embarrassment, and will require efforts by both rich nations and poor to spread prosperity more widely.

Even within rich countries like the United States, rapid technological change in the 21st century may create a privileged class of Robert Reich's "knowledge workers," and we will have to find ways to spread the wealth more widely by education, training, and retraining.

A CLOUD ON THE HORIZON: WORLD PROTECTIONISM

"If this bill is enacted into law...we will have a renewed era of prosperity in which all of the people of the United States will share, which will increase our wealth, our employment, our comfort, promote our trade abroad, and keep the name of the United States still before the world as the premier nation of solid finance."

—*Rep. Willis Hawley (June 14, 1930)*

Wrong. The Smoot-Hawley tariff became law in 1930 and helped plunge the world into the Great Depression. World trade almost completely dried up as our trading partners retaliated against America's increased tariffs with higher tariffs of their own. This history lesson, and the writings of almost every reputable economist of this century, are ignored by many Americans who still believe, as Hawley did, that by "protecting" our industries from foreign competition we are somehow going to make ourselves better off.

It seems the American public is somewhat gullible, or is just misled by the basically foolish arguments in favor of protection. Protection can save jobs only by raising the prices consumers pay for imported and, usually, domestic goods. Economists have calculated that the cost of protection, in terms of extra dollars spent per job saved, is often $50,000 to $100,000.[4] Even worse, protectionism tends to spread through the economy like a cancer. First, each successful attempt to win protection will embolden other industries to seek protection, since it is easier to seek protection than it is to reduce costs and compete. More important than this "copycat" effect, however, is a direct input-cost effect. If American car makers are forced to buy high-priced American steel, their costs will rise and their cars will be even less competitive versus the Japanese, requiring even more or longer protection. The auto import quotas we "forced" the Japanese to accept in the 1980s had a third, more perverse effect: The Japanese maintained total profits by selling midsize and luxury cars with higher

4. As the immortal Casey Stengel said, "You could look it up." See the Hufbauer reference at the end of this chapter.

profits per unit. Since the Japanese did not surrender this market, American car makers lost market share as a result of automobile import quotas.

There are valid arguments for protection. Industries vital to national defense, for example, must be supported. Yet it is very difficult to determine just when national security is at stake. For example, must we have a merchant marine to transport troops and supplies in a war? I doubt it, and we have paid dearly for this standby navy.

The spread of protection to more industries in the United States will have the short-term effect of increasing employment of workers in the protected industries at the expense of workers in other industries and all consumers, who pay higher prices. If other nations retaliate against us, which is quite likely the farther we go down this slippery slope, the effects are much worse, of course. Our exports will fall, which will reduce incomes and destroy jobs. Another general worldwide descent into massive protectionism will sharply reduce the amount of world trade and lower living standards for many of the world's citizens. Ironically, poor countries may be hurt the most: their export earnings provide the funds to repay their debts to the advanced countries. We cannot in good conscience demand repayment when at the same time we prevent poor countries from earning the dollars to pay us back!

Creeping protectionism can damage the economy in still other ways. First, dynamic industries such as electronics may be driven to seek protection, which will inevitably slow our rate of technological change as the pressures of competition weaken for these firms. A number of semiconductor firms have in the past sought protection from Japanese electronics imports. (Computer firms correctly pointed out that increasing prices for American chips would just drive their assembly operations offshore.) American high-tech firms have also pressured our government to "get tough" with the Japanese, and force them to import more American products. If our products are technologically superior, why should we worry if the Japanese foolishly choose to handicap themselves?[5] Second, protection will slow the

5. It is unfortunate that the Japanese do not practice the open markets that they preach. Many industries are protected in Japan, partly because there are powerful interest groups that can win protection from more efficient producers abroad. Much of the protection is cleverly concealed under the guise of safety standards, inspections, and the like—non-tariff barriers that foreign goods are unable to pierce. This protection is misguided because it makes Japanese consumers worse off and invites retaliation by an enraged United States, which will then make both countries even worse off. The solution is bilateral or multilateral negotiations and concessions reducing the trade barriers of all parties. It is our only real hope.

movement of resources out of declining industries and into new, dynamic industries, making our growth rate suffer. Admittedly, there are losers in this shift, or protection would not be an issue. Workers in declining industries may be unable to get jobs in expanding industries. I believe these workers should be helped with income supplements, job retraining, and other such programs. Nevertheless, we should not guarantee their jobs in declining industries with escalating levels of protection.

American industries that claim they have been "injured" by foreign competition can petition the ITC (International Trade Commission) for protection from this competition. In theory, the industry will receive temporary protection in the form of tariffs or quotas or both, during which time the industry will retool, modernize, slim down, or whatever, to prepare it to meet foreign competition to the benefit of all. This is not what usually happens, unfortunately. Protection from competition is a narcotic that is difficult to give up: Many industries, including steel, sugar, textiles, and shipping, have remained heavily protected from the rigors of world competition for decades.

The nations of the world can act in concert to overcome the dangerous urge to raise barriers against foreign goods and services. Multilateral negotiations, under the auspices of the General Agreement on Tariffs and Trade (GATT), have reduced the level of tariff barriers repeatedly in the past, and the successful Uruguay Round of negotiations initiated a serious multilateral effort to reduce the world's many "non-tariff" barriers to trade. It is in the best interests of all countries to move toward freer trade. Back at home, the President can veto any suggestion for protection for petitioning industries made by the ITC, but even better would be rejection of petitions by the ITC. The President can also veto any protectionist measures passed by Congress. So-called "domestic content" legislation is even worse than quotas, and we can only hope that it never becomes law. It takes political courage to confront powerful interest groups like the automobile and steel companies, and the United Auto Workers and United Steel Workers. It remains to be seen whether any American president can consistently do so.

While the reduction of trade barriers in Europe (the European Union) and North America (NAFTA) are strong evidence of the trend toward worldwide economic integration, it will be very tempting for all to view the world as coalescing into trade blocs, thus justifying protection of "bloc" industries against the products of "non-bloc" countries.

It is also an open question whether the world's great powers have the will to resist this form of protectionism.

STILL ANOTHER CLOUD: THE ENVIRONMENT

Even an incorrigible optimist must come to terms with the worldwide problem of environmental degradation. We cannot expect free markets to give us cleaner air, cleaner water, or a place to put our trash, radioactive or otherwise. Markets work best when the drive for private gain benefits all. The maker of the better mousetrap may be driven solely by a lust for personal gain, but the better mousetrap will improve the lives of many others. On the other hand, if the production of the mousetrap pollutes the water around the mousetrap factory, who will take this "social cost" into account? Not the mousetrap maker. Not the mousetrap buyer. No one will, but many may be made worse off. Economists refer to these all-too-common outcomes as market "failures." The general prescription for these types of market failures is a tax that forces markets to take the social costs into account. In theory, we will then get the "right" amount of pollution, which is, of course, more than zero. In practice, governments have more often legislated the "right" amount of pollution. In any event, however, we can reduce the amount of pollution to a more acceptable level. We can also expect the market to help us "solve" environmental problems like our trash problem: As landfills close and citizens pay more and more for refuse disposal, recycling will become economical in more and more cases. And we can expect the mousetrap makers, again driven by personal gain, to develop new products and techniques that will help us solve the trash problem.

While we can, in theory, get our own environmental house in order, many pressing environmental problems are international in scope. Acid rain, for example, may fall in Canada even though it was created by industrial activity in America. At the same time, some American acid rain carries the label "made in Canada." Reductions in industrial and vehicle emissions, which cause acid rain, will require international cooperation, a scarce commodity.

Nonetheless, acid rain, pollution, radioactive waste disposal, and atmospheric ozone depletion all pale in comparison with the big bugaboo of the 21st century: global warming. While it will probably take at least several more decades for the earth to heat up enough to have any measurable impact on human affairs, a substantial rise in the earth's temperature could cause catastrophic economic dislocations on a scale not seen before. Unfortunately, we may not have a clear idea of the precise causes of global warming, let alone a reasonable projection of the consequences, or a program for dealing with them, until well after the year 2000. Rather than make idle and depressing speculation without concrete scientific facts, I will merely note that this small cloud on the horizon could eventually make life on earth difficult for PAD investors and all other Earthlings.

TECHNOLOGY AND OUR FUTURE

We have driven away most of the economic clouds overhead and on the horizon. I foresee them providing only occasional rainfall on the otherwise mostly sunny voyage into the future. Technological change will play a key role in making the voyage sunny. While it is no doubt true that technology can be used for good or evil—and this most pointedly applies to space technology and genetic engineering—I have ruled out the cataclysm as far as investors are concerned. We generally live our lives on the assumption that it will not happen, and I think we will continue to do so.

The electronic revolution will continue to change the way we live and work, and its effects could easily be as great as the first industrial revolution. Although we only see through a glass darkly, some of the outlines of the future are not hard to perceive even now. The basic underlying force of change is that the costs of computing and transmitting information are falling continuously. This process should continue for many more decades. There are a number of applications of ever greater computer power available at lower and lower cost that are already evident; rather than try to make an exhaustive list, I will present a few which, although relatively mundane, are under way now.

Medicine

While genetic research gets all the headlines and may dramatically change our lives in the future, other changes in medicine have been brought about by advances in computing and information transfer. The explosion of medical knowledge requires the storage of information and its retrieval to be done electronically, and there is no conceptual difficulty with computers being used to do routine diagnostic work on human patients. While it is certainly true that computerized medicine can be dehumanizing (and that is a problem with all the technological changes I will discuss), consider the following possible scenario for the not-too-distant future. You awake one morning and you notice that you have a runny nose and some red spots on your face. Instead of picking up your telephone to make an appointment with the family doctor, you dial a medical information number that gives you access to a computer diagnostician. You are queried about your symptoms, and the computer can check hundreds of thousands of case histories for comparison with your symptoms and background in an instant. It can order lab tests, inquire about other possible symptoms, and check to see whether "it's been going around." It should also be easy to program the computer to say, "Take two aspirins and call me in the morning." It is usually pretty good advice anyway.

Many other uses of the computer and microelectronics have already changed medicine dramatically. CAT scanners have become commonplace, and magnetic resonance imaging (MRI) and positron emission tomography (PET) may come next to your local hospital. Robots can already perform simple surgery under the direction of human surgeons at a remote location. Medical laboratories also use an ever increasing number of sophisticated instruments and computers in the battle against disease and in the search for a deeper understanding of how the human body works. Our progress in this area is so great and so fast that it can legitimately be called a "biological" revolution. Already biotechnology companies have used gene-splicing techniques to induce bacteria to produce insulin for human use. A host of new genetically engineered products will be appearing in the next 20 years, some of which may prolong and improve human existence to a degree never before possible.

The most important breakthrough, however, may make products like insulin obsolete: if life scientists are successful in mapping the entire human genome (all of our genes carried on the DNA double helix), we may be able to "correct" the faulty gene or genes that make a person a diabetic.[6] Using the same techniques, we may also be able to engineer better food crops, as mundane as a frost-resistant tomato or as revolutionary as a plant able to use nitrogen in the air. It may be possible to "build in" many desirable qualities: high yield, storability, pest resistance, and taste, to name just a few. The possibilities are endless.

6. While this form of genetic "repair" may be uncontroversial for many, possibilities for abuse of genetic research are legion. Even if we decide to limit ourselves to genetic diagnosis rather than repair, we will face complex ethical and moral riddles that may resist all solutions.

Meteorology

We are all affected by the weather, probably more than we know, and I doubt that we can change this in a hundred years. I even doubt that we will be able to change the weather, except unintentionally, in the foreseeable future. We can, however, learn to predict it much better than we do now, and improvements in prediction would be of enormous value. Bigger and faster computers are the answer. The earth's weather systems are incredibly complex, and the models that describe these systems push today's largest and fastest computers to their limits. In the future, though, computers will certainly be much faster and larger, and our weather forecasting ability should improve. The saving in lives and crops will be enormous. In fact, it is only with these new and even more powerful computers that we will ever be able to model the earth's atmosphere and then forecast the potential climate changes induced by global warming.

Everyday Life

Microchips, which are really tiny computers, are already everywhere. Our automobiles are filled with them, and so are most of our new appliances. What will change in the future is our ability to communicate with our cars, appliances, computers, each other, and yes, even our VCRs, which in many homes still flash "12:00." Steady progress in speech recognition and the relentless fall in the cost of computing will finally give us, early in the next century, truly smart machines to work with. Computers will become as easy to use as telephones (and perhaps as inexpensive), and may even merge with them and other appliances in a "networked" home.

All of the networked homes may themselves be connected to the "information superhighway," a national or even international electronic network connecting individuals, businesses, and governments. Of course "the devil is in the details," and fortunes will be made and lost as battles are fought to create, install, and standardize all of the new technology. It is sobering to remember that there were once over a hundred automobile manufacturers in the United States alone.

Many Americans are already connected to the Internet, which may function as a key part of the information superhighway of the future.[7] Others are already using the "information toll roads" provided by America Online, Compuserve, and Prodigy. Still others have discov-

---

7. I am connected to the Internet. Readers can send "E-mail" to DSEIVER @ SBA-LAWS.SBA.MUOHIO.EDU (Note: The dash is not an underscore!)

ered true electronic banking: Electronic deposit of paychecks and electronic payment of bills using household financial software. Advances in global communications technology have shrunk the world down to McLuhan's global village. In the future, all of us will be as closely tied together as we wish. This phenomenon could make the world a little safer to live in: The uncontrollable spread of information and ideas is the lifeblood of pluralistic societies and the slow poison undermining autocratic and totalitarian regimes.

All of these changes are quite likely, since they are already under way. Many more changes, which no one can predict, will no doubt take place in future decades. It is also quite likely that there will be sufficient demand for all the new products that technology will create. As their prices fall, the amount demanded will increase. This is, of course, the first principle of microeconomic theory, but many predictions in the past did not consider just how "elastic," or responsive, demand is to a fall in price. Retailers know this principle very well. A fire sale in which "everything-must-go, all-items-drastically-reduced" will bring the customers out of the woodwork. Filene's Basement in Boston has occasionally been as dangerous to life and limb as the scrimmage line in an NFL game as customers battle for the best bargains. People can be driven to riot by low prices.

Remember that we are constantly reducing the cost of computation of all kinds. This downward trend may continue indefinitely. The price of a new electronic component that is smaller and faster than its predecessors will invariably fall over its lifetime, which gets shorter and shorter for each new product. What many observers, often including electronics executives, do not realize is just how much extra demand is created by the falling prices of the components and the falling prices of the machines that use the components. The examples of this mistaken "elasticity pessimism" are far too numerous to catalog here. A few classic examples should suffice.

The first complete cycle I am familiar with is the hand-held calculator.[8] The first hand-held calculator was produced by Hewlett-Packard in the early 1970s and cost several hundred dollars. Even at this price, there was an unexpectedly large demand for it. Steady advances in technology put even more power into the hand-held calculator at a steadily falling price. Few analysts predicted the fall in price or the expansion of the market. Today, hand-held calculators costing $40

---

8.   The anecdotal version of this story can be found in Rochester and Gantz, *The Naked Computer*, p. 24 (see Sources section, this chapter).

have amazing capabilities, but they do not have much of a future. The personal computer, which can easily be made to function as a calculator, will continue to fall in price, while becoming faster and more powerful. In this respect, it is following the same pattern as the hand-held calculator. Every new electronic innovation that reduces computer prices will expand the market. When IBM, Apple, and their competitors cut the prices of computers, the entire computer market expands (although pricing pressures may cut into the profit margins of all firms). Yet firms and industry observers still underestimate the market-expanding effects of falling prices. I have two favorite examples of insiders underestimating the elasticity of demand. First, the chief executive of IBM once suggested that the world market for mainframe computers was "about 50." Executives of Cray Research, the leading builder of supercomputers, once estimated the entire world market for these machines at "about 50." Cray itself eventually installed more than 500.[9]

While no one, and certainly not the executives of these firms, can predict where the demand will come from, we can safely guess that it will grow beyond anyone's predictions as the price of computing continues to fall.

Innovations will reduce the time we must spend in household drudgery, such as paying bills, or filing our tax returns. This time can then be spent in productive work or more satisfying leisure. Innovations that make us more productive in the workplace give us the same pleasant alternatives. In either case, the standard of living of most Americans rises, and that is good for all of us. Our rising standard of living will make it easier to help those who do not participate in this growth: It is much easier to give the disadvantaged a larger slice of the economic pie when the pie is growing. This idea applies to the peoples of the poor countries of the world also. We can afford to be more generous when our economy is healthy and growing. The wellsprings of this growth are the dynamic sectors of the American economy. PAD investors, especially technology investors, can invest in tomorrow today.

SOURCES FOR THE PAD INVESTOR

Drucker, Peter, *Post-Capitalist Society*. New York: HarperCollins, 1993. Drucker sees the knowledge revolution as the key force

9. Unfortunately, the performance of Cray's stock has been less than super for many years (see Figure 4.2).

remaking the world in the next century. Well written, and filled with insights.

Hufbauer, Gary, Diane Berliner, and Ann Elliott, *Trade Protection in the United States: 31 Case Studies*. Washington, DC: Institute for International Economics, 1986. Read 'em and weep.

Kahn, Herman, *The Coming Boom*. New York: Simon and Schuster, 1982. If you think I am too optimistic about the future, compare me with the late, great Kahn. He was a worthy counterpoint to the Casey-Ruff-Granville "bad is beautiful" crowd.

Kennedy, Paul, *The Rise and Fall of the Great Powers*. New York: Random House, 1987. A thoughtful discussion of what makes empires and nations great, and how they lose their greatness. Americans certainly have to be concerned about Kennedy's concept of "imperial overstretch," which helped do in the Soviets.

Reich, Robert, *The Work of Nations*. New York: Alfred Knopf, 1991. Although Reich has only a limited understanding of economics, he makes several good points about the increasing importance and power of "knowledge workers," the scarce resource of the next century.

Rochester, Jack and John Gantz, *The Naked Computer*. New York: William Morrow, 1983. A fascinating, albeit dated, collection of anecdotes and facts about the world of computers. Not that well written or organized, but these are the people who gave us "config.sys" and "win.ini."

CHAPTER 9
EFFICIENT MARKETS?

"In practical terms, the evidence suggests that if an investor or investment counselor only has access to publicly available information, then the hypothesis that the market is efficient is an appropriate approximation to the world. If prices fully reflect publicly available information, then such information cannot be used to beat the market."

—Eugene Fama
(Professor of Finance, University of Chicago),
Foundations of Finance (1976)

"The efficient-markets hypothesis is the most remarkable error in the history of economic theory."

—Robert Shiller
(Professor of Economics, Yale University)

INTRODUCTION

Many academic economists do not believe that the advice I am giving in this book is of any real value to investors. I, of course, disagree with them, or I would not have written the book or devised and (successfully) followed the PAD rules myself. Many investors have heard of the theory of "efficient markets," which is the basis for the academic belief that investors cannot beat the market consistently. If this theory is true, investors should ignore all books, systems, and techniques that promise superior performance.

While most Wall Street professionals deny, somewhat self-servingly, that the efficient-markets theory (EMT) is true, EMT believers have had an impact on Wall Street. Mutual fund families and money managers have created many "index" funds, which are managed passively: The sole objective of these funds is to match the performance of the general market, as measured by broad market indexes like the Wilshire 5000 or the Standard & Poor's 500. Investors who believe that it is in fact impossible to beat the market consistently can thus invest in an index fund, a diversified portfolio that will always do just about as well as the underlying market index, no better and no worse.[1] Since even the most diehard EMT proponents are willing to admit that there is a very long-term upward drift to stock prices, it makes sense even with efficient markets to buy the market and then hold it indefinitely. (This will certainly reduce commissions!)

Although I reject much of the EMT as a theory based on false assumptions and inadequate testing, I accept some parts of it as essentially true. I therefore believe that it is vitally important for the PAD investor to understand what the EMT is and what its flaws are. This understanding will enable you to both resist succumbing to the "the market can't be beaten" psychology and to avoid the dangerous attempt to beat the market with short-term trading strategies.

I also provide in this chapter the theoretical basis for belief in the PAD System. The fact that my rules are sensible and that I have profited by them and endorse them is not sufficient. I go on to demonstrate in a nontechnical way how the PAD System is firmly grounded in well-supported theories of human behavior, which most economists have ignored. I consider this grounding in theory a much more compelling argument for my system, and it awaits those readers with the patience and discipline to read this chapter.

EFFICIENT-MARKETS THEORY

The efficient-markets theory can actually be "purchased" in three different strengths. In its "weak" form, it can be stated very simply: *It is impossible to predict future stock prices from data on past prices.* If true, this hypothesis is an indictment of all "systems," such as charting, which rely on an analysis of patterns in prices. A head-and-shoulders top, for example, does not increase the probability that the price of the stock will go down. The patterns of stock prices, which are interpreted by chartists, are the result of random changes in stock prices. Even though these random changes often form pretty patterns

---

1. Index funds actually do slightly worse than the indexes they track, since index funds have costs of operation, and indexes do not.

like "pennants," "islands," and "diamonds," they contain no information that can be used to forecast future changes in prices. This version of the theory is sometimes called the "random walk"; that is, the next price change in a stock is as likely to be up as down, regardless of what has happened before. This claim is correctly amended to allow for a very long-term upward drift in prices.

Defenders of charting and other similar "technical" systems argue that stock prices do not follow a random walk, but almost all of the evidence that has been gathered shows that they do. (Readers who wish to delve further into this academic literature should consult the Sources at the end of this chapter.) Many systems that have been tested rigorously by academics do not make profits large enough to offset significant commission costs and are therefore useless. I accept these findings for the most part, with the one possible exception noted in Chapter 4. The major significance of the weak EMT for the PAD investor is that it highlights the near impossibility that short-term and technical stock trading strategies can be pursued profitably by the ordinary investor. (A humorous example of the pitfalls of charting appears in Burton Malkiel's book cited at the end of this chapter.) However, the weak EMT does not imply that investors cannot beat the market; it implies only that *a stock's price history alone will not enable an investor to beat the market.* A wealth of other potentially useful information about a company and its stock is available, which could be exploited successfully.

It is also important to realize that the weak EMT (and its stronger sisters) in fact does not rule out the possibility that some investors can achieve above-average performance. Thus, the fact that you or I know someone who consistently beats the market does not invalidate the weak EMT. Consider the classic example of a room full of coin flippers. All flip their coins once, and those who flip "tails" must leave the room. All remaining (probably about half of the group) flip again, and again the "tails" leave the room. Eventually only one or a few individuals are left who have flipped an unbroken and perhaps quite long string of "heads." They may actually believe, and so may you, that they have an ability to flip "heads," and indeed the odds of flipping (say) 10 "heads" in a row is quite small, about one in 1,000. Yet the result was surely accidental! With repeated testing, it would become clear that a fair coin is going to be flipped heads about half the time, and the champion "heads" flippers will not beat this average by much. If we now substitute stock-picking for coin-flipping, and stock winners for "heads," we can fully expect that some individuals and some systems will beat the market by sheer luck. This will happen if the weak EMT is true, and also if the "semistrong" and "strong" variations are true.

The "semistrong" EMT states that stock prices correctly reflect all publicly available information[2] about a company that could affect the price of its stock. In other words, all that is known about a company that could affect its stock price is already accounted for in the price. New information, which by definition cannot be predicted, can and will change the price, of course, but the company's balance sheet, earnings prospects, or Value Line ranking, for example, cannot be used to select one stock over another because the information is already reflected in the market price of the stock. In other words, the stock market is "semistrong" efficient. (Since the new information must arrive unpredictably, stock prices will change in a random fashion, thus ensuring that the weak EMT is also true.) The semistrong version of the EMT, if true, would mean that the PAD System, along with all other schemes and advice designed to provide persistently better than average market returns, must fail in the long run, except for successes based on luck. If the semistrong version is false, then the market may have "inefficiencies," or valuation errors, that, when discovered, will lead to above-average profits for the finders.

The semistrong version of the EMT is based on two foundation stones: (1) a theory of investor behavior that leads to efficient markets, and (2) a large variety of tests for efficiency using real-world data. I discuss these in turn.

The assumptions that underlie the EMT are not always spelled out by its proponents, but they can be sketched without mathematics, beginning with a few definitions. An *economic actor* is a producer, consumer, or investor who engages in economic activity. Economists ascribe *rationality* to all economic actors, in a very special sense of the term; that is, economic actors know what they want and behave so as to get it, limited only by the means at their disposal. For a consumer, this means purchasing those goods and services that yield the highest satisfaction achievable with a limited budget. For a firm, it means behavior aimed at maximizing profits, given a set of constraints within which the behavior must occur. And for an investor, it

---

2. Those with private, or inside, information could still profit by trading before the inside information became public. This phenomenon is too common to even merit discussion, except to point out that it is illegal. The strong version of the EMT denies even the possibility of insider trading profits, and thus there is no point in discussing it further.

means maximizing satisfaction, also, presumably through maximizing expected profits, given the willingness to take risks. While economists have developed many unusual variations on these themes, such as the economic theory of fertility and the economic theory of crime, rational maximization behavior by investors is the essential building block of the EMT. Profit-maximizing investors will ferret out any useful information on a company and will, through purchases or sales, drive the company's stock to the level that best represents the company's value at that time.[3] If somehow the stock price were to rise above or fall below this value, these superbly astute investors would instantaneously restore it to its proper value. Now this, of course, borders on the tautological in that we are saying, in essence, that the market is efficient because the market is efficient: Whatever stock price exists at this moment must be correct, or rational investors would immediately make it correct. This is, of course, not a falsifiable proposition, which is why most EMT proponents fall back on empirical tests of the theory. Before we turn to these tests, however, I should point out that there are alternative assumptions we can make about investor behavior that are just as reasonable and that lead to very different conclusions about market efficiency.

Testing the Theory

Perhaps the most celebrated tests of the semistrong EMT are the performance evaluations of mutual fund managers. It has been repeatedly shown that mutual fund managers, as a group, have not outperformed the stock market averages over long periods of time. Since these managers have access to superb research staffs, pay very low commissions, are well trained in portfolio strategy, and are paid handsome salaries to manage money, one might expect them to be able to outperform the market. The fact that they do not is taken as evidence that the market is efficient, and perhaps it is these very individuals that make it so. Any undervalued stock is quickly discovered and bid up by one or more of these managers to its correct value. If the professionals are unable to beat the market, what hope is there for the (amateur) individual investor? There may be some inefficiencies that the professionals can discover, but, since the "little guy" does not have the resources to find them, they are not exploitable by the small investor. The small investor should then behave as if the market were efficient.

---

3. Information is often costly to aquire, but this does not change the substance of the discussion.

The performance of investment advisors has also been monitored by the academics, again with sobering results in almost all cases. (One notable exception, the *Value Line Investment Survey*, is discussed below.) Other studies have shown that new information, when it arrives in the marketplace, is reflected in stock prices in a matter of hours, allowing for no persistent inefficiencies.

The bulk of the evidence suggests that those whom we would expect to beat the market cannot do it consistently, except for the lucky coin flippers. Even if there are some minor inefficiencies in the market (and there are some troubling academic findings), these are probably not exploitable inefficiencies for the ordinary investor. For example, certain arbitrageurs may make consistently above-average returns with complex strategies involving simultaneous buying and selling of stocks, options, warrants, convertibles, and the like. But these inefficiencies that the professionals exploit are not available to the rest of us. The story is the same for the little-researched company that is overlooked by the professionals. Enormous effort and skill must be employed to root these special situations out, and again the individual investor will not have the time or resources to succeed in finding these pockets of inefficiency. Must we give up, then, and just buy the market and hold? No. Both the underlying theory and the testing of the EMT are seriously flawed. Not only is the market semistrong *inefficient,* but the PAD System makes the inefficiencies exploitable by the average investor. I show why in the following paragraphs.

The major weakness in the testing of the semistrong EMT has been pointed out by Professor Lawrence Summers. In nonmathematical terms, Summers's argument is as follows. If we perform an experiment (examine some data) that produces results that are consistent with the EMT, there is a possibility that we will accept the EMT as true even if in fact it is incorrect. The "power" of a test is its ability to discriminate among competing theories, avoiding this type of error. A commonplace example can clarify the argument: Pregnancy tests are not infallible. A positive pregnancy test does not guarantee that a woman is pregnant, nor does a negative pregnancy test guarantee that a woman is not pregnant. The more "powerful" the pregnancy test, the fewer false positives and false negatives that will be given. The ultimate in power is a test that is 100 percent reliable. What Summers argues is that the statistical tests of EMT are not very powerful tests and that major inefficiencies could exist in the stock market for long periods of time and not be detected by these tests, just as some pregnant women receive (false) negative pregnancy test results. Summers concludes:

The preceding analysis suggests that certain types of inefficiency in market valuations are not likely to be detected using standard methods. This means the evidence found in many studies that the hypothesis of efficiency cannot be rejected, should not lead us to conclude that market prices represent rational valuations. Rather, we must face the fact that our tests have relatively little power against certain types of market inefficiency. In particular, the hypothesis that market valuations include large persistent errors is as consistent with the available empirical evidence as is the hypothesis of market efficiency.[4]

This finding casts doubt on many of the studies of stock price fluctuations that purport to show efficiency.

Second, there is the Value Line anomaly. Financial economists have carefully and repeatedly documented the ability of the Value Line ranking system to successfully discriminate among stocks in terms of future performance. This should not be possible, since Value Line is using publicly available information and its rankings and success are widely publicized (in part by Value Line itself). How could Value Line consistently pick winners and losers if the market has already incorporated the information in prices? Clearly, Value Line is exploiting a persistent inefficiency, and the PAD System uses Value Line for just that reason.

The third major weakness in the testing of the EMT is contained in one of the bulwarks of the theory, a scholarly tome written by Clive Granger and Oskar Morgenstern (see the Sources cited at the end of this chapter). The bulk of their evidence is that the market is efficient, especially with respect to short-term fluctuations, and yet they admit in Chapter 5 of their book that they did find persistent trends in stock prices over periods of several years or more. In other words, the day-to-day or week-to-week movements of prices are unpredictable, but there are longer-term trends that should *not* exist in an efficient market. Granger and Morgenstern claim that these trends go beyond the time horizons of most investors. This rather lame explanation is probably right. Again, this is precisely why the PAD System is a long-term strategy for stock market profits, since above-average profits can be made!

---

4.   Summers, 1982, p. 14.

A fourth major weakness of the EMT is that, in recent years, a rising number of academic researchers have reported on anomalies in stock prices, over both short and long time horizons, which should not exist if the market is semistrong efficient. The best-known of these findings are the "January effect" (stocks of small companies in particular perform inexplicably well in January), the "weekend effect" (do not buy stock on Friday afternoon), and the "first-half-of-the-month effect" (a huge portion of the stock market's total return occurs in the first half of each month). These and other studies that show major, long-term, exploitable inefficiencies in the market are listed at the end of the chapter. New studies documenting inefficiencies appear every year, and the pace is accelerating.

These disquieting results may be sufficient to convince the reader that the PAD System can work, since the stock market is not really semistrong efficient. But there is more: The theoretical underpinning of the EMT—the rational, satisfaction- and profit-maximizing investor—is also suspect, undermined by a few pioneering economic theorists who have been publishing their findings in leading journals in the economics profession. I present just a handful of papers from a growing body of work. Two more papers by Nobel-prize-winning economists, which also attack EMT, are listed at the end of the chapter. All of the papers cited refer to still more articles on the subject.

Recent Research

In a 1981 pathbreaking article in the *Journal of Political Economy* (see Sources), Richard Thaler and H. M. Shefrin (T-S) suggest that rational man is actually subject to conflicting desires. This is, of course, no news to anyone except economists, and it is a very old hat to psychologists. T-S posit two selves, called a planner and a doer, which bear a striking resemblance to the ego and the id of Freud. The planner has a long time horizon and must constantly restrain the doer, who wants immediate gratification; that is, "do it, eat it, buy it, now!" The planner knows that this shortsightedness will ruin the organism, and so it takes defensive action to restrain the doer. This self-control, which we are all taught, and a few learn, manifests itself in ways that are inexplicable with conventional maximizing theory. For example, Christmas Clubs were very popular with savers even though they offered no interest. Why? Clearly, this kind of forced saving enables the planner to keep the doer from spending it all now and having nothing left when Christmas arrives. Obviously, the doer has no patience or discipline! T-S present much additional evidence that their model of behavior is supported in the real world. While their planner-doer is still rational in that he or she is maximizing satisfaction given a limited budget and an internal conflict, it is quite instructive to consider the effect that "two-self" investors will have on the stock market. Those investors who are unable to restrain their doers will buy it now, and sell it now, looking for the quick killing, and not exercise patience and discipline. If inefficiencies remain uncorrected for long periods of time, these T-S investors will be unable to reap the gains from waiting. The PAD System is designed to enable you to control your doer with a set of rules and thus profit from waiting.

I believe that most market participants cannot control their doers. Money managers often admit that they are striving for short-term performance, although the real pressure is coming from their clients. Money managers fear, often with justification, that one poor quarter of performance will mean the loss of the managed account to a manager who is "hot." Under this kind of pressure it is much too dangerous to buy and hold stocks for the long term, since they may do poorly in the short term. At the same time, there is tremendous pressure to conform to what the other managers are doing. If everyone else is buying stocks in industry X, you cannot afford to be left out if this industry is going to outperform the averages. In fact, institutional buying could be so strong that the industry does for a time outperform the averages. This self-fulfilling prophecy only reinforces the herd mentality. The reverse is also true: When every other manager is dumping stocks in industry Y, you cannot afford to hang on in the hopes that eventually you will be right. The most publicized example of this phenomenon occurs at the end of every quarter of the year, when mutual funds and other institutions (pension funds, bank fund managers, insurance companies) engage in "window dressing," i.e., purchasing stocks that have done well in the current quarter to show them in the portfolio, and selling stocks that have done poorly to keep them out of the portfolio.[5] There are more objective measures of the short-term approach of many money managers. A good example is the turnover rate for growth-oriented mutual funds: This figure exceeds 100 percent for many funds, which means that on average their stocks are held for less than a year.

---

5.   There are a number of exceptions to this bleak picture, among them John Neff of the Vanguard Group and John Templeton of the Franklin/Templeton Group. Both buy undervalued stocks, according to their criteria, and then hold them until they are no longer undervalued. They have been extreemly successful for many years, which is further evidence in support of the PAD System approach.

This shortsightedness describes the average investor just as well. One of the great advantages of Las Vegas, the race track, and legal and illegal numbers games is that the payoffs are quick. Sports betting in the United States, a true growth industry, also offers short-term pay-offs. This passion for the quick payoff pervades American life, where time is highly valued. Americans in general are loath to postpone consumption compared to many other countries, and even our own in earlier times. Many investors are unwilling to hold stocks for years at a time, and will sell at the first disappointment or the first big rally. For some, the excitement of calling the broker and switching from one horse to another is as important as making profits. I rest my case with one more example. In the 1980s, brokers lobbied Congress very hard to get the long-term capital gains holding period reduced from twelve months to six. They knew this would probably increase trading volume and hence their profits, since the quick kill would get favorable tax treatment in half the time. It is doubtful that any benefits to the economy accrued from this change. The doers rule the roost.

Another pathbreaking paper was published by Daniel Kahneman and Amos Tversky in *Econometrica,* although a later, more readable paper by the same authors appeared in *The American Psychologist* (see Sources for both). In their papers, Kahneman and Tversky (K-T) point out that experimental subjects do not behave in accordance with the rational maximization principle of conventional economic theory. K-T find that subjects make systematic and repeated errors in choosing among risky alternatives, which are exactly what investors face in the stock market. These errors exhibit several interesting patterns, but the most significant for our purposes is called "loss aversion." In non-technical terms, most experimental subjects will accept a gamble with a potentially large loss to avoid a sure but smaller loss, while the same subjects will take a sure gain rather than gamble on a larger one in which there is the possibility of no gain at all. For example, suppose you are given a choice between winning $500 for sure, and a chance to win $1,000 with 50 percent probability. If you do not win the $1,000, you get nothing. If you took the gamble many times, you would win $500 on average, winning $1,000 half the time and nothing half the time. Most subjects take the sure $500 rather than gamble on the $1,000. This "risk aversion" has been well documented for many years and poses no problems for economic theory or efficient market theory. The plungers, who are "risk lovers," take the gambles, and the conservative investors, who are risk averters, buy safe stocks. The problem arises in the following experiment. Suppose now that you have a choice between losing a sure $500, or losing $1,000 with 50 percent probability. If you do not lose the $1,000, you lose nothing. If you took the gamble many times, you would lose $500 on average, using the same reasoning as before. But if you have already displayed risk aversion, you should take the sure $500 loss rather than risk losing $1,000. But this is not what experimental subjects do! Most who took the sure gain will gamble, or take the risk, to try to avoid the sure loss. The aversion to loss overcomes the aversion to risk. (Technically speaking, loss aversion means that risk-taking behavior is even more pronounced with potential losses than risk-avoiding behavior is with potential gains.) This behavior, which K-T document very carefully in their papers, is quite inconsistent with rational maximizing behavior in risky situations; yet it is quite consistent with observed investor behavior. Rather than take a loss on a stock, the K-T investor holds on valiantly, hoping to "get out even" while arguing "how much lower can it go?" This is a clear example of the loss aversion documented in the laboratory by K-T. At the same time, the K-T investor will point out that "you can't go broke taking a profit" and then sell a stock at a small profit rather than holding on for a really large gain. This risk aversion on the gain side has also been documented by K-T in the same subjects. These behaviors are so common among investors that Wall Street long ago coined the adage, "Cut your losses and let your profits run." K-T investors, if left to their own devices, do just the opposite, cutting their profits and letting their losses run.

The third pathbreaking paper was published in the *American Economic Review* by John Haltiwanger and Michael Waldman (see Sources). This research is the most disquieting of all for EMT believers. All of the arguments against the EMT that I have presented up to this point could still be dismissed by EMT proponents with the following counterargument: Granted that some investors are naive, suffering from T-S or K-T disease, for example, and that their decisions about stocks would not give us an efficient market, but there are still sophisticated investors in the market who can keep prices "right," and they have the dollars to do it. Haltiwanger and Waldman show, however, that a market with both sophisticated and naive participants can be influenced by the naive ones. By definition, sophisticated participants have correct expectations about the future, while naive participants do not. Haltiwanger and Waldman put these two kinds of players together in two different types of markets. The first kind of market is characterized by "congestion." What this means, in nontechnical terms, is that this market is much like a city's street system at rush hour. The naive drivers will clog up the main arteries as they always do. The sophisticated drivers are the ones who know that this will happen and adjust either their times of departure or their routes in order to reduce their own delays. These efforts by the sophisticated drivers will reduce the level of congestion, and offset to some degree the effects of the naive drivers. (Technically speaking, the sophisticated drivers will have a favorable effect on the outcome or equilibrium disproportionate to their numbers.)

The second type of market is characterized by "synergy." Again, in nontechnical terms, this means that the market is much like the market for personal computers or videocassette players. The more purchases made of one type of machine, the more software or tapes will be available for that machine. For example, when IBM was dominant in personal computers in the 1980s, those makers with machines incompatible with IBM suffered for just this reason. Software writers want big markets for their products, so they tended to write software for the IBM. As Osborne Computer, among others, lost market share, software writers stopped writing new software for Osborne computers, which reinforced the downward spiral toward Chapter 11 bankruptcy. Apple Computer is an exception that proves the rule: Continuing sales of the outmoded Apple II family were fostered by an enormous library of available software. Similarly, as Beta lost the battle with VHS for the videotape recorder market, it became harder to rent movies recorded in the Beta format, which is incompatible with the VHS format. This trend was also self-reinforcing, as new purchasers of VCRs bought VHS to guarantee the broadest selection of movies, and so on.

This synergy in the market means that sophisticated participants, the ones who correctly figure out who will win the market share battle, will *reinforce* rather than offset the behavior of the naive participants. Sophisticated players know that naive participants will display some preference for the less expensive VHS and therefore that VHS will win over Beta. Thus, they all buy VHS to ensure themselves a good supply of rentable movies, compatibility with friends, etc. The result is that the naive participants have a major impact on the outcomes of the battles, since their choices are reinforced by the sophisticated participants.

The best example of synergy is the stock market itself. If you, the sophisticated investor, know what the next fad will be, whether it be restaurants, casinos, electronics, or emerging markets, you will buy the appropriate stocks, regardless of reasoned investment considerations, before the thundering herd of naifs discovers them. As prices are driven to outrageous levels, you will sell your shares before the bubble bursts. Similarly, those stock groups that are about to go out of favor with the naive players will be sold by the sophisticated players. Accordingly, prices will be driven down, again with no regard for reasoned investment considerations. (The much-maligned chartists argue that their squiggles on graph paper are supposed to detect exactly this behavior by those with superior knowledge.) The bottom line is that sophisticates reap abnormal profits, naifs lose, and market prices are efficient only for brief moments of time. Thus, successful investors must solve the beauty-contest problem of Keynes: Pick the faces that others will judge the prettiest.

This theory of inefficiency has been repeatedly tested in a laboratory setting by Professor Vernon Smith of the University of Arizona. Smith, who is one of the pioneers of experimental economics, discovered in one set of experiments that "inexperienced traders never trade consistently near fundamental value, and most commonly generate a boom followed by a bust."[6] The clever traders in the group profited at the naifs' expense. Although after three trading sessions, the participants did learn to trade near fundamental value, real-world learning can take many years. There is also an endless supply of new lambs to be shorn. Although I lost all my wool many years ago, I participated in one of these experiments at the University of Arizona in 1993. Even though all of the participants were university economists, the group's trading created a bubble in which the experimental stock price repeatedly exceeded its maximum possible fundamental value!

Admittedly, a demonstration that naive investors can affect stock prices even if sophisticated investors are present has one weakness. Certainly, mutual fund managers must be among the most sophisticated investors. Why, then, doesn't their performance reflect their sophistication? I believe the answer is that mutual fund and other money managers are constrained by clients who demand short-term performance. As mentioned before, if a performance shortfall in any quarter is likely to be immediately followed by the loss of many accounts and thus a substantial reduction in the amount of money under management, it is dangerous to look for undervalued stocks that may not be "discovered" for many months or years. It is much safer to run with the pack. When many managers dump the same stock at the

6. *The Wall Street Journal*, November 17, 1987.

same time, which is common, the effects on the price are truly dramatic. In the 1970s the victims were known as "air-pocket" stocks, since they fell as fast and as suddenly as a jet that hits an air pocket. In the 1980s, a stock "cratered." In the wry humor of the 1990s, a stock that fell by one-third or one-half in one day was said to have had an "unannounced stock split." The colorful descriptions change, but the herd mentality stays the same.

INEFFICIENT MARKETS AND THE PAD SYSTEM

Who, then, is making the above-average profits in the inefficient stock market? Not the day-to-day traders, since they are playing against the random walk of the weak EMT. Not the big money managers either, since they are constrained by their clients to play a short-term, imitative game. Not the T-S two-self investors with weak planners, or the K-T investors, either. The answer, of course, is the PAD investors and others like them, who have the patience and discipline to buy stocks cheap and hold them until they are dear, acknowledging inevitable mistakes, but with eyes always on the long term. Even PAD investors can be subject to the whims of the marketplace, but a strong set of rules keeps us under control. If our planners cannot do it, our rules will. This chapter has shown why these rules are so important.

SOURCES FOR THE PAD INVESTOR

Ariel, Robert, "A Monthly Effect in Stock Returns," *Journal of Financial Economics* (March 1987). The first report on the "first-half-of-the-month" effect.

Arrow, Kenneth J., "Risk Perception in Psychology and Economics," *Economic Inquiry* (Jan. 1982). A Nobel prize winner expresses doubts about efficiency.

Bishop, Jerry E., "Stock Market Experiment Suggests Inevitability of Booms and Busts," *The Wall Street Journal* (Nov. 17, 1987). An excellent newspaper story on Vernon Smith's experimental research.

French, Kenneth, "Stock Returns and the Weekend Effect," *Journal of Financial Economics* (March 1980). A classic article that confirms the Wall Street wisdom of "Blue Monday."

Granger, Clive and Oskar Morgenstern, *Predictability of Stock Market Prices*. Lexington, MA: D. C. Heath, 1970. A difficult book for the nonspecialist. It makes the case for efficiency, but see Chapter 5.

Haltiwanger, John and Michael Waldman, "Rational Expectations and the Limits of Rationality," *American Economic Review* (June 1985). For the specialist only.

Kahneman, Daniel and Amos Tversky, "Prospect Theory: An Analysis of Decision Under Risk," *Econometrica* (March 1979). For the specialist only.

————. "Choices, Values, and Frames," *American Psychologist* (April 1984). Much more readable.

Keane, Simon, *Stock Market Efficiency.* Oxford: Philip Allan, 1983. A well-written book for the nonspecialist that makes the case for market efficiency, but also discusses many anomalies.

Keim, Donald, "Size-Related Anomalies and Stock Return Seasonality," *Journal of Financial Economics* (June 1983). One of the first reports on the "small firm" and "January" effects.

Malkiel, Burton, *A Random Walk Down Wall Street.* 5th edition. New York: Norton, 1990. A well-written book about the stock market, by an economist, with a humorous send-up of charting.

Romer, David, "Rational Asset-Price Movements Without News," *American Economic Review* (Dec. 1993). A "middle way" between the EMT and pure irrationality, in which levels and changes in stock prices do convey information to market participants, which leads to a new explanation of the crash. Highly technical.

Samuelson, Paul A., "The Judgment of Economic Science on Rational Portfolio Management: Indexing, Timing, and Long-Horizon Effects." *Journal of Portfolio Management* (Fall 1989). This Nobel prize winner stoutly and wittily defends EMT.

Saunders, Edward M., Jr., "Stock Prices and Wall Street Weather," *American Economic Review* (Dec. 1993). Strong statistical evidence that stocks do better on sunny days in New York, which is hardly rational.

Schelling, Thomas C., *Micromotives and Macrobehavior.* New York: Norton, 1978. Schelling has created models, especially the "dying seminar," which bear a family resemblance to markets with synergy. Quite readable.

Schleifer, Andrei and Lawrence H. Summers, "The Noise Trader Approach to Finance," *Journal of Economic Perspectives* (Spring

1990). "Noise" traders, who may be responding to fads, charts, or the weather, push the market away from fundamental value and create opportunities for sophisticated players (the PAD investors). Accessible to the nonspecialist.

Shiller, Robert J., *Market Volatility*. Cambridge, MA: MIT Press, 1989. Important work by a leading critic of the EMT. Hard going for the nonspecialist, but the section discussing investor behavior during the 1987 stock market crash is quite revealing.

Smith, Vernon and Arlington Williams, "Experimental Market Economics," *Scientific American* (Dec. 1992). A thorough and readable account of experimental "bubbles" and crashes.

Summers, Lawrence H., "Do We Really Know that Markets Are Efficient?" Working Paper No. 994. Cambridge, MA: National Bureau of Economic Research, 1982. Not for the nonspecialist.

————. "Does the Stock Market Rationally Reflect Fundamental Values?" *Journal of Finance* (July 1986). A later and more accessible version of the same research.

Thaler, Richard and H. M. Shefrin, "An Economic Theory of Self Control," *Journal of Political Economy* (April 1981). Accessible to the nonspecialist.

Tobin, James, "On the Efficiency of the Financial System," *Lloyd's Bank Review* (July 1984). Another Nobel prize winner casts doubts on efficiency.

CHAPTER 10
OPTIONS, FUTURES, AND INSURANCE FOR THE PAD INVESTOR

The explosive growth in new financial instruments (often called "derivatives") in recent years has created new opportunities for the PAD investor, as well as new risks. In this chapter I review some of the actively traded instruments that can improve a PAD investor's performance, mainly by providing some insurance against market declines. The advent of discount commissions has made this insurance relatively cheap.

In the sections that follow, I first review the mechanics of individual stock options and their uses. I then explain how options trading has been expanded to stock indexes like the S&P 100. After mastering this material, the reader will arrive at the section on index put-option insurance, in which I explain how to use put options in a conservative fashion. I have also included a glossary of technical terms at the end of the chapter.

This chapter may be particularly difficult for the novice investor. However, since the techniques can be applied successfully only to portfolios of $30,000 or more, a skimming of the chapter should be sufficient for novice or small PAD investors. When your portfolio has grown to $30,000, and you have earned some investment "stripes," you will be ready to give the chapter a more thorough reading. Experienced investors with large portfolios may wish to skip directly to the section on put-option insurance.

Drawing by M. Stevens; © 1985, *The New Yorker* Magazine, Inc.

STOCK OPTIONS

The oldest form of option is the option on a common stock. The holder of an option has the right to buy or sell a particular stock at a specified price for some time period in the future. There are two kinds of options: *call options* and *put options*. I discuss calls first. Call options give the purchaser of the option the right to buy the stock at a specified price, called the "striking price," until some point in the future, which is known as the expiration date. For example, suppose stock X is selling for $61 a share in June. If there is a market in call options for this stock, there will be someone willing to sell you a call option with a striking price of $60 a share and an expiration date of September for (say) $3. Once you have purchased this option and paid the $3, which is known as the premium, you have the right to buy the stock at $60 at any time until the end of September. If you decide to buy or "call" the stock, it must be sold to you by the writer of the option at the striking price. Obviously, if you just wanted to buy the stock, it would be cheaper to buy it at $61 on the open market rather than pay $60 plus $3 (= $63). The excitement begins when you consider what will happen to the value of the option itself if the stock begins to go up. Suppose stock X suddenly rises to $70 a share in July. If you own the stock, you have made a quick $9 on each share. But what about an option to buy it at $60? The option must be worth at least $10, since the stock is selling for $70! If the option was priced below $10, anyone could make a riskless profit by buying the option at, say, $9, then "exercising" the option, that is, forcing the writer of the option to sell the stock to you for $60, and then selling the stock on the open market for $70. Since your cost is $60 plus the $9 for the option, you make $1 a share in no time at all with no risk. So it should be clear that the option must be worth at least $10, and probably more. If you owned the option instead of the stock, and there was a place you could go to sell the option to someone else after it appreciated from $3 to $10, you could more than triple your money, instead of settling for the stodgy 15 percent gain you would have if you owned the stock and it rose to $70 from $61.

If this is truly your first introduction to options, your hands should be trembling by now. I suggest you sit on them for a minute until I finish the story. Let's see what happens if stock X declines to $55 a share and remains there through the end of September. In that case, the value of the $60 call option will decline slowly and steadily to zero. At the expiration date, it will be worthless, because no one will pay for the right to buy a stock at expiration at $60 when it is selling for $55. The $3 you paid for the option has become $0, which is a 100 percent loss. If you held the stock, you have suffered a minor 10 percent loss, which looks quite good by comparison. The magnified gains and losses are the result of leverage. Your small investment in the premium is tied to the movements of the much-higher-priced stock. This leverage is, of course, a double-edged sword, since both gains and losses are magnified. Most options have lives shorter than a year, which also appeals to those looking for the "quick killing." Not surprisingly, many unsophisticated investors have been attracted to the options markets on individual stocks. (The put/call indicator of Chapter 6 has worked well in the past because it measured the sentiment of these investors quite well.)

Now let's go back to the simple example and fill in some missing details. First, who is the mysterious writer of the option you purchased? This individual is often a sophisticated investor or institutional stockholder who is trying to increase the return on his or her stock portfolio in a conservative manner by writing options on stocks in the portfolio. The writer receives that $3 premium you paid for the right to buy at $60. If the stock stays around $60 for a long time, the writer can receive a whole series of $3 premiums from speculators like you who are looking for the fast leveraged profit. It is not hard to earn 10–15 percent on your money this way in a flat market. If the market falls, the writer of the call option is still $3 better off than otherwise. Only in a rising market does the writer lose out: While receiving the $3 premium, he will be forced to sell you his stock at $60 when the market value is $70. You or someone else will exercise your right to buy the stock, or "call it away."

Call writing is a conservative strategy, because it trades away the potential for a big capital gain for steady income in a flat or declining market. But some writers of call options do not own the underlying stock. These writers write "naked" options that are not "covered" with the underlying stock. Their potential losses are infinite since, if the stock is "called," they must go into the open market and buy it in order to deliver it to the caller. This is clearly a very risky strategy that is not suitable for PAD investors.

The preceding examples have been simplified in a number of ways. First, brokers charge a commission for every options transaction. Discount stockbrokers (see appendix to Chapter 4) also charge reduced rates for options, so commission charges are fairly small, although not nearly as small on a percentage basis as stock commissions. Second, options are generally traded in 100-share units, that is, a single call option quoted at $3 a share gives you the right to buy 100 shares at $60, and you pay $3 for each share in premium, or $300 ($3 times 100). Third, an option that last traded at $3 may have a bid price of $2\frac{7}{8}$ and an ask price of $3\frac{1}{8}$. What this bid-ask spread means is that if you are buying "at the market," you pay the higher price, and if you are selling "at the market," you receive the lower price. The difference usually accrues to the market-makers for the option. In general, the more actively traded the option, the narrower the bid-ask spread. This spread reduces the profitability of all options strategies. Fourth, our example used an "in-the-money" option for simplicity. A call option is in-the-money when the underlying stock is selling for more than the striking price. Thus, the option has some immediate or intrinsic value. In the previous example, a $60 call on a $61 stock has an intrinsic value of $1 at that very moment. The other $2 of the premium represents the market valuation of the likelihood that the stock will appreciate before expiration of the option. This part of the premium is called the "time value." Thus, more volatile stocks have higher premiums, everything else being equal, and options with longer lives also have higher premiums. Options with other striking prices will trade at the same time as our $60 call. A $65 or $70 call is "out-of-the-money" since the underlying stock can be purchased for less than the striking price. A $70 call on stock X will probably have a very small premium when the stock is at $61. But there is some chance that the stock will rise over $70 before expiration of the option, and even if it doesn't, it may rise enough to increase the premium on the $70 call, making a profit for the buyer. In our example, however, if a $70 call were purchased and held to expiration, by which time the stock would have risen to $70, the option will still expire worthless! The probability and magnitude of profit thus depend on more than just a rise in the price of the stock: out-of-the-money options are cheaper to buy and offer greater leverage, but are more likely to expire worthless.

Since the creation of the Chicago Board Options Exchange (CBOE), it has been possible for individual investors to trade options on an organized exchange. This has helped spur the tremendous growth of options trading, which is now carried on by the other stock exchanges, including the NYSE, the AMEX, and the regional exchanges, as well as the CBOE, which is still the largest options exchange. In 1985, options trading expanded to OTC stocks traded on the NASDAQ system. Although listed options have been subject to abuses by floor traders and large investors (often at the expense of the ordinary investor), they are still a vast improvement over the old options trading system, which had no resale market and a much smaller set of choices of options.

The mirror image of the call option is known as a put option. When you purchase a put option from the writer, you have purchased the right to sell a stock at a specified price, the striking price, until the expiration date of the option. Using the same example as before, you might buy a put option for $3 on stock X, with a striking price of $60, with the stock trading at $61. (This is an out-of-the-money option, since it has no immediate realizable, or intrinsic, value.) If you own the stock, and it declines to $55 before the expiration date (September again), the value of the put option will increase to at least $5. Using the same logic as in the call option example, if you can sell a stock to someone at $60 when you can buy it at the same time at $55 in the open market, you would make a riskless profit of $5 a share. Anyone would pay up to $5 for the privilege of doing this, so the option, which gives you this privilege, will sell for at least $5. Now, if you own the stock, the decline in the stock price will be offset to some degree by the increase in the value of the put option. This is a form of insurance, which pays off when the market declines. Of course, this insurance is not free, either. The premium on the put option is just like an insurance premium: You pay it in advance and do not get it back. In a rising market, stock X may rise to $70 a share, but you have not made the full $10-a-share profit, since you bought put-option insurance for $3 a share. This state of affairs is still preferable to the bear market alternative, much as paying fire insurance premiums is normally preferable to collecting on your policy after your house has burned down.

Buyers of put options do not have to own the underlying stock either. Buying "naked" puts is extremely profitable when the market declines. In the example above, the put buyer would see the value of his option on stock X rise from $3 to over $5, which is a large percentage gain, much more than could be achieved by selling short on 50 percent margin. (As noted in Chapter 6, when stocks are falling, unsophisticated investors often buy put options in large numbers, and a sharp rise in the put/call ratio has often signaled a short-term market bottom.)

The writers of put options are sometimes conservative investors. You can "lock in" a price for a stock you want to buy by writing a put option. If the price rises, the put option will become worthless, and the option writer keeps the premium. Using our example again, when stock X is selling for $70 and the September $60 put option is about to expire, who will pay for the right to sell the stock to someone at $60 when the stock can be sold in the open market for $70? No one will, and the option expires worthless. If the stock declines to $55, the writer of the option may get the stock "put," or sold, to him. Remember that a put option gives the buyer the right to sell the stock to the writer for $60. You may want to do this when the market price is $55, since the writer must then pay you $60. His net cost is, however, lower, since he received a $3 premium from you at the outset. When the stock was $61, the writer "locked in" a price of $57 a share ($60 – $3 premium). Many put writers have no desire to have the stock put to them. They are simply hoping to pocket the premium. Other put writers may be employing complex strategies involving multiple stock and options positions.

Unfortunately, though, some of the put writers are writing "naked" puts with no realization of the risks involved if the market declines. After the crash of 1987, *The Wall Street Journal* reported that some of the biggest losers in that debacle had been ordinary investors who had been writing naked puts during the last stages of the bull market. Their losses in many cases wiped out their entire life savings. If we use our put option example, the poor soul collects the $3 a share premium on stock X, which falls from $60 to $40 on October 19, 1987. The $60 put option is now worth more than $20. The hapless put writer has two choices: either buy back the option for more than $20 and suffer a loss about seven times as large as the premium, or prepare to buy 100 shares of a $40 stock for $60 a share. The moral of the story is simple: When your broker begins pitching naked options, it is time to pitch your broker.

The organized markets for options on individual stocks have grown in size for more than a decade. Most actively traded stocks (including many PAD stocks) have options traded on them. In addition, at any point in time, there are different call and put options being traded for the same stock. Thus, for stock X, there may be simultaneous trading in call options expiring in September with striking prices of $50, $55, $60, and $65, and additional sets of options may be trading with expiration dates in December and March. An entire set of put options may be trading, too.

For those investors who wish to study options trading in more detail, there are several books and booklets cited at the end of this chapter that are good introductions to the subject. They explain a variety of complex multioption strategies, and the books contain valuation models for option pricing. Our purpose in presenting just a bare-bones description of the option market is to set the stage for discussion of stock index options, which can be used by the PAD investor as portfolio insurance.

INDEX OPTIONS[1]

In the early 1980s the Chicago Mercantile Exchange (CME), once better known for pork belly and cattle futures, began trading futures contracts on the S&P 500 stock index. This trading also spawned a "futures options" market, in which traders could buy and sell put and call options on the stock index futures as still another, and even more leveraged, way to bet on the market. Although these options closely tracked the S&P futures, which in turn closely tracked the S&P 500 itself, it was not long before the futures were bypassed completely and "index options" were born. A new index was created by Standard & Poor's and the CBOE to serve as the basis for index option trading on the CBOE. Called the S&P 100 (OEX) Index, it is composed of

---

1.   In previous editions, I discussed index futures and futures options, and recommended S&P 500 futures put options for hedging. As I explain in the text, I now use and recommend S&P 100 Index put options.

100 of the 500 S&P stocks in the S&P 500. These stocks were chosen in part to make the 100 Index follow the movements of the 500 as closely as possible, while giving small investors a chance to place their bets with small stakes: The value of a CBOE S&P 100 Index option is only $100 times the option price, which is one-fifth the cost of a CME S&P 500 futures option. In addition, the CBOE set options expirations one, two, and three months from the current month every month, to appeal to those looking for the quick killing.

Since the index call-option buyer is not buying the right to buy a futures contract, what is he or she buying? In effect, one buys the right to "buy" the S&P 100 index at expiration, since when trading stops, all options accounts are settled in cash and the options then have only intrinsic value. Before expiration, the price of each option will reflect its intrinsic value, if any, and a time value for the leveraged bet of the option. These innovations have made the S&P 100 options so popular that volume has exceeded 800,000 contracts in a single day, and the open interest, or number of contracts outstanding at the end of the day, has exceeded one million. This success has bred imitation, so that most other exchanges have instituted index option trading.

Index options like the S&P 100 have finally given the small investor or speculator the chance to bet on the market for small stakes. Critics of this trading explosion have argued just that: What economic purpose is served by legalizing pure gambling on the stock market? I would not deny that much of this trading is pure gambling, but the nation now tolerates and even encourages gambling on state lotteries, and barriers to casino and riverboat gambling are falling fast. Remember that pork-belly futures have an economic function: To spread the risk of price fluctuation, allowing market participants to "hedge" against an uncertain future. Yet a buyer of February pork bellies may be strictly interested in a one-day gamble on the price of pork bellies. In the same manner, stock index options can provide insurance to investors large and small, as well as opportunities for pure gambling. I recommend that PAD investors use these markets solely for insurance rather than gambling, and I explain the insurance technique in the following section.

INDEX PUT OPTIONS AS INSURANCE: A CONSERVATIVE STRATEGY

We have already seen that put options increase in value when the underlying stock declines in value. By the same token, an index put option also increases in value when the underlying index declines. This insurance aspect of options can be used by the PAD investor to protect a PAD portfolio against a decline in value. If we knew exactly when the market was going to reach a cyclical peak, it would be easy to liquidate all our stocks at the appropriate moment. To paraphrase an old Wall Street adage, "No one rings a bell when the market reaches a top." The phased liquidation of Chapter 4, combined with the long-term market-timing rules of Chapter 6, will help you liquidate gradually when stocks are no longer cheap. But the market may continue to rise after you have liquidated all of the stocks that meet the rules for a general selling program. If you justifiably fear a temporary but sharp decline in the market, it may be more profitable to buy insurance on your remaining portfolio, rather than liquidate your remaining stocks, which may very well continue to rise if the bull market rages on.

There are several ways to "buy" the insurance you need. In the past I have bought, and recommended buying, S&P 500 CME puts (futures options), which tended to have smaller premiums than S&P 100 puts (index options). Since the most liquid market by far is now the CBOE S&P 100 option, the option premiums are now essentially identical, and index options can be purchased through discount stockbrokers, I now use, and recommend, S&P 100 Index options for hedging.

An example of a daily summary of S&P 100 Index options trading is reproduced in Table 10.1. (Summaries like this one appear in newspa-

TABLE 10.1:   S&P 100 Index Options Trading

Strike		Volume	Last	Net Change	Open Int
May	435c	1,403	7¾	–⅝	4,371
May	435p	803	8⅝	+⅛	4,488
June	435c	27	9¾	unch	0
June	435p	163	10½	unch	0
May	440c	6,599	5	–⅛	12,616
May	440p	480	11¼	+¾	4,478
June	440c	7,971	4⅛	unch	3,538
June	440p	88	13¼	unch	3,143
July	440c	80	9	unch	0
July	440p	3	15¼	unch	0

pers like *The Wall Street Journal* and the *New York Times*, and include many more options and strike prices.) On this particular day, the S&P 100 Index closed at 435, down about two points. The first column of the table shows the type of option ("c" for call and "p" for put), month of expiration of the option, and its strike price. The first option listed is a May call option with a strike price of 435. Volume for this option was 1,403 contracts, and the last trade of the day was at $7\frac{3}{4}$, down $\frac{5}{8}$ of a point from the previous day. The fall in the S&P Index made this option less valuable. Open interest of 4,371 contracts means that at the end of the day there were 4,371 May 435 call options outstanding. All of these options will expire in late May. The

CASE HISTORY: Put Options and the 1987 Stock Market Crash

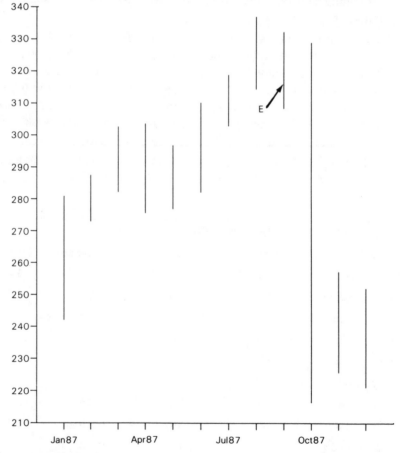

Figure 10.1: S&P 500 Index

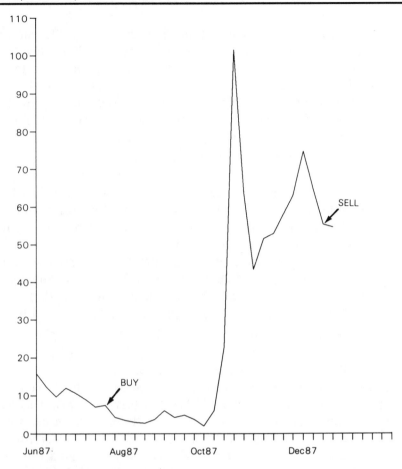

Figure 10.2: S&P 500 December Put (300)
It would be nice if we could buy insurance only when we "needed" it, but of course insurance companies might object. I began purchasing put options in early 1987, after the market had risen enough to put the VL MAP indicator firmly in the sell range. Although I also continued to raise the cash percentage in my portfolio to the PAD maximum of 50 percent, I felt strongly that I wanted to protect stocks I still held with CME S&P 500 futures options and CBOE S&P 100 Index options. While I was mainly stuck with worthless insurance in the first half of the year, the "house burned down" in the fall. Figure 10.1 shows the levels of the S&P 500 in 1987. Figure 10.2 shows the actual market price of the December 300 put option on the S&P 500, which I held until expiration in December. The gain on this option helped offset big losses on my portfolio and provided extra cash for reinvestment after the crash. Note also, however, that three S&P 100 put options were allowed to expire ("E" in Figure 10.2) at the end of September 1987. If I had rolled these over, I would have lost nothing in the crash. "For all sad words of tongue or pen, / the saddest are these: 'It might have been!' " (Whittier)

second line shows the same information for the May 435 put option, which rose slightly in value as the S&P dropped. The May 440 put option rose more, since it is an in-the-money option. Note the wide range in volume and open interest among the options listed. All else equal, the options with higher volume and open interest will have smaller bid-ask spreads, and thus cost less to buy and sell. These options are almost always those closest to expiration.

In the following example, let's assume that your stock portfolio is worth $30,000, the absolute minimum for which hedging is appropriate. Let's assume, as in Table 10.1, that the S&P 100 is at 435, and based on the level of VL MAP and the technical indicators of Chapter 6, you feel it is now time to insure your remaining portfolio against a 10 percent correction, which would take a nasty bite out of your assets (remember that you have already completed a general selling program and raised your cash reserve to 50 percent). Suppose you purchase one June 440 S&P 100 put option, which is trading, according to Table 10.1, at $13\frac{1}{4}$ (5 points intrinsic value + $8\frac{1}{4}$ points time value). This option would cost $1,325 ($13\frac{1}{4}$ × $100) plus commission. Suppose the market does decline by 10 percent before June. If the S&P 100 falls to 400, nearly a 10 percent decline, your stocks, which generally rise and fall at least as fast as the broad market averages, may fall in value from $30,000 to (say) $26,000. This $4,000 loss in your portfolio will be offset by the increase in the value of your put option, which will be worth about 40 points more, its exact value depending on the size of the option's remaining time value. This 40 points is worth $4,000, and thus your overall loss has been eliminated. Hence, one put option on the S&P 100 has given your $30,000 portfolio 100 percent insurance protection; in other words, one S&P 100 Index put option insures a $30,000 portfolio. A $60,000 portfolio would be 50 percent insured with this one put option, or fully insured with two options. Of course, if the market continues to rise, the value of your put option(s) will fall, and your put(s) may expire worthless. But the value of your portfolio will also rise, and it is likely that it will rise faster than the value of your put option(s) will fall. For example, a 10 percent rise in the market will increase the value of your portfolio by (say) $4,000, while your put option will fall to zero for a loss of $1,325. The situation is analogous to homeowner's insurance: You do not get your insurance premium back just because your house did not burn down!

It may also happen that the stock market remains flat until option expiration in late June. In this case your put option will decline in

value slowly but, in the example here, will still have five points of value at expiration. (If you still fear a market decline, you can "roll over" your put insurance by selling your June put and buying an August or September put.) This residual value of your option is not unlike a policy dividend. Unfortunately, the insurance analogy breaks down at this point. If you had purchased a 435 put instead, which was cheaper at $8\frac{5}{8}$ since it had no intrinsic value, it would expire worthless and there would be no "dividend."

We have made a crucial assumption in this example that your stocks will follow the direction of the market. This is not always a safe assumption, especially for a PAD-A investor holding only technology stocks, which fall out of favor with investors periodically (as do most stock groups). When these stocks are "in the doghouse," the market could rise while technology portfolios lose ground. In this worst of all possible cases, your option insurance will decline in value at the same time that your stocks decline in value, so that the insurance role of the put will have been destroyed by this divergence in performance. It is more likely, however, that technology stocks, rather than be left behind, will lead a raging bull market. And it is during a raging bull market that a PAD investor is likely to turn to put options for insurance.

Let me review the key elements of this section. When, during a bull market, the PAD investor has completed a selling program in accordance with the rules of Chapters 2–6, and wishes to protect his or her remaining stocks and mutual funds against a sharp market decline, put options on the S&P 100 can be purchased as insurance. Up to 100 percent "coverage" can be obtained, although the insurance will not "pay off" if your portfolio declines while the general market rises. (If the market falls while your portfolio increases in value, you of course receive an extra dividend.) The protection you actually get will depend on how closely your portfolio tracks the movements of the S&P 100.[2]

---

2. PAD investors concerned about divergence between their portfolios and the S&P 100 Index can use the CBOE's somewhat less liquid market for S&P 500 Index put options. These index options are identical to the 100s except for the underlying index. A PAD investor with just a few stocks (and no mutual funds) left in his or her portfolio could also hedge directly by buying put options on the individual stocks themselves, if such options exist.

GLOSSARY OF TERMS

Bid-Ask Spread   The difference between the buying (ask) and selling (bid) prices for an option.

Call Option   The right to buy the underlying security, index, or index future.

Cash Price   The current level of the stock index itself.

Covered Option Writing   Writing (selling) of options on stocks or futures contracts you own.

Expiration Date   The last day of trading for an option or future.

Futures   Contracts for future delivery of a commodity or financial asset of some kind, including a stock index.

Futures Option   The right to buy or sell a futures contract until the expiration date.

Index Futures   Futures traded on stock indexes.

Index Options   Options on stock indexes in which settlement is in cash rather than in stock index futures.

"In-the-Money" Option   An option that has intrinsic value, that is, a call option with a striking price below the market price or a put option with a striking price above the market price.

Intrinsic Value   What an option is worth if exercised.

Leverage   Any technique that increases the magnitudes of gains and losses.

Naked Option Writing   Writing a call option without owning the underlying stock, or writing a put option without holding a short position in the underlying stock.

"Out-of-the-Money" Option   A call option with a striking price above the market price or a put option with a striking price below the market price.

Premium   Total payment for an option, composed of intrinsic value and time value.

Put Option   The right to sell the underlying stock, index, or future.

Spot Price   Another term for cash price.

Striking Price   The price at which an option can be exercised.

Time Value   Any premium in excess of intrinsic value.

SOURCES FOR THE PAD INVESTOR

"Characteristics and Risks of Standardized Options." A booklet prepared jointly by the major exchanges. Published 1994. An introduction to the basics.

Cox, John and Mark Rubinstein, *Options Markets*. Englewood Cliffs, NJ.: Prentice-Hall, 1985. A thorough and well-written book. For those with training in finance or economics.

Daigler, Robert T., *Advanced Options Trading*. Chicago, IL: Probus Publishing, 1994. Covers all types of options trading, including synthetics and exotics.

Fullman, Scott H., *Options: A Personal Seminar*. New York: New York Institute of Finance, 1992. A good book for the beginner.

CHAPTER 11
SELLING SHORT (PAD-S)

"There is certainly good money to be made on the short side of the market, but you can't learn how to do it with the PAD System."
—*Outperforming Wall Street*, 2nd edition (1991)

"It is only an error of judgment to make a mistake, but it argues an infirmity of character to adhere to it when discovered."
—C.N. Bovee

Most investors have a visceral dislike of short selling and short sellers. Most books on investing either completely ignore it or advise against it (see above). I have now concluded, however, that short selling, properly timed and in modest amounts, can actually improve an *experienced* investor's returns without increasing risk. More importantly, I think it is possible to use the PAD System to find those overvalued stocks that are most likely to suffer in a market decline, and thus are ideal candidates for short selling. In the sections below, I lay out a set of rules for short selling, with justifications and examples. (If you have never sold a stock short before, or are unsure of the mechanics of short selling, please study the appendix to this chapter, "An Introduction to Short Selling.")

RULE 1: The VL MAP must be in the SELL range before short selling can be undertaken.

RULE 2: Cash reserves must be at 50 percent before short selling can be undertaken.

Although there are stocks that fall even during the most powerful bull markets, the odds of success are clearly greater when short selling is undertaken near a market top. While the VL MAP indicator (see Chapter 6) is by no means an infallible indicator of market tops, it is true that in the last 25 years, every bear market has started after the VL MAP reached the SELL range. Of course, many months or even years can pass before the market starts down in earnest. Thus, Rule 2 is designed to further limit short sales to the later stages of a bull market, since the PAD investor, in a normal market cycle, will have a fully invested portfolio when the VL MAP first reaches 65 percent, the "true" demarcation of the SELL range. With the VL MAP at 65 percent, it is time to construct a "Sell List" as described in Chapter 4, and begin a selling program, which should continue as long as the market stays in the VL MAP SELL range. Once cash reserves have reached 50 percent, however, and the market remains in the SELL range, the time is ripe to create a Short Sale List and begin a limited program of short sales using the rules set out below.

RULE 3: A short sale candidate must be selling above the low end of its three- to five-year appreciation potential.

This is the fundamental rule I use for ferreting out overvalued stocks. Although Value Line would be the first to admit that projecting earnings and stock price three to five years in the future requires much educated guesswork, a stock selling above the low end of its three- to five-year appreciation potential has already discounted much of Value Line's "guesstimated" growth, and is thus more likely to fall sharply when the market declines. In fact, research discussed in Chapter 6 suggests that three- to five-year appreciation potentials are on average too optimistic, making it even more likely that Rule 3 will uncover good short sale candidates. It is occasionally possible to find stocks that are selling for more than the *high* end of their three- to five-year appreciation potential. This represents an extreme of overvaluation that is often corrected even if the overall stock market continues to rise. Figure 11.1 illustrates this rare occurrence.

The only difficulty I have encountered in following this rule is that Value Line does periodically alter three- to five-year appreciation potentials. While many stocks receive a boost in three- to five-year appreciation potential when Value Line "rolls out" its estimates in spring or summer (see footnote 3 of Chapter 6), the regular, quarterly, full-page review is also a common time for a change in a stock's three- to five-year appreciation potential. If I have already sold a stock short, I

CASE HISTORY: Biomet

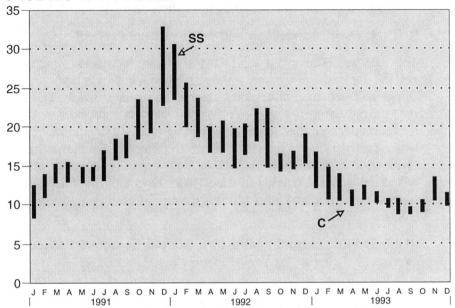

Figure 11.1
Biomet first came to my attention in early January 1992 when the "medical" stock bubble was about to burst. As I was leafing through the weekly Value Line "Summary and Index," I noticed that Biomet, a high-growth medical appliance maker, was selling for 31, while Value Line was projecting its appreciation potential for 1995–97 at 20–30. Thus, even under the most wildly optimistic scenario, the stock had no appreciation potential left for the next three to five years! Shortly after discovering this, I gave a speech on investing to the Cincinnati chapter of the American Association of Individual Investors (AAII). During the speech I singled out Biomet as a short sale candidate (point "SS" on the graph). The stock began an immediate decline (there were stock brokers in attendance) that did not really stop until the price hit 10, at which point the stock had 100 percent appreciation potential to the low end of its three- to five-year range, and was thus a "buy" using Rule 1 of Chapter 2. I consider this the perfect time to "cover," or buy back, the shares sold short (point "C" on the graph). My only regret is that I did not sell the stock short myself.

will continue to stay short even if Value Line raises the stock's three- to five-year appreciation potential. If I am ready to sell a stock short, and the three- to five-year appreciation potential is increased, I will adjust upward my minimum sell price based on Rule 3. Normally the stocks I am watching as potential short sales will not have their three- to five-year appreciation potentials reduced, but if this were to happen, I would be governed by the new lower range, which would make the stock an even better candidate for a short sale.

RULE 4: Dividend yield should be low or nonexistent.

This rule will eliminate many high-yielding utility stocks, which may not fall far even in a major market decline. Since all high-yielding stocks will get some downside "support" from their dividends, I prefer to avoid them in my search for good short sale candidates. While it is certainly true that some high-yielding stocks will decline sharply when their dividends are cut, I prefer to "short" a stock that has no dividend at all to support its price in the event of a market downturn. All of the stocks discussed in Case Histories in this chapter (with the special exception of Philip Morris) have paid zero or minimal dividends.

RULE 5: Price-earnings ratio (P/E) should be above the market average.

It is much harder to make a case that a stock is overvalued if its P/E does not even exceed the market norm. It is fairly common in the late stages of bull markets for many stocks to sell at inflated P/Es of 40, 50, or even 60 times earnings. Before the 1973–74 market collapse, the "Nifty Fifty" stocks had P/Es as high as 100 times earnings. These extreme multiples leave no room for the slightest disappointment in a quarterly earnings report, or even for a downgrade by a brokerage house from "strong buy" to just "buy." Tandycrafts, which was bid up to an extreme P/E before falling back to earth, is a prime example of the market's repeated bouts of temporary insanity.

RULE 6: Diversify. Sell more than one stock short, preferably in more than one industry.

Diversification makes sense on the short side of the market, too. If you can identify several promising overvalued stocks, the odds improve that the group as a whole, as opposed to any single stock, will underperform the market and decline rapidly once a bear market begins in earnest. It is often common, though, that a number of stocks in an industry will become overvalued by the above rules at the same time. Selling all of them short will not provide diversification, while picking one stock from each of several overvalued industry groups will spread your risk without diluting your potential return.

CASE HISTORY: Tandycrafts

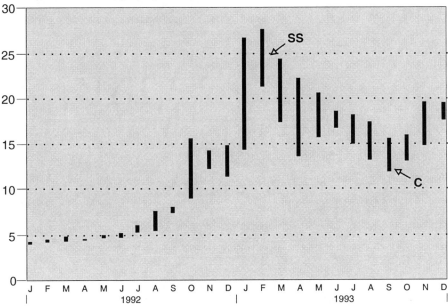

Figure 11.2
Tandycrafts was recommended as a short sale by the *PAD System Report* in February 1993 ("SS" on the graph) when it was selling for 25½. The stock had had a fabulous run-up from 4 in just 12 months, and once it shot up to the midpoint of its three- to five-year appreciation potential of 20–30 with a P/E ratio approaching 40, I decided the stock price movement must be a speculative "bubble," since there was no earthshaking development to account for the price surge of such a mundane supplier of hobby and handicraft items. Sure enough, earnings could not justify the price and the bubble burst shortly afterward. The stock then traded as low as 12½, which satisfied Chapter 2's 100 percent rule for purchase, and was thus an ideal point to cover ("C" on graph) the short sale. (All prices adjusted for 2-for-1 stock split.)

RULE 7: Limit short sales to approximately 10 percent of the total value of your portfolio (including cash reserves).

Not all short sales will work out as nicely as the ones I have discussed so far. Short selling requires nerves of steel, since you are fighting against the long-run trend of the market and selling short the very stocks that are among the most popular on Wall Street. There is no obvious upper limit to Wall Street's enthusiasm for a stock, and thus you must limit your short selling to conserve your hard-won profits from the previous bull market.

CASE HISTORY: International Game Technology (IGT)

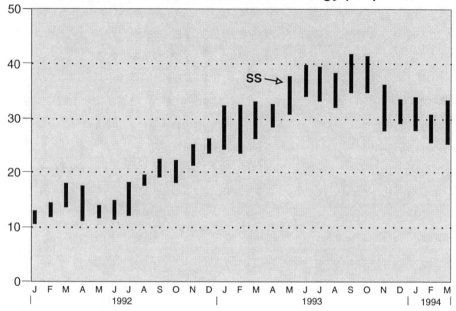

Figure 11.3

Gambling was one of the major fads of the 1990–1994 bull market. Every company with "gaming" or "casino" in its name was bid up to unsustainable levels. I picked IGT for my Rule 6 bet against the gambling stocks because it temporarily traded above the high-end of its three- to five-year appreciation potential, and had a P/E approaching 50. Both the *PAD System Report* and I sold the stock short in May 1993, in the low to mid 30s ("SS" on the graph). The stock did rally as high as 41 later in the year, but then dropped to 17½ in 1994, leading me to cover my short sale. (All prices adjusted for 2-for-1 split.)

RULE 8: For additional comfort, wait until the price of your short sale candidate has stabilized, and place a stop-loss order above the previous high price. This is especially wise if the stock is ranked "1" for year-ahead performance.

An old Wall Street adage, which is also useful in everyday life, is "Never step in front of a moving train." What this really means is that when a stock is cannonballing skyward, stand aside until there is some sign that the "train" is running out of steam. Stocks almost invariably go sideways for a period before heading back to earth. Although I have no hard-and-fast rule, a month with no forward progress after a surge to the midpoint of a stock's three- to five-year appreciation potential is very tempting. Unfortunately there is still no

CASE HISTORY: QVC Network

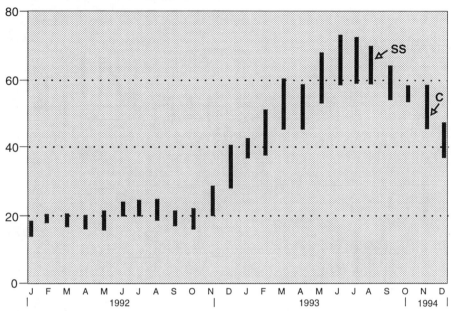

Figure 11.4

In December 1992, QVC Network, a relatively obscure cable shopping channel, was taken over by Barry Diller, the former CEO of Fox Broadcasting. Diller's reputation on Wall Street as a media superman was soon reflected in QVC's stock price, which rose from under 20 to 67 by the summer of 1993. Since 1993 earnings were estimated by Value Line at $1.70 per share, and three- to five-year appreciation potential was 60–105, I highlighted the stock in the *PAD System Report* as a short sale candidate in June 1993. I did not sell it short at this time, however, because there was no way to tell how far Wall Street would bid up the stock solely on the strength of the name Barry Diller. By August 1993, the stock appeared to have finally stabilized around 70, and I sold it short at that price ("SS" on the graph). I could not use a stop-loss order in this case, although a natural point for a more nervous PAD short seller to place a mental stop would have been at 74, above the all-time high. The stock began to drop almost immediately (always a good sign) even before QVC decided to enter the well-publicized Paramount bidding war. I covered my short sale at 49½ ("C" on the graph) although some subscribers to the *PAD System Report* may have covered as low as 40, based on my instructions in that newsletter. My reason for covering even though the stock had not reached its price target was that I felt there was a chance QVC would not win the bidding war (it didn't) and thus the stock price would bounce back sharply (it did, briefly).

guarantee that the train was not just taking on fuel for a new surge to even more exalted levels. I will use a stop-loss order if I am particularly concerned that another surge is on the way. A stop-loss order

CASE HISTORY: Cisco Systems

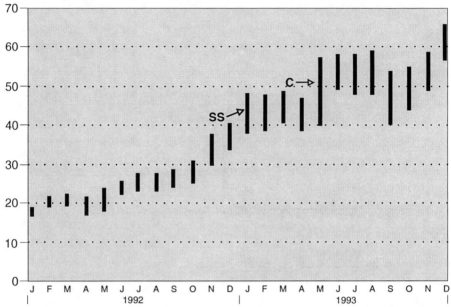

Figure 11.5
Cisco Systems is a computer networking company, which was another fad industry of the 1990–94 bull market. All agreed that Cisco's earnings were going to grow rapidly during 1993 and beyond, but when the stock price reached 45, which was nearly 40 times current earnings and well within the three- to five-year appreciation potential for the stock, I decided to sell it short ("SS" on the graph). I instructed subscribers to the *PAD System Report* to place a stop order at 50, just above the all-time high, so that they would not be "run over" if the train moved out of the station in high gear. I was particularly concerned about this possibility since Cisco was ranked "1" for year-ahead performance by Value Line. After a few months of sideways movement, Cisco broke out to new highs, and my subscribers were stopped out for a small loss at 50 ("C" on the graph). (All prices adjusted for 2-for-1 stock split.)

instructs your discount broker to buy back your shares when the stock reaches a predetermined price. If the specified price is reached, the order becomes a market order and is normally executed at or near the level of your stop loss. Although stop-loss orders can be entered for exchange-listed stocks, it may be necessary to place a "mental stop" for NASDAQ stocks. If a mental stop would require more than the available self-discipline, you must limit your search to exchange-listed issues or find a broker who will accept stop orders on NASDAQ stocks. Unfortunately, it is not illegal or unheard of for a stock to trade at your stop-loss price and then fall sharply just as you predicted.

RULE 9: Cover your short sale when the stock has appreciation potential of 100 percent to the low end of the three- to five-year range.

This is, of course, the ideal outcome for a short sale. Any stock that has become suitable for purchase based on its current price is clearly not overvalued any longer. Biomet, Tandycrafts, and International Game Technology (see above) were covered based on this rule.

RULE 10: Cover all short sales when the VL MAP reaches 100 percent.

This is another rule that follows naturally from earlier chapters. If stocks are now "OK to Buy" under Rule 1 of Chapter 6, it is time for the PAD investor to get back to the main order of business, which is buying and holding reasonably priced stocks with good growth prospects, and good mutual funds.

An investor who is comfortable with short selling can use the above set of rules to build a small portfolio of short sales during the late stages of a bull market. These short positions will normally show gains when the market is falling and losses when the market is rising, and thus tend to offset the gains and losses of the remaining stocks in your portfolio. This partial offset will tend to reduce the volatility of your portfolio while at the same time providing a way to profit from inevitable bear markets.

SELLING SHORT WITHOUT VALUE LINE

While my short-selling system is based on Value Line, it is also possible to find good short sale candidates without the aid of Value Line. I doubt the typical PAD investor has either the time or the inclination to actively pursue the necessary research, à la Peter Lynch, to find overvalued stocks that Wall Street (and Value Line) have missed. Yet chance favors the well-prepared. When, in the course of your work, your reading, or your discussions with friends, you are presented with information that Wall Street has overlooked, but which could fundamentally affect a stock or an industry, be prepared to act.

CASE HISTORY: Philip Morris

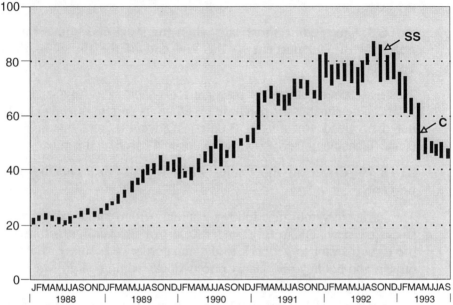

Figure 11.6

For many years I have made an annual contribution to Action on Smoking and Health (ASH), an organization that I felt was fighting the good, albeit quixotic, fight against the tobacco industry. For most of this time, of course, tobacco stocks were providing outstanding returns for investors. Industry leader Philip Morris was considered an ideal and safe investment by almost everyone on Wall Street, since it was obvious that a leadership position in a highly concentrated industry selling an addictive product would lead to steadily higher prices and profits. By the summer of 1992, however, my monthly ASH newsletter was filled with more and more reports of scientific research documenting the hazards of second-hand smoke, new restrictions on smoking, and potential legal reverses for the once legally impregnable industry. I concluded also from discussions with friends that the glamor of smoking was completely gone, and that almost all smokers would gladly quit if they could. Yet every major source of investment advice I consulted (including Value Line) seemed blissfully unconcerned about an industry that looked to me like the asbestos industry of the 1990s. I recommended selling Philip Morris short in the September 1992 issue of the *PAD System Report*, and sold it short myself soon afterward at 80 ("SS" on the graph). I covered my short position too soon ("C" on the graph), but once the bad news started coming out I thought it was fully reflected in the stock price. I have since increased my contribution to ASH, and expect to sell MO short again in the future, when Wall Street again decides that all is well with tobacco.

SOURCES FOR THE PAD INVESTOR

Caes, Charles J., *Tools of the Bear: How Any Investor Can Make Money When Stocks Go Down.* Chicago: Probus Publishing, 1993. This book provides some useful source and background material for an investor preparing to make a first short sale. Also contains information on options and options strategies.

Mamis, Justin and Robert Mamis, *When To Sell: Inside Strategies for Stock Market Profits.* New York: Farrar, Straus Giroux, 1977. Although somewhat dated, this book is fun to read with lots of good advice. Chapter 10 is devoted exclusively to selling short.

Staley, Kathryn, *When Stocks Crash Nicely: The Finer Art of Short Selling.* New York: Harper Business, 1991. An excellent collection of short-selling stories, based on the actual experience of author Staley and short sellers like Chanos and the Feshbachs. Full of gems of Wall Street wisdom, such as the quote at the beginning of the appendix to this chapter.

Walker, Joseph A., *Selling Short.* New York: John Wiley & Sons, Inc., 1991. A good book for beginners. Chapters 4–6 contain the basic short-selling material. Later chapters discuss options strategies.

APPENDIX 11
AN INTRODUCTION TO SHORT SELLING

"Short selling can be much like a cat waiting outside a mousehole—the level of persistence, patience, and attentiveness is not for everyone, especially over sustained periods of time."
—Kathryn Staley, *When Stocks Crash Nicely* (1991)

Most investors are unfamiliar with short selling, even though the mechanics are fairly simple and the potential profits are large. In the paragraphs below I have tried to provide enough background information to prepare an experienced PAD investor to take the plunge. Readers who desire a more thorough introduction to the subject should consult the sources previously listed.

Short sellers are no different from the rest of us. They want to buy low and sell high. The trick is that the "shorts" just reverse the order of the transactions, selling high first and then buying low later. Of course to sell a stock you do not own requires you to first "borrow" the stock from someone who does own it. Once you have borrowed it, you can sell it in the hopes that you can replace (buy) the stock you borrowed later at a lower price. Some investors balk at this point because they envision borrowing a friend's car and then selling it. This would be an unfriendly act, to say the least. But when you borrow stock, the lender does not know, let alone care, that you borrowed it! Your discount brokerage firm has many thousands of shares of stock which it is holding in street name for its customers. (PAD investors are not supposed to leave their stock in street name, but to take delivery.) Your broker then borrows the shares for you from among those on deposit and sells them on the open market, as you instruct. You receive a confirmation of the transaction (Figure 11A.1), which looks very similar to an ordinary sale of stock.

There are several key differences, however. During the time you are holding a short position, any dividends paid on the stock must be transmitted by you to the rightful owner, but the brokerage firm will handle this automatically. Since you are supposed to be selling short only low- or no-dividend stocks (see Rule 4 in text) this is a very minor matter.

Also, you must sell short in a "margin" account, even though I have stated elsewhere never to *buy* on margin. The risk of course with buying or selling short on margin is that an adverse move can trigger a margin call (funds you must send the broker to protect his loan to you), and you must then either send the funds or the broker will close out some or all of your short position. This should not be a problem if you are following the rules set out in this chapter, which require you to raise cash reserves to 50 percent before selling short, and limiting your short sales to 10 percent of the value of your portfolio. I have been short as many as six stocks at the same time, and my cash reserves have always been large enough that I earned interest every month on my cash balance.

Your monthly brokerage statement may also look different when you have short sales. Expect as much as a full page of daily "mark-to-market" entries, which are simply bookkeeping entries that the PAD short seller can safely ignore.

Figure 11A.1

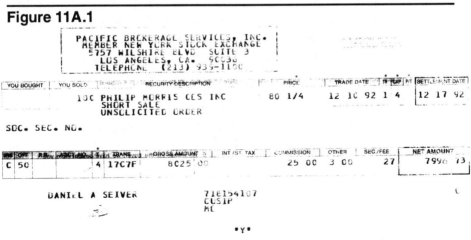

A trickier reporting problem will occur if you have short positions open at the end of the calendar year. Your brokerage firm will send you a "1099" summarizing the total gross proceeds you received from stock sales during the year. The broker will include any short sales, even if you have not completed the transaction by "covering," or buying the stock back. Schedule D of your federal income tax return requires you to report all completed transactions during the year and total the gross proceeds received. It will now be necessary to add a "reconciliation" note to explain to the IRS why your Schedule D total gross proceeds does not match what the broker sent to you and the IRS. If you close the short position in the following calendar year, your gross proceeds will again not match up, since your Schedule D will now show the proceeds from the short sale, while the brokerage firm's total gross proceeds for the year will not.

It may also happen that a discount broker, especially a small one, may not be able to find stock to borrow and sell short for you. My solution to this problem is to open a second account with another (and larger) discount broker, which can then be a backup when this problem arises.

A still rarer but not unknown problem can arise with exchange-listed stocks. A little-known rule called the "(zero) uptick rule" requires that a stock must trade on an uptick (usually one-eighth of a point) before a short sale can be made. This rule was designed to prevent the "bear raids" of old, when a group of shorts would conspire to beat down a stock with wave after wave of short sales, and thus panic the "longs" into selling and driving the stock even lower. With the uptick rule in place, a short seller can't pounce when the price on consecutive trades has gone straight down from 50 to $49\frac{1}{2}$ to 49 to 48 and so on. Until someone steps up and buys and pushes the price up by at least one-eighth, the short seller will have to wait on the sidelines. Usually this type of price collapse only occurs when the overall market is in a 1987-type free fall, and since crashes usually come after long bull markets have pushed prices to extremes, PAD investors will already have their short positions in place. If you just happen to begin your short selling during a market crash, put aside your plans and begin preparing a Buy List!

CHAPTER 12
SPECIAL TOPICS

This chapter contains a broad range of advice for PAD investors. There is no particular order to the presentation of topics, and in many cases each topic is an introduction to a complex subject. I suggest the reader browse through those topics that are of special interest or concern. The choices lie among taxes, tax reform, ethical investing, computers and investing, managing information flow, and PAD no-no's (commodity futures and Ponzi schemes).

TAXES

General Strategy

Near the end of every calendar year, daily columns on stock market activity often mention "tax-loss selling" as a factor in the market's behavior, and at the very end of the year the end of this selling is also frequently mentioned. In this section I explain the tax-loss selling phenomenon and present a few rules to help you do your buying and selling in a way consistent with keeping your taxes low. The most important lesson of the section, however, is to avoid letting your tax strategy control your portfolio strategy. You can take advantage of stock market bargains created by others who make this mistake.

The 1986 tax law revision eliminated the favorable tax treatment of long-term capital gains, which had been part of the tax code for many years. PAD investors reaped many benefits from this preference item, since successful PAD investing will result in long-term gains. Preferential treatment of long-term gains, for high-income individuals only, was restored in 1993 as part of the Clinton deficit reduction program. Whatever the social and economic merits of a tax break on capital gains (it is either a sop to the rich or a good deal for everybody), it is a bonus for the long-term investor. Even without favorable treatment, investors can adjust the timing of their realizations of gains and losses to reduce their current or future tax bills.

In fact, any set of tax rules will encourage investors to adjust their portfolio strategies for tax purposes. The pervasiveness of the tax system and its rules drives some individuals to arrange their lives—and even their deaths—so as to minimize taxes. I do not recommend this approach to life or to the stock market. What a PAD investor can do is make slight adjustments to strategy that can reduce taxes or postpone tax payments while keeping the essential PAD strategy intact.

My first rule is to have a housecleaning of your portfolio at least once a year. This is probably best done at the time of a general review of your portfolio. August is my favorite month, because I prefer to do my housecleaning before the majority of investors do theirs. In particular, any stocks on your Sell List, which you are keeping in accordance with the rules of Chapters 2–4, should be sold by the early fall. I cannot emphasize too strongly that these sales should be undertaken only because you have decided to "bail out" of a company's stock, not because you "need" tax losses to offset gains. This latter type of selling is an example of tax strategy ruling portfolio strategy.

If the VL MAP indicator of Chapter 6 is not in the sell range, all of the proceeds from your sales can be reinvested in companies that meet the criteria of Chapters 2–4. If there are not sufficient stocks that meet these criteria, maintain cash reserves until there are.

Sale and Repurchase

If in fact you have not lost confidence in a stock on which you have taken a loss, you can undertake another strategy to reduce current taxes. Any stock you sell for a tax loss can be repurchased 31 days later without the transaction being considered a "wash sale," that is, a transaction undertaken solely to reduce taxes. (Losses on wash sales do not qualify as tax losses.) The main drawback of this approach is that it is always possible that the stock will rise during the 31-day waiting period. Thus, I recommend this strategy for only a limited number of stocks, and only when the market is relatively expensive by Chapter 6's standards.

It is also possible, although the commission costs will begin to mount up, to follow more complex strategies that will protect you against a sudden upsurge in your stock while you are counting off the 31 days. The purchase of a call option (see Chapter 10) on your stock can lock in a price at which you can get back into the market. Some stocks still do not have exchange-traded options, and regular use of the options markets for individual stocks requires additional time and expertise, which I do not think is necessary for most PAD investors. More importantly, the IRS might conclude that your trading scheme is the equivalent of a wash sale. Only with exquisitely bad timing will a stock you have suffered with for six months or a year explode in the one month you do not own it, especially if your market timing is better than average. In fact, if you houseclean ahead of the pack, you may be able to buy back when others are selling, and repurchase at a price below your sale price.

We can hope that more of your efforts will be devoted to timing the realization of your gains. If you sell stock for a profit in January, it is possible to defer paying income taxes on the gain for 15 months. Capital gains taxes for a sale in the first few days of January are not due until April 15 of the following year. This delayed payment is equivalent to an interest-free loan from the IRS.[1]

Most investors sell their losers from October through December, so this is not a good time to sell yours. Some stocks on your Buy List may need just a little decline, induced by tax-loss selling, to exceed the minimum-appreciation-potential hurdles of Chapter 2 or the equivalent total return hurdle of Chapter 3. Be prepared.

Short-Term Gains

A stock that rises rapidly shortly after purchase can also create a dilemma for the PAD investor, especially if the market as a whole appears overvalued. On the one hand, if you continue to hold the stock to avoid tax liability in that year, the bubble may burst. On the other hand, if you sell and pay tax now and the market does not decline, you have paid much more in taxes than necessary—with perfect hindsight, of course. Again, one way out of this pleasant predicament is with an option, in this case a put option (full details are presented in Chapter 10). A put option on a stock gives you the right to sell it at a stated price for a fixed period of months. The IRS does not consider the stock sold, however, until you have actually sold the stock to someone, and the option only gives you the right, not a binding con-

---

1. If you must pay quarterly estimated tax, the value of the tax deferral is not as great, although you pay no penalty if your total tax payments are at least 90 percent of your liability, or 100 percent of the previous year's taxes. (These percentages can, of course, be changed by Congress at any time.)

tractual obligation, to sell. This right, which will increase in value if the stock price falls, may not be cheap to buy: you must pay the option seller for the privilege, and the broker will charge you a commission. Extra time and learning will be required on your part, and the strategy cannot be applied to stocks that have no options trading. A put option will provide you with a hedge against a market decline while you wait for your gains to carry over into the new year.

A simpler alternative is to sell part of your holdings, lock in the gain, and pay your taxes. If the market does go down while you are waiting for the new year, you could easily lose more than you would have paid in higher taxes! If you refuse to sell because of the tax consequences, you have begun to let tax strategy rule portfolio strategy, which, I repeat, is a major error. In this example, the danger may be relatively small, but many investors use the tax argument to justify holding stocks with large capital gains long after they should have been sold.

Tax Shelters for the PAD Investor: IRAs, Keoghs, etc.

The individual retirement account (IRA) was the best tax break given to the middle class since the home mortgage interest deduction was created. PAD investors who can still qualify for IRA deductions should continue to take them, if at all possible. Many PAD investors

CASE HISTORIES: Texas Instruments and Genrad

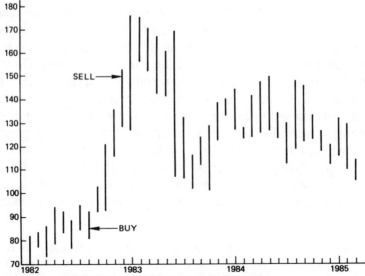

Figure 12.1: Texas Instruments (NYSE-TXN) 1982–1985

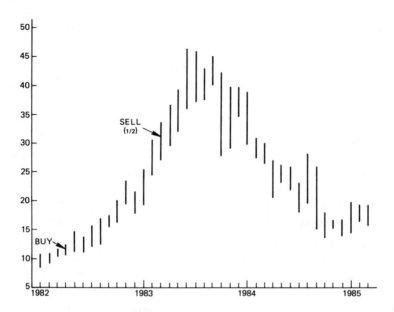

Figure 12.2: Genrad (NYSE-GEN) 1982–1985

I was faced with a short-term gain dilemma in 1983 in two stocks: Texas Instruments (TXN), which, with a little luck, I had purchased in August 1982 at 84. The subsequent bull market carried it to 150 in less than a year, and I decided to take my profits, even though they were taxed at the full rate, rather than wait for preferential tax treatment. The stock did rise to 170 after I sold it, but then the company's failure in home computers drove the stock down to 100. I was happy to get out.

I had purchased Genrad (GEN) at 12 in the spring of 1982, and by the spring of 1983 the same bull market had driven it to 30. I wrestled with the short-term gain problem and decided to sell half of my holding. It subsequently rose to 45 after becoming a long-term gain, but slower earnings growth and the bear market of 1984 dragged it to under 20, and mounting losses for the company in 1985 pushed the stock back below 12. I sold the remaining shares at 12, months after it had been downgraded to "5" for short-term performance by Value Line. I broke my own rules and paid the price!

(Both of these examples are drawn from the "good old days" of highly preferential tax rates for long-term gains.)

(including me) quit contributing to our IRAs when the deduction rules were tightened. Universal IRAs were popular enough that they, or suitable substitutes, could be resurrected at any time. (The IRA is supposed to encourage saving in the United States, and since we do precious little of that, I consider it one of the more justifiable tax breaks.) Even without new contributions, however, PAD investors must manage the IRAs they already have. Patience is crucial, since under normal conditions, IRA funds cannot be withdrawn without penalty until age 59½.

There are several alternatives for managing this money. If you are a full-fledged PAD investor, you can manage it yourself through a discount brokerage firm, but there are fees and commissions to pay, and these can be significant when the account is small. A better alternative for small accounts is to set up an IRA with either Fidelity, Schwab, or another firm offering no-fee transactions for a wide variety of no-load mutual funds, and then use the rules of Chapter 5 to find funds with good, long-term total returns achieved with moderate risk. You can use the market-timing techniques of Chapter 6 to switch your money from money-market to stock funds and back, and the costs are generally quite low. Annual IRA fees are very small, and all dividends and capital gains will be automatically reinvested for you. The switches between funds are usually free, although the number of switches per year may be limited. Investors covered by a 401(k) plans at work, or self-employed individuals with Keogh plans, may be able to use these same strategies.

Employees of educational institutions, and others who can qualify under section 403(b) of the tax code, are entitled to pay pretax dollars into a tax-deferred annuity (TDA) plan. The money compounds tax-free until it is withdrawn, but some plans do restrict withdrawal or charge extra fees for premature withdrawal. In many cases, the switching options available are similar to the mutual-fund switching options previously mentioned. Annuity firms that allow more flexibility in investments are more desirable, other things being equal. I must also point out that these tax-shelter plans are only as safe as the underlying insurance company. Most are quite safe, although nothing is absolutely safe in today's world. Baldwin-United investors discovered the risks involved. Holders of the firm's single-payment deferred annuities lost much sleep, if not principal and interest, when the company plunged into Chapter 11 bankruptcy in the mid-1980s.

Of course, there are many other schemes, legal and otherwise, designed to reduce taxes. Most of these only make economic sense for the rich and near-rich. Successful tax reform eliminated a number of these shelters, which often have no economic function. If you are determined to invest in oil-drilling participations or suburban shopping malls, you will have no trouble finding assistance. Our tax code spawned an entire industry to serve you.

TAX REFORM

Many American presidents have tried to reform the American tax code, often with little success. Everyone wants to see unfair tax breaks eliminated, except for the ones they use! If we start from first principles to design a simple and "fair" tax code, we would choose, first, a small number of tax brackets for simplicity; second, progressive tax rates, that is, higher tax rates for higher incomes; and third, horizontal equity, that is, equal taxes for equal incomes. The latter two items also give us fairness and simplicity: poor people would pay no taxes, rich people would pay plenty of taxes, and those of us in between would pay the same taxes on a (say) $40,000-a-year income whether the source was wages, capital gains, interest, or shares of corporate profits. It would not matter how many children we had, whether we owned our home, gave to charity, or drilled for oil. This ultimate in simplicity and fairness would save massive administrative costs, eliminate all activities designed to shelter income, and permit us to raise the same dollars from individual income taxes with much lower marginal tax rates.[2]

Of course, such a plan will never become law. First, some deductions are "sacred," that is, they have existed for so long and benefit such a large group that lawmakers will not risk making a change. Home mortgage interest is an excellent example of such a sacred cow. Many others are nearly as sacred, and once we agree that some deductions or exemptions are justified on equity or economic grounds, we open the door for the "special interests," which include you and me. Tax reform in 1986 followed this pattern. The simplest plans became more complex and less "fair" in order to improve chances of passage into law. The final outcome in 1986 was a "grand compromise," which could always fall apart. By 1993, the unraveling had begun, as the number of tax brackets increased; there was no evidence that the tax changes made that year simplified the system. I doubt that we can resist using the tax code for social engineering, and thus major reform efforts are doomed to failure. We can hope that minor reforms, such as eliminating abusive tax shelters, can be made and kept on the books.

There is little reason, then, to plan in advance for major tax reform. Even if investors may discover that the maximum tax rate on capital

---

2. I have simplified matters for the sake of argument. The costs of earning income should be deductible even in this system, and knotty problems such as the "marriage penalty" would still have to be resolved.

gains will be raised or lowered a bit, or that maximum contributions to IRAs or other tax plans are increased or reduced, the PAD System will not require modification. If the corporate tax code is modified, Value Line will incorporate the changes into its long-term projections, and judicious application of the rules of Chapters 2–4 will still enable the PAD investor to select equities that will outperform the market in the long run.

ETHICAL INVESTING

A growing number of investors are concerned about the activities of the firms in which they own shares, and a number of "socially conscious" mutual funds have appeared to cater to these investors.[3] Rather than simply buy those stocks they think will best meet their monetary objectives, ethical investors refuse to purchase shares in companies whose lines of business or behavior they find ethically unacceptable. Ethical investing is a very personal matter, however, as there is very little in the area that is purely black or white. I define an ethical investor as anyone who has ever managed his or her portfolio on any basis other than maximum monetary gain. Yet ethical investors disagree about which companies should be avoided for ethical reasons. My opinion in this matter is that you should let your conscience be your guide. If the company's business makes you uncomfortable, don't buy the stock. (If your standards are so high that the universe of potential stocks approaches or equals zero, the stock market is not for you!)

I have been an ethical investor for many years, and my past concentration on technology was partly a result of my own ethical considerations. I readily admit that the firms of Silicon Valley are far from perfect in behavior. Pollution from high-technology manufacturing entered some local water supplies, for example. I was willing to live with this peccadillo. Industries I will not invest in include the tobacco and liquor industries, because I think their products do much harm in the world, and because they have done little to control this damage. I also refuse to invest in the defense industry, mainly because I would be overjoyed to see an end to war and the threat of war in the world, and it would be a shame to have the joy of this unlikely event spoiled by an enormous decline in my defense stocks. Evidence of corporate wrongdoing by major defense contractors has served to harden my

3. The January 7, 1994 Summary section of *Morningstar Mutual Funds* lists 18 socially conscious funds, with styles and phone numbers, in a short piece on page 7.

opinion on these stocks, since I do not choose to own shares of companies whose executives violate the law. My ethics on defense are not absolute: Many firms I have owned sell products to the Pentagon, either directly or indirectly. I find this tolerable up to the point where the Pentagon has become one of the firm's biggest customers. The percentage of sales to the U.S. government, if significant, is actually reported by Value Line in the same small section of the individual stock report that contains the R&D percentage.

Firms in other industries are also unsuitable for my ethical portfolio for a variety of reasons. For example, my holdings in General Instrument (Chapter 4) made me uncomfortable because gambling became an important indirect source of their revenues. I would not buy the shares of Grolier, Inc., because I was exposed to and disapproved of their door-to-door sales tactics for their encyclopedias. I am sure the reader has his or her own ax to grind with a particular company, and it is relatively painless to indulge yourself and refuse to buy their stock no matter how highly it is recommended by Value Line.

In sum, if you despise the merchants of sin and death, don't buy their stocks. You have not reduced the universe of stocks that much unless you enforce your guidelines quite rigidly. The stocks of many growth companies, except for those whose main customer is the U.S. government, are relatively "clean" by generally accepted ethical standards. For further advice on this topic, I would consult the book by John Simon listed in the Sources section at the end of this chapter.

COMPUTERS AND INVESTING

The information revolution is changing the way we invest. Computers have made it possible for the New York Stock Exchange (NYSE) and its member firms to manage volume in excess of 600 million shares per day. Computers enable the National Association of Securities Dealers' (NASD) NASDAQ system to trade over 300 million shares in a single day without a central trading floor or face-to-face trading. These numbers are truly astounding when we recall that average daily trading volume on the NYSE was five million shares at the beginning of the 1960s. Information on trading is transmitted instantaneously around the world, and individual investors can purchase portable hand-held computer/receivers that can provide up-to-the-second quotations on thousands of stocks, futures, and options contracts. A personal computer owner can review the same information over telephone lines or via FM broadcast signals. These technological marvels are not of direct interest to the PAD investor, however, since trading is relatively infrequent with the PAD system, and up-to-the-second quotations are unnecessary. Even the eventual linkup of exchanges around the world, permitting around-the-clock trading, would have little impact on the PAD investor. I suppose if you had made up your mind to buy or sell a stock today, and then the press of work or other activity caused you to forget until after 4 p.m. Eastern time, it would be useful to be able to call your broker after dinner and have your transaction carried out that evening in Tokyo or Hong Kong. Waiting until the next day would not be that painful or costly in most situations, however.

The computer revolution has also made it possible to bypass the human side of your brokerage firm altogether, entering your buy or sell orders via computer and telephone line. It certainly does not pay to purchase a computer, modem, and accessories just to partake of this service, but I admit that surly or uncooperative stockbrokers can drive an investor to prefer the subservience of a computer monitor. I have recently switched to placing buy and sell orders through my broker's on-line service, because the broker offers a further break on commissions, and the on-line service never gives me a busy signal. Others may still prefer the human touch. To each his own.

Portfolio analysis is also simplified by the computer. A wide variety of software is available to help you keep track of your transactions, dividends, portfolio value, and investment performance. This software has now become powerful enough to be a worthwhile investment for an active investor who is comfortable with computers. The best programs will also write checks for you and transfer relevant data to your tax preparation software.

James Feldhouse and I have updated our own PAD software, now known as the PAD Stock Selector Program II[4] (copyright 1994 by James Feldhouse and Daniel A. Seiver), which can be obtained free with the order form found at the back of this book. PAD investors familiar with PC software should have no trouble loading and using the program. (Please follow the instructions on the diskette label.) The program will store information on up to 100 stocks, and print out a PAD information sheet showing which of the PAD rules are met or not met based on raw data supplied by the user. Price data can be

4.   The program requires an IBM PC or compatible. (A Macintosh version is being developed.) PAD Stock Selector II is available from the author in 5-1/4 inch and 3-1/2 inch format. Readers should write to P.O. Box 554, Oxford, OH 45056, and enclose a copy of the order form found at the back of this book.

entered manually or via ASCII files created from on-line databases. Stocks stored in the system can be placed in a portfolio for which summary statistics are generated, such as yield, portfolio average year-ahead performance ranking, portfolio average appreciation potential, etc. PAD Stock Selector II will also store data on mutual funds and help you build a portfolio of mutual funds meeting all of the requirements of Chapter 5. The program will also generate a Buy List of stocks meeting all the requirements of either section of Chapter 2 or Chapter 3, and a Sell List of stocks based on criteria suggested in those chapters. The program has also been updated to track short sales and short-sale candidates selected with the rules of Chapter 11.

Another program that deserves special mention is Value/Screen III, a product of Value Line. Value/Screen software enables the user to select stocks from the Value Line universe using criteria similar to those laid out in Chapters 2 and 3. It also contains a portfolio information module, which lets you store key information about your portfolio. While this product could automate much of the PAD System, it has several drawbacks, namely, it is only available at *reasonable* cost on a monthly basis,[5] and the "screens" do not match up with the precise rules of Chapters 2 and 3. For example, it is impossible to select stocks based on R&D percentage or price growth persistence, or on the basis of appreciation potential to the low end of the three- to five-year range. Nonetheless, this program is the forerunner of more flexible software that will appear in the future. Once a PAD investor can cheaply "interrogate" the complete Value Line database with a computer, the time that must be devoted to stock-screening elements of the PAD System can be reduced to minutes per week.

MANAGING THE INFORMATION FLOW

Until the computer revolution is complete, however, PAD investors must deal with a significant burden of paper. In the following sections I give suggestions that can keep the paper flowing smoothly, with a minimum of confusion. Once a household robot can do these chores, as well as serve drinks and ward off intruders, buy it.

Recordkeeping

If you are ever audited by the IRS, you will quickly discover that you are at a major disadvantage without good records. Good recordkeep-

---

5. Weekly updates are available, but are very expensive.

ing will also help you in preparing your annual Schedule D, "Capital Gains and Losses," with a minimum of pain and suffering. Accordingly, keep a record of every transaction you make. Your discount broker will provide you with an extra copy in addition to the remittance copy for every transaction. Keep a stock record book of some kind (purchase price may be tax-deductible) or use a financial software program in which you can list your holdings, dates of purchases and sales, amounts of profits and losses, and dividends. One inexpensive loose-leaf book that will do this for you is listed at the end of this chapter. If you record your transactions as you make them, with a separate listing of gains and losses for the year, you can see at a glance what your tax situation is in August. Also, when tax time arrives, you (or your preparer) can copy your entries directly onto Schedule D. As noted above, good financial software can transfer this data directly to your tax-preparation software.

One additional piece of information you will want to keep for every stock you own is the name and address of the transfer agent for the common stock. Banks usually handle this work, and every stock certificate has the name of the transfer agent on it. Corporate annual reports also contain this information. If your securities are ever lost or stolen, you must contact the transfer agent. The transfer agent will want to know the serial numbers on your certificates, so you should write down these numbers also. Keep your securities in a safe place (see below), since replacing them can be a lengthy and expensive process.

If you keep your certificates and maintain your records as I have suggested, you can use the "identified cost" method for calculating your taxable gains and losses. This method is more flexible than either the "first-in, first-out" (FIFO) or "last-in, first-out" (LIFO) methods of accounting. The identified cost method makes it much easier to postpone gains when that is advantageous and to convert short-term gains to long-term ones. To use the method, every purchase and sale must be "identified" with stock certificate numbers. Then, when it is time to sell some stock, you can select which block or blocks of shares to sell based on purchase date and price. Here is an example.

Suppose you bought 100 shares of stock X at 45 on May 6, 1996, another 100 at 35 on July 27, 1996, and a final 100 at 60 on November 1, 1996. Suppose that it is now April 22, 1997, the stock market has risen sharply, and it is time to sell some stock. Stock X, at 65, is one of those you decide to sell. To minimize the tax paid, you can sell the shares bought at 60, on which you have the smallest gain. This minimizes your tax now and leaves more of your gains to be taxed later. (If there is a minimum holding period for preferential treatment of capital gains, your bigger gains may end up being taxed at a lower rate.) If the stock had declined instead, the sale of the stock bought at 60 would provide the largest tax loss. While in this case LIFO accounting would provide the same result, the next sale under LIFO would be the stock bought at 35, whereas with identified cost, you could sell the stock bought at 45 next if you wished. If you know that your tax bracket in the current year will be either much higher or much lower than the following year, you can use the identified cost method to push more taxable income into the lower tax-rate year. In the example here, suppose also that this year is a low-tax year for you. You might then want to sell the 100 shares bought at 35 instead, so that the biggest gain is taxed at the lower rate. This strategy also works if capital gains are ever indexed for inflation (minimize tax by selling the shares with the smallest inflation-adjusted gain), since a tax postponed is money in the bank.

Even investors who leave stock in "street name" rather than taking delivery of the certificates can use the identified cost method, although you need your broker's cooperation. When you have decided which shares to sell, instruct your broker to put *on the sale confirmation slip* "versus purchase (date)" where (date) is the day you bought the shares you want to identify as being sold.

This flexibility of the identified cost method does require extra work, but it is well worth it. Note also that in this example we have stuck to the advice given earlier in the chapter: Our tax strategy has not dictated our portfolio strategy.

Safekeeping of Securities[6]

The identified cost method is simpler if you take possession of your securities. Even if you do not want or need to use this method, I still recommend that you take possession of your securities rather than leave the certificates on deposit with your broker. If you have your securities on deposit, your broker will mail them to you at your request. Brokerage houses do fail, and when they do, customer balances and securities can be tied up for long periods of time, even though customers are insured by the Securities Investor Protection Corpora-

6. Wall Street, under pressure from the SEC, is planning to switch to computerized and "paperless" trading of stocks on June 1, 1995. If this comes about, it may become impossible to take delivery of certificates.

tion (SIPC). Do not keep your securities at home. They will be safer in a safe deposit box at your local bank, and the small fee for the box may be tax deductible. Selling your stock will now entail a trip to the bank, a visit to your safe deposit box, and the mailing of the certificates to the broker. This extra time and effort raises the "cost" of trading in and out of the market and thus may help make you a patient investor. In addition, placing your securities in a bank vault may create an aura of permanence, which will militate against short-term trading. The risk that your securities will be stolen in the mails is minimal if you mail them unendorsed at the same time that you mail a "stock power" form to the broker separately. Your broker can instruct you on even simpler endorsement procedures, which will also keep the risk of theft to a minimum.

Where to Keep Your Cash Reserves

Where should you keep your funds awaiting reinvestment? I would not leave them on deposit with your broker, because I believe this creates a subtle pressure to reinvest them. I recommend a money-market mutual fund (MMMF) with free check-writing privileges and low fees for wiring money. It is quite simple to deposit money in an MMMF, and it is just as simple to write a check against your MMMF balance to pay for stock purchases. There are many good-quality funds with the features I have mentioned, and there are services that rate the safety of funds if you are in doubt. Whenever possible, I limit myself to those which invest in Treasury securities only. The yield is lower, but the loss of a fraction of a percent is well worth the extra security for me. For this reason I would pay no attention to the comparative yields listed in the newspaper, since the differences are often too small to be significant, and they may reflect different degrees of risk or temporary subsidization of expenses. For example, some MMMFs buy commercial paper, which usually has a higher yield than many other short-term instruments. But commercial paper is an unsecured IOU. When Penn Central failed in 1970, holders of their commercial paper lost their entire investment. Although a number of MMMFs have had commercial paper "go bad" on them since that time, the parent of the fund family has taken the loss and protected investors in the MMMF. There is no guarantee this will always be the case, though.

PAD investors in the highest tax bracket can keep their cash reserves in a (federal) tax-free fund investing in short-term municipal obligations. Many of the major fund groups offer this type of investment. In some cases the interest could also be at least partially exempt from state and local taxes.

Mail

The other kind of paper that can overwhelm you is provided free by the companies in your portfolio. Every year you will receive quarterly reports, and an annual report and proxy statement from each company in which you own shares. If the firm pays dividends, you may also receive four separate dividend checks. Additional materials may appear in your mailbox regularly—a report on the annual meeting, for example, or press releases, or, when a proxy fight or takeover battle is looming, seemingly endless missives from the antagonists. If you have always felt that you never received enough mail, investing can help solve your problem. If you already spend as much time with your mail as you like, I have a few time-saving suggestions.

First, remember that corporate reports are essentially self-serving and that all of the information has been disseminated on Wall Street by the time you read it. Remember also that your proxy means very little, since, like a citizen of the old Soviet Union, you can only vote for the nominees or withhold your vote, with few exceptions. If the firm is performing in accordance with expectations, I routinely sign and mail the proxy card. I would not bother to vote against any proposal that management favored, unless it would make the company a difficult takeover target. Since most takeovers tend to benefit stockholders, I do not like to see them made too difficult. I ignore the proxy statement itself unless it contains some of these anti-takeover provisions. The annual report, which often comes in the same package, is much more pleasant to read, although it is often filled with self-congratulatory kudos in good years and pious platitudes in bad. (Technology companies, however, are more likely to have pictures of new technology, which are fun to look at. Consumer product companies may provide coupons or free samples.) *Never* make a buy or sell decision about a company based on the annual report. Although I keep the most recent annual report of each company whose shares I own, my pile of reports gathers dust. A PAD investor can safely throw them away, along with the quarterly reports. It can be dangerous to know your companies too well, since objectivity is quickly lost.

If you want to study the numbers in detail beyond the level of Value Line, write for the company's 10-K report if it is not included with the annual report. Write to the address that is normally listed at the end of the annual report. The 10-K has more detail and no fluff. One feature of the 10-K that can be valuable to a PAD investor is the section on business competition. The stock of the chief competitor of your company may also be a good investment!

Mutual fund investors will also receive their share of mail, some of which is vital to keep. Most PAD mutual fund investors will be reinvesting their capital gains and income distributions in additional shares of their funds. Keeping a record of all of these reinvestment transactions is essential for determining the tax cost basis of your shares when you sell. Annual and quarterly fund reports can be illuminating, although Morningstar gives many funds low grades for the quality of their shareholder reports.

WATCHING YOUR STOCKS AND THE MARKET

PAD techniques do not require a large amount of time. Review of the *Value Line Investment Survey* should take at most an hour or two a week. *Morningstar Mutual Funds* is published every other week, and fund ratings are only updated once a month. The only additional required time is for occasional quiet contemplation of the market's condition and direction, and the performance of your portfolio. I recommend that this time be spent on weekends, when your pace of life can be a little more relaxed.

It is possible, however, to spend all your waking hours reading financial publications, watching financial programs on television, and using your computer to "log on" to an online financial database and news service.[7] I cannot recommend this to anyone without a will of iron, because it is so tempting to listen to the siren song of one market expert or another who says "buy this" or "sell that." A Patient and Disciplined investor must limit exposure to prevailing market wisdom.

There is also no reason to call your broker (or computer database) for quotes on the market or your individual stocks. This practice wastes your valuable time. It is akin to social drinking by reformed alcoholics. It is dangerous.

A TIME-SAVING ALTERNATIVE

Your time commitment can be reduced to one hour per month by subscribing to my monthly market letter, the *PAD System Report*, P.O.

---

7.   I tried a news retrieval/quote service in 1994. I found it addictive, time-consuming, and expensive.

Box 554, Oxford, OH 45056. (Readers of this book are entitled to a free recent issue and a special discount. See the order form at the end of this book.) The *PAD System Report* highlights one or two stocks or mutual funds of interest each month, monitors four portfolios constructed and managed with the rules of Chapters 2–6, reports on economic conditions and their impact on the stock market, and periodically includes updates and modifications of the PAD System itself (Figure 12.3 offers a sample cover page of this newsletter). The *PAD System Report*'s portfolios have been tracked by the *Hulbert Financial Digest* for five years. For the five-year period ending in December 1993, Model Portfolio-C, a broadly diversified portfolio based on the stock selection rules of Chapter 3, significantly outperformed the broad market with below-average risk. Model Portfolio-A, based on Chapter 2's rules, has outperformed the market since April 1993. Model Portfolio-I, a relatively new portfolio that follows the "income" rules of Chapter 3, outperformed the market, on a risk-adjusted basis, in 1993. Model Portfolio-M, a mutual fund portfolio based on the rules of Chapter 5, commenced operations in the fall of 1993. Readers who request a free sample issue will also receive an updated report on the performance of all four portfolios.

PAD NO-NO'S: COMMODITY FUTURES AND PONZI SCHEMES

Commodity Futures

Don't do it. If you don't want to take my word for it, here is the opinion of a professional futures trader as reported in *The Traders* (p. 143) by Sonny Kleinfeld (see Sources section):

Over a late lunch, Stone tells me that the public probably shouldn't fool around with futures. He imparts this advice even though professional traders derive a good chunk of their profits from dull-witted trading by Mr. Average Investor. To the professional, members of the public are looked on as lambs available for fleecing.

Ponzi Schemes

Every year investors are bilked out of millions of dollars by clever con men who use variations on the Ponzi scheme. Ponzi himself produced phenomenal gains for his first investors, and money poured in as the stories of sudden fabulous gains spread. Unfortunately, the gains to the first investors were financed by the payments of the late-

Figure 12.3: The PAD System Report

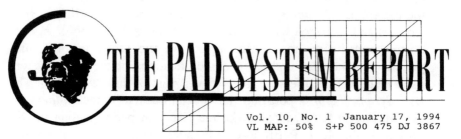

Vol. 10, No. 1   January 17, 1994
VL MAP: 50%   S+P 500 475 DJ 3867

ANNUAL FORECAST ISSUE

The market is now within days of a close above 4000 on the Dow. If this is really the final gasp of the bull, we should be able to observe the signs of excessive optimism. First, we expect substantial press coverage of the historic event, with casual predictions of Dow 5000. Second, the public should be drawn in further with new record inflows into stock mutual funds combined with another surge in the IPO market. Third, the technical condition of the market should deteriorate: the advance should appear "ragged," with almost as many stocks falling as rising on up days, while the CBOE put/call ratio is falling toward 0.4, a level usually associated with short-term tops. Fourth, some well-known bearish investment advisers should capitulate and turn bullish. Fifth, and perhaps most important, interest rates should continue their gradual upward creep without meriting any headlines. It is true that "no one rings a bell at the top," but if all these come to pass, stay away from the bell tower.

Some of Wall Street's optimism is based on new strength in the economy. Our annual forecast (see page 5) argues that this time the economic strength is for real: the economy should grow at 3.5%-4.0% this year. Our reserves of excess capacity and unemployed workers are already shrinking, and thus this growth will put some upward pressure on prices and wages. The Fed will respond by gradually "snugging up" (as Paul Volcker once described it) on interest rates. Wall Street wisdom also suggests that "bull markets don't end until interest rates are rising." Well?

CONCLUSION: Hold at least 50% cash and any short positions. New subscribers: if you are fully invested, raise cash now. If VL Composite Index (geometric) closes above 300, we will take further defensive measures. (Call the MessageLine for details at that time.) [1/17]

INSIDE: Our 1994 Forecast page 5   Janus Fund page 6

THE PAD SYSTEM REPORT IS PUBLISHED 12-18 TIMES A YEAR BY PATIENCE & DISCIPLINE INC. P. O. BOX 554 OXFORD OHIO 45056. PRES: DANIEL A. SEIVER. ANNUAL SUBSCRIPTIONS $195 (3 MO TRIAL: $35). SUBSCRIPTIONS NOT ASSIGNABLE WITHOUT CONSENT; PRO-RATA REFUNDS ON ANNUAL SUBSCRIPTIONS GIVEN WITHOUT QUESTION. PATIENCE AND DISCIPLINE IS REGISTERED AS AN INVESTMENT ADVISER WITH SEC.

comers. Ponzi's scheme and all others like it end when the supply of fools no longer can grow fast enough to finance the growing number of existing players. Always assume you are a latecomer to these deals that seem too good to be true. They probably are.

SOURCES FOR THE PAD INVESTOR

Kleinfeld, Sonny, *The Traders*. New York: Holt, Rinehart and Winston, 1984. Watch the little porkers end up in the supermarket.

J. K. Lasser's *Stock Record Book*. Published by Chartcraft/Investor's Intelligence, 30 Church St., New Rochelle, NY 10801. A cheap, easy-to-use loose-leaf binder to record all your stock transactions and related data.

Simon, John G., *The Ethical Investor*. New Haven: Yale University Press, 1972. The classic in the field.

The Wall Street Journal. Published by Dow-Jones and Co., 200 Liberty St., New York, NY 10281. The *Journal* has just about all the tax information you will ever need.

CHAPTER 13
CONCLUSIONS

"...when you once learn a thing, you must never give it up until you have mastered it...when you inquire into a thing, you must never give it up until you have thoroughly understood it...when you once try to carry out a thing, you must never give it up until you have done it thoroughly and well. "

—The Wisdom of Confucius

You are now ready to start a new life as a PAD investor. Before you jump in with both feet, however, I want to review briefly the elements of the PAD System for outsmarting Wall Street. First and foremost, you must follow the rules. These rules, which have evolved over many years of experience, will keep you from running with the pack. This instinct, which we have all inherited, had survival value eons ago. But on Wall Street today the herd instinct will lead you to ruin. The PAD rules will also overcome the desire for a quick profit, which, if unchecked, will soon have you running with the pack again. As I argued in Chapter 9, it is almost impossible to beat the market except over the long term, and the PAD System is a long-term system.

The rules of Chapters 2 and 3 will help you select growth stocks that have the potential to double or triple. These rules, and the rules of Chapter 4, will also force you to hold those stocks patiently. Chapter 5 will help you pick mutual funds that are likely to continue to provide high total return without high risk. The one rule of Chapter 6 will improve your long-term market timing, so that your buying of growth stocks and mutual funds is more likely to coincide with periods of pessimism and good value, and your selling of them is more likely to coincide with periods of optimism and excessive valuations.

If you buy PAD stocks and mutual funds at market tops and sell them at market bottoms, you will not profit from the PAD System.

Many systems have little to say about selling. The PAD rules will help you sell winners, forcing you to lighten up rather than hold forever, and sell losers, because there is a time to give up and look elsewhere. You must be prepared to take losses.

If you follow these rules and limit yourself to the universe of Value Line stocks and Morningstar mutual funds, you may be able to resist the temptation to buy the local startup firm on which you just got a hot tip from your uncle's brother-in-law. You will also be forced to pass up all the new mutual funds created just to cash in on the latest investment fad.

I believe it would be a mistake to ignore the other chapters of the book, however. Without some understanding of the vicissitudes of the economy and economic policy, you will be at the mercy of monetarists, gold bugs, and other strange creatures who may convince you that the sky is falling. A strong dose of Chapter 7 can keep you from turning into Chicken Little. J. M. Keynes, an economist who understood financial markets, said it best: "Practical men, who believe themselves to be quite exempt from any intellectual influences, are usually the slaves of some defunct economist." Chapter 7 will also help you cast a discerning eye on the Federal Reserve, the money numbers, and the budget to determine whether the economy is headed for rough sailing before reaching the Valhalla of the electronic revolution. A little economics goes a long way.

If you have accepted the PAD System wholeheartedly, you have accepted my vision of the future outlined in Chapter 8. My vision of the future could be wrong. No one has a good record of predicting the future in any detail. If you disagree with my rosy scenario, then Chapter 3 can help you apply the PAD System to a non-technology portfolio. But if my vision of a benign electronic and biologic revolution is right, many PAD-A stocks have a very bright future. Indeed, as the future unfolds, Chapter 8 can help you spot the new and important trends in the ongoing electronic revolution. Entire new industries may spring up in the next century that we cannot imagine now. You will have to decide whether they are PAD-A industries for the new century.

Readers who foundered in Chapter 10 are forgiven. An experienced PAD investor with a substantial portfolio should review Chapter 10 carefully, however. Large portfolios can be "insured" cheaply with Standard and Poor's index options strategies. The small or inexperienced PAD investor can save Chapter 10 until his or her portfolio has reached the requisite size.

I am fully aware that many readers will but scan Chapter 9. It provides no advice for making money. But it is a very important chapter. Not only does it explain why a book like this can provide superior returns for readers, but it also shows how the PAD System is grounded in the same economic theories that are slowly undermining the notion of "efficient markets." John Maynard Keynes knew that markets were not efficient in 1936. I am sure he would endorse the arguments of Chapter 9, since they echo Chapter 12 of his monumental *General Theory of Employment, Interest, and Money.* Even though past performance is no guarantee of future success, there is good reason to believe that the PAD System will continue to work in the future as well as it has in the past.

FINAL WORDS OF ADVICE (FOR THE SKEPTIC)

It took me many years and many mistakes to develop the PAD System to its present form. It thus took me many years to become a full-fledged PAD investor. If you also prefer the gradual approach, start with the PAD System on a "trial" basis. Start with the following three rules:

1. Don't buy stock when Chapter 6 says sell.
2. Don't sell stock when Chapter 6 says buy.
3. Use Value Line and Morningstar to build and monitor your portfolio of stocks and mutual funds.

These three rules alone can turn an average investor into a superior investor. (They also saved PAD investors many thousands of dollars in 1987 and 1990.) If you like it, try the whole system. And good luck to you!

EPILOGUE

Although *Outsmarting Wall Street* does not come with a warranty, the PAD System should provide many years of trouble-free operation. It will work in bull markets and bear markets, helping you pick good growth stocks when the market is cheap, and then forcing you to hold them until the market is dear. Value Line and Morningstar are the only external sources of information required, and they may be available in your local library.

The purpose of this epilogue is to clarify a few points, on a variety of topics, in light of events too recent to be included in the preceding chapters of this book. For ease of exposition, I have arranged my commentaries by issues rather than chapters.

WORLD EVENTS

Although the West need not fear the East anymore, the world has a large supply of swords that have not yet been beaten into ploughshares. Heavily armed outlaw countries like North Korea, Iraq, and Iran have the potential to create serious world crises, while Somalia, Bosnia, and Rwanda show just how horrid "local" conflicts can be in the post-Cold War Era. Neither the U.S. nor the United Nations is up to the task of punishing the guilty or protecting the innocent. The world will remain dangerous for many years to come.

HEALTH CARE

The system may be broken, but it is not obvious anyone has a politically acceptable means of fixing it. Any changes that mandate universal coverage or expansion of benefits will be expensive. The key is to find a way to harness market forces to improve the allocation of medical resources.

MONETARY POLICY

The Federal Reserve began a new round of monetary tightening in 1994. This process could continue for many months, or even years. While the economy can continue to grow in an environment of monetary restraint, an overvalued stock market may face rougher going.

THE STOCK MARKET

The 1990–94 bull market may have ended in January 1994. Even if the bull market does resume and the Dow surges to new highs, PAD investors must remain heavily in cash until the VL MAP returns to 100 percent.

PAD STOCKS

Technology stocks have been among the leaders of the 1990–94 bull market. While this strength could continue for many years, a PAD investor should prudently diversify using the rules of Chapter 3. I do.

PATIENCE AND DISCIPLINE

A system based on patience and discipline will not provide instant results for new converts. Many months, and perhaps years, of the PAD regimen may be necessary before its full fruits are realized. "The secret of success is constancy to purpose."

LISTING OF ALL RULES

CHAPTER 2 (PAD-A)

Part 1 (*Value Line Investment Survey*)

1. Appreciation potential must be at least 100 percent to the low end of the range.

2. Estimated future earnings must be at least 100 percent higher than earnings of the most recently completed year (or the estimate for the year in progress).

3. A financial strength rating below "B" or a safety rating of "5" (lowest) disqualifies the company.

4. Research and development (R&D) percentage must be at least 7.5 percent.

5. Short-term performance ranking must be higher than "5" (lowest).

6. Diversify!

Part 2 (*Value Line OTC Special Situations Service*)

1S. A special situation must be rated at least a "buy/hold."

2S. A special situation must have a three- to five-year appreciation potential of at least 200 percent.

3S. Purchase one-half of your eventual investment when Rules 1S and 2S are satisfied. Then wait at least three months before completing your investment.

4S. Do not purchase additional shares more than once.

5S. Sell all of your holdings of a stock that is rated "switch" by Value Line.

6S. Sell one-fourth to one-half of your holding when the stock has tripled in price.

7S. Sell additional fractions of your holdings at higher multiples of your cost.

8S. Sell all of your shares when a merger or buyout is announced.

9S. Select stocks rated "hold" with low appreciation potential for your Sell List.

10S. Do not "churn" your specials portfolio.

11S. Diversify!

CHAPTER 3 (PAD-C)

1C. Average annual total return must be at least 19 percent to the low end of the range.

2C. Estimated future earnings must be at least 50 percent higher than earnings of the best year of the last five years (including the year in progress).

3C. A financial strength rating below "B++" or a safety rating below "3" (average) disqualifies the company.

4C. Research and development (R&D) percentage must be at least 2 percent.

5C. Short-term performance ranking must be higher than "4" (below average).

6C. Diversify!

Income (PAD-I)

7I. If the dividend is not covered by earnings for two consecutive years, the company is disqualified.

8I. If Value Line suggests a dividend cut is possible, the company is disqualified.

CHAPTER FOUR

Buying

1. Use a discount broker exclusively.

2. Buy stocks on your Buy List at fixed intervals.

3. Do not buy on margin.

4. Use market orders only.

Selling

1. Sell between one-fourth and one-half of your holding when it has tripled, and then sell additional fractions at higher multiples of your cost. Use stock splits to ease the pain of parting.

2. If a stock has declined 50 percent from purchase price, or has performed significantly worse than the market for six months, or has dropped to a "5" for short-term performance, it must be reevaluated carefully.

3. If a stock reviewed under Rule 2 survives a reevaluation, cash reserves can be committed to it. If the price has fallen, this will enable you to "average down." This rule should be invoked only once for any stock and does not apply to a short-term "5."

4. Do not use stop-loss orders.

5. Use market orders only.

6. Sell when a merger or buyout is announced.

7. Review every stock in your portfolio at least once every three months.

8. Sell stocks on your Sell List at fixed intervals.

CHAPTER FIVE (PAD-M)

1M. Morningstar's (relative) return must be at least Above Average.

2M. Morningstar's (relative) risk must be no higher than Average.

3M. Morningstar's star rating must be at least four stars.

4M. Average Historical Rating must be at least 3.0 stars.

5M. The fund should be a pure "no-load" fund.

6M. Diversify (especially internationally).

7M. If Morningstar's star rating drops to two stars, or the Average Historical Rating drops below three stars, or risk rises to "Above Average," or return drops to "Below Average," sell at least half of your fund holding.

8M. (OPTIONAL) When the VL MAP reaches the SELL range (65 percent), begin selling shares in your mutual funds and raising cash reserves. Continue raising cash reserves as long as the VL MAP stays in the SELL range, with an upper limit of 50 percent cash reserves.

9M. (OPTIONAL) When the VL MAP returns to the BUY range (100 percent), begin reducing cash reserves, and if the VL MAP stays in the BUY range, reduce them to zero.

CHAPTER SIX

1. The market is OK to buy if Value Line Investment Survey Median Appreciation Potential equals or exceeds 100 percent. Selling should be undertaken when this potential is below 70 percent. From 70 to 95 percent is a neutral area.

CHAPTER ELEVEN (PAD-S)

1. The VL MAP must be in the SELL range before short selling can be undertaken.

2. Cash reserves must be at 50 percent before short selling can be undertaken.

3. A short-sale candidate must be selling above the low end of its three- to five-year appreciation potential.

4. Dividend yield should be low or nonexistent.

5. Price-earnings ratio (P/E) should be *above* the market average.

6. Diversify. Sell more than one stock short, preferably in more than one industry.

7. Limit short sales to approximately 10 percent of the total value of your portfolio (including cash reserves).

8. For additional comfort, wait until the price of your short-sale candidate has stabilized, and place a stop-loss order above the previous high price. This is especially wise if the stock is ranked "1" for year-ahead performance.

9. Cover your short sale when the stock has appreciation potential of 100 percent to the low end of the three- to five-year range.

10. Cover all short sales when the VL MAP reaches 100 percent.

LISTING OF ALL CASE HISTORIES

Index

SOFTWARE ORDER FORM

To receive your free PAD STOCK SELECTOR PROGRAM II software (available on an IBM 3 1/2" diskette), just fill out the mailing label below and mail a copy of this entire page to:

THE PAD SYSTEM REPORT-PSSP2
P.O. BOX 554
OXFORD, OH 45056

Please print clearly; this is your mailing label!

NAME _____

ADDRESS _____

CITY_____ STATE_____ ZIP_____

MARKET LETTER OFFER

If you would like to receive a FREE copy of the *PAD System Report,* a monthly market letter written by Daniel Alan Seiver, just fill out the mailing label below and mail a copy of this entire page to:

THE PAD SYSTEM REPORT
P.O. BOX 554
OXFORD, OH 45056

Please print clearly; this is your mailing label!

NAME _____

ADDRESS _____

CITY_____ STATE_____ ZIP_____